The Engineer's Contribution to Contemporary Architecture

HEINZ ISLER

Series editors
Angus Macdonald
Remo Pedreschi

Department of Architecture
University of Edinburgh

The Engineer's Contribution to Contemporary Architecture

John Chilton

Thomas Telford

Endorsed by

RIBA Publications

Published by Thomas Telford Publishing, Thomas Telford Ltd, 1 Heron Quay, London E14 4JD.
URL: http://www.thomastelford.com

Distributors for Thomas Telford books are
USA: ASCE Press, 1801 Alexander Bell Drive, Reston, VA 20191-4400, USA
Japan: Maruzen Co. Ltd, Book Department, 3–10 Nihonbashi 2-chome, Chuo-ku, Tokyo 103
Australia: DA Books and Journals, 648 Whitehorse Road, Mitcham 3132, Victoria

First published 2000

Also available from Thomas Telford Books

The Engineer's Contribution to Contemporary Architecture – Eladio Dieste. R. Pedreschi ISBN 0 7277 2772 9
The Engineer's Contribution to Contemporary Architecture – Antony Hunt. A. Macdonald ISBN 0 7277 2769 9
The Engineer's Contribution to Contemporary Architecture – Peter Rice. A. Brown ISBN 0 7277 2770 2

The Architecture of Bridge Design. D. Bennett ISBN 0 7277 2529 7
An Introduction to Cable Roof Structures. Second edition. H. A. Buchholdt ISBN 0 7277 2624 2
Shell Structures in Civil and Mechanical Engineering: Theory and closed-form analytical structures. A. Zingoni ISBN 0 7277 2574 2

A catalogue record for this book is available from the British Library

ISBN: 0 7277 2878 4

© John Chilton and Thomas Telford Limited 2000
Heinz Isler retains the copyright for his photos, drawings and designs.

All rights, including translation, reserved. Except as permitted by the Copyright, Designs and Patents Act 1988, no part of this publication may be reproduced, stored in a retrieval system or transmitted in any form or by any means, electronic, mechanical, photocopying or otherwise, without the prior written permission of the Publishing Director, Thomas Telford Publishing, Thomas Telford Ltd, 1 Heron Quay, London E14 4JD.

This book is published on the understanding that the author is solely responsible for the statements made and opinions expressed in it and that its publication does not necessarily imply that such statements and/or opinions are or reflect the views or opinions of the publishers. While every effort has been made to ensure that the statements made and the opinions expressed in this publication provide a safe and accurate guide, no liability or responsibility can be accepted in this respect by the author or publishers.

Designed by Acrobat
Printed and bound in Great Britain

Acknowledgements

First, my heartfelt thanks must go to Heinz Isler for agreeing to be the subject of this book and for giving me every assistance in its preparation. Last summer (August 1999) he gave a full week of his valuable time to show me his office, examples of his work and modelling techniques, and to discuss his philosophies and influences. The conversations that I recorded at that time have formed the basis for this text. He has read and corrected the manuscript and made many invaluable suggestions for its improvement. He has also provided more than half of the illustrations and drawings that enrich the following pages. Without his generous help and encouragement the task of assembling all this information would have been impossible.

I wish also to thank Maria, Heinz's wife, not only for making my wife and me so welcome last year but also for the support and help that she has, I am certain, given Heinz during his work on the manuscript. For their abundant hospitality during our visit I thank them both.

To my wife Gloria, who accompanied me on my visit to Heinz in Switzerland and then patiently deciphered and typed my badly written transcripts of the taped interviews and conversations, I must give my warmest thanks. Not least, she tolerated my self-inflicted incarceration in my study over Christmas and New Year 1999/2000, as I feverishly completed the first draft of the manuscript. Subsequently, she cheerfully edited the text in accordance with my own and Heinz's numerous amendments.

Finally I would like to thank Neil Jackson and Michael Balz for kindly permitting me to use their photographs and drawings and Glyn Halls for his skilful processing of my own photographs.

John Chilton
August 2000

Preface

There are two principal ways of approaching the general theme of this book series, the Engineer's Contribution to Contemporary Architecture. Perhaps the first direction that springs to mind is to contemplate how the efforts of a particularly innovative engineer have influenced and enhanced the work of nationally or internationally renowned architects. The second approach is to consider the unique work of an exceptional engineer whose work transcends the definition of mere structural engineering to the extent of becoming structural art. In this sense the engineer's accomplishments contribute to contemporary architecture by their inspirational qualities, which appeal to both architects and other engineers. This volume describing the work of Heinz Isler falls into this second category.

Isler is a structural artist and his primary medium of expression is the reinforced concrete shell. But, where most shell designers use precise mathematical formulae to describe the shell's surface and analyse its behaviour, Isler revels in physical modelling both to determine the form and subsequently to investigate its stability. Harmonious, natural and inspiring structures are the result.

Surprisingly, it was not until September 1989 that I first encountered the amazing free-form shells of Heinz Isler. Having only just started teaching structures at a School of Architecture earlier that year, I attended the 30th Anniversary Congress of the International Association for Shell and Spatial Structures (IASS) in Madrid. Here, Heinz Isler showed how his shell structures had developed over the 30 years since he had presented his innovative form finding methods at the first IASS Congress in 1959. A dazzling display of enticing shell forms culminated with the, then just recently completed, Sports Halls at Norwich Sports Village (location of the only Isler shells in the UK). Inspired by what I had seen, in the break that followed I talked to Heinz and discovered that another shell was scheduled for construction at the same site, in the following year. When I showed interest in the imminent creation of that swimming pool shell, Heinz took my card and said that he would let me know when the concrete pour was to take place. Anticipating that such an eminent and occupied engineer would not recall a brief conversation at an International Congress, I thought it unlikely that I would hear from him. However, how wrong could I be? Just over a year later I received a telephone call inviting me to the Norwich Sports Village Hotel to stay overnight and to see the shell being concreted at the adjacent site the following day. I went, of course. A highly enjoyable meal that evening, with Heinz and his wife Maria, led to a friendship that has grown over the intervening years and which has ultimately resulted in the writing of this book.

I hope that the (still undiminished) thrill that I experienced on first discovering Heinz Isler's shells and on witnessing the creation of the Aquapark shell in Norwich will be communicated to the reader over the succeeding pages.

Contents

One   Shells, the man, his philosophy and influences   11
- Historical shells   12
- The great concrete shell builders   12
- Thin concrete shells   12
- Heinz Isler   13
- Isler's first polyester shells   16
- First Congress of the International Association for Shell Structure   16
- Influences of Torroja, Lardy, Hauri and Candela   20
- Munich Olympic Stadium   22
- Design philosophy   22
- Creative play   28
- The future of the practice   29

Two   Finding the form and proving its strength   31
- Why shells?   32
- The process of form-finding   32
- 'Bubble' shells   33
- Expansion forms   35
- Free- form shells from hanging membranes   35
- Forces in the shell   38
- Model tests   40
- Instability   41
- Measuring the form   42
- Construction   44
- Monitoring of lifetime performance   44
- Is the physical model dead?   46

Three   'Bubble' shells   49
- Architectural considerations   50
  - Planning   50
  - Shell thickness   52
  - Façades   52
  - Daylight and ventilation   52
  - Artificial lighting   54
  - Moser, Lyssach, 1964   54
- COOP, Wangen bei Olten, 1960   54
- Recent applications of the bubble shells   58
  - Warehouse Formex, Bubendorf, 1994   60
  - Bus depot, Müllheim, 1996/7   61
  - New office building, W. Bösiger AG, Langenthal, 1998   62
- Co-operation with contractors   62
- Demolition of bubble shells   66

Four   Free-form shells   69
- Wyss Garden Centre, Solothurn, 1962   70
- Soc. Migros, Bellinzona, 1964   77
- Garden Centre Florélites Clause SA, St. Appoline, Paris, 1965   80
- Kilcher Factory, Recherswil, Solothurn, 1965   83
- Bürgi Garden Centre, Camorino, 1973   86
- Sports and Ski Centre, Chamonix, 1970–75   86

Five   Inverted membrane shells   91
- Motorway Service Station, Deitingen Süd, 1968   92
- Factory for Sicli SA, Geneva, 1969   97
- Open-air theatres at Stetten auf den Fildern, 1976, and Grötzingen, 1977   102
  - Stetten   102
  - Grötzingen   105
- Tennis halls and swimming pools   106
  - Tennis halls   106
  - Swimming pools   108
- Aircraft Museum, Dübendorf, 1987   109
- Norwich Sports Village, 1987–91   110
  - Formwork   113
  - Shell thickness   114
  - Concrete   115
  - Pouring the shell   115
  - Prestressing   117
  - Surface protection of the shell   117
  - Environmental considerations   118

Six   Hypars, domes and sculptures   121
- Holy Spirit Church at Lommiswil, 1967   122
- Inflated 'ball' houses   128
- Balz House, Stetten auf den Fildern, near Stuttgart, 1980   130
- Villa, near Geneva, 1986   134
- New Church, Cazis, 1996   135
- Sculptures   138

Seven   Translucent shells of ice and plastic   141
- Sky domes and vaults   143
- Translucent plates   145
- Translucent cantilever shells   147
- Structures in ice   148

Eight   Influence of Heinz Isler's work and the future of thin concrete shells   155
- Heinz Isler's contribution to contemporary architecture   156
- Working with architects   156
- IASS and structural morphology   156
- Future of shells   157

Endnotes   160

Selected List of works   165

Bibliography   167

Index   168

Chapter One
Shells, the man, his philosophy and influences

Chapter One
Shells, the man, his philosophy and influences

Historical shells

For around 2000 years single and double-curved shells structures, such as barrel vaults and domes, have been used to cover large spans in buildings. Until the twentieth century these were generally constructed either from masonry or some form of unreinforced concrete, materials strong in compression but relatively weak in tension. Well-known examples such as the Pantheon[1] (AD 120–124), in Rome, and Hagia Sophia[2] (AD 532–537), in Constantinople, now Istanbul, Santa Maria del Fiore (1420–1434) in Florence and St. Peter's Basilica[3] (1585–1590) in Rome have a span to thickness ratio of less than 50 to 1, which is relatively thicker than the shell of a typical hen's egg. However, the stone vaulting of the magnificent medieval Gothic cathedrals of Europe demonstrate the mason's art in the construction of quite complex masonry shells.

With the advent of reinforced concrete, a mouldable material strong in both compression and tension, it became possible, from around the beginning of the twentieth century, to construct thin shells with much higher span to thickness ratios. Since then many thousands of thin reinforced concrete shells have been built all over the world. These commonly have span/thickness ratios in the region of 500 to 1.

The great concrete shell builders

If asked to record the most significant reinforced concrete shell builders of the twentieth century, the list of most architects and engineers might contain the names Eduardo Torroja (1899–1961), Félix Candela (1910–1997), Heinz Isler (1926–), Pier Luigi Nervi (1891–1979), Ove Arup (1895–1988), and Nicolas Esquillan (1902–1989). The majority of these designers worked with geometrical shells where the curved surface is defined by a mathematical formula, which allows the engineer to calculate by hand the stresses within the shell. Alone among these sits Heinz Isler whose free-form shells are of a shape that cannot be defined by simple geometric formulae as they have continuously varying double curvature across the whole surface and they obey physical laws. These forms carry shell building to the level of structural art.

Thin concrete shells

As thin shells are economical in the consumption of materials and of steel in particular, which is used only for reinforcement and usually at quite a low density, they were used widely for medium and long-span roof structures from the 1920s until the 1970s. For example, the works of Torroja, Candela and Nervi were mainly constructed during this period when steel was often in short supply. Since the 1970s the use of reinforced concrete shells has declined in developed countries and this has been due to several factors. One reason is that, traditionally, shell construction is labour intensive, which makes it expensive in high wage economies. Another reason is that large quantities of structural steel sections are now available at competitive prices together with many new long-span structural systems suited to steel construction. Further, the high cost of the formwork and falsework required to produce shell forms (which is often used only once or a limited number of times) has also reduced their acceptability. More recently, tensile membranes have enabled architects and engineers to cover large areas with lightweight, translucent structures, which have taken much of the potential market for shells. However, tensile membranes may be inappropriate for some architectural applications. They have a limited life span, depending on the material used, and are difficult to insulate without sacrificing the appearance of lightness which is their hallmark. There are also problems with their acoustic performance as they have such a low mass compared to that of even the thinnest concrete shell.[4]

Moreover, many developing countries do not produce their own steel (or produce less than they consume) and can ill afford to import large quantities of structural sections for building construction. In these countries labour is often very cheap and most construction materials expensive, therefore, the economic argument in favour of using thin concrete shells for long-span roofs still holds true.

The use of Heinz Isler's concrete shells has endured longer in the more competitive economic environment of Europe due to their superior aesthetics, performance and more reasonable cost.

They are very durable and require minimal maintenance as they use well-compacted concrete, of good quality, which is maintained in compression to eliminate cracking. This is achieved by a good choice of shape, sometimes assisted by prestressing. Sprayed insulation materials can be used to achieve the final shape of the shell formwork without having to resort to expensive timber lining. Improvements in concrete technology have also made the task of placing, compacting and finishing his shells easier.

Heinz Isler

Heinz Isler (*Fig. 1.1*) was born on the 26 July 1926, at Zollikon, which is now a suburb of Zürich, where his father Jakob Isler, a graduated land surveyor, worked as a municipal engineer in the supervision and maintenance of roads, water supplies and sewerage systems. Heinz pursued his early studies first at primary school then, from 1939, at the high school. There were only a few subjects that he did not like at school and he believes that although he had many talents they were nothing extraordinary, 'just normal talents, a bit more a bit less so I could have chosen ten professions'.[5] One particular talent that Heinz Isler had, and still has, is his skill in sketching and watercolour painting. This was recognised by his teachers and in 1944 he was encouraged — the first time that this had happened in this school — to mount an exhibition of his work (much of it having been done when he was just 16 years old). The sketches and paintings were

Fig. 1.1. Heinz Isler in his office reading John Chilton's draft of this book.

Photo: Heinz Isler

Chapter One
Shells, the man, his philosophy and influences

mainly of the Swiss countryside, displaying his love of nature, a love that endures to this day. This sensitivity and feeling for the natural world is expressed in the quiet beauty of the shell forms that Isler has designed and the way that they merge more easily into the landscape than most modern buildings.

However, the young Heinz Isler had no idea which profession he wanted to pursue, as he felt that everything both interested him and did not interest him. He believes that he might have become a clergyman, a judge, a teacher, a painter or an engineer; almost anything was possible. Many issues caught his attention and when he encountered something new he got pleasure from it and found new topics for exploration. School life was stimulating and he enjoyed it but some day he had to choose a career. The only speculation about the future direction of his life that Heinz Isler remembers was in a conversation with a school friend, when he was about 17 years old. He distinctly recalls that one day when walking round the school playground, while he and his friend were passing along the south side of the square, he turned and said, 'I think I may do research'.[6]

His first passion was for painting and art but his father did not consider that to be an appropriate career and declared that he would only allow his son to take this up once his son had acquired a proper profession. Before making a final decision, on leaving school in 1945, Isler went to enlist for his compulsory national service where he spent four happy months assisting in erecting military construction projects in the open countryside. Having enjoyed these activities, the young Heinz Isler decided to follow some way in his father's footsteps and study civil engineering at the Swiss Technical University (Eidgenössische Technische Hochschule — or ETH) in Zürich.[7] Choosing to study thin shells as his dissertation project, which was supervised by Prof. Pierre Lardy (1903–1958), he became fascinated with the subject that was to become his life's work. Although at that time he was not aware of the profound influence his choice of project would have on his future.

Once Isler had graduated, Professor Lardy (who was a musician and mathematician as well as an engineer) invited him to work as his assistant, for teaching and consultancy, at the ETH. Here for over two years, from January 1951 to May 1953, Isler gained valuable experience of the behaviour of structures as he assisted Lardy in his investigations of failed structures. After Isler, in this capacity, there followed the renowned bridge designer Christian Menn, for whose work Isler has a great respect. Commenting about one of Menn's bridges over the River Aare in Bern, a simple three span concrete tapered box girder, Isler said that the form was 'perfect and very elegant, you could not remove ten centimetres from anywhere.'[8] It was during this time as assistant that Isler was exposed to the use of model tests as a method of exploring the behaviour of structures, as Lardy set up a laboratory to carry out such testing, following his visit to Torroja's research facilities in Madrid.

However, Isler was still tempted to follow a career as a painter. He applied to art schools and was accepted at the Academy in Munich, on the basis of the work that he had produced when he was just 16 years old. In order to earn money to finance his art studies, he decided to work for some months and was offered a job in Burgdorf (ostensibly to design a bridge) but when he arrived he was asked to work on a project for the roof of a concert hall at the Hotel Kreuz, in Langental. This was the venture that was to launch him on his lifelong exploration of the fascinating world of thin shells.

Isler struggled for months, working days and nights in the office and in his lodgings (a room that he was renting in a mansard roof). The problem he was trying to solve is shown in the sketch on the blackboard in his office basement (*Fig. 1.2*). This shows the real beginning of his new enterprise, his new calling. He had to design a roof where the architect wanted just a cylindrical vault but with domed end sections over a tapering rectangular plan. However, Isler did not like the straight line joining the two curved ends so he began to change the architect's concept,[9] which, in section, had been a radius, a straight line and then another radius, a segment of a slight cone.

On the drawing board Isler tried to elaborate the new shape by sections, mainly in the longitudinal direction but with some in the transverse and diagonal sense. The shape of the wooden formwork was to be defined by the 'z' co-ordinates (or height above a fixed datum) of 400 points. However, the task that Isler undertook was really an impossible one because when one point or one curve had to be altered or adapted to new cross-sections, all the other 399 points also changed. At that time no numerical method or computers existed to find or define such a free shape. Using a model made of wood, an approximation was checked and, finally, the form of the curved girders was established in tables.

The worst thing was that work on the building site was advancing steadily and the foreman asked every morning for a new set of curves, and this before Isler had concluded his work, in order to see if the exact curves fitted together. However, naturally, the curves fitted, the shell was successfully built and still exists today in good condition after 46 years of service. During that time it has survived three fires and for the last 15 years has carried an additional load of 50 tonnes of gypsum, the decorative ceiling of a dance hall, which hangs from it.

At the end of this unnerving task to find the new, more organic, shape one thing was clear to Isler: this was the first but evidently also the last free-form shaped shell he would ever build. Worse still, the shape, as built, of the concert hall shell, in spite of its excellent technical performance, did not please Isler aesthetically. It was arbitrary or as he describes 'something like a plum'.

However, just near the end of the painstaking definition of the shape something happened, which would have a decisive impact on Isler's professional career. One night, returning from the office to his lodgings in the early hours of the morning (exhausted from struggling with the geometry of the shell), Isler was suddenly struck by the shape of the plumped-up pillow on his bed. This was just what he had been searching for, a form with a continuously curved surface. He had been seeking such a shape for months, yet the pillow made it automatically, instantly and without any effort.

Isler realised immediately that this was the solution. Not the drawing board, not imagination, nor a mathematical formula but a physical model was the way.

If he made a technical pillow with the necessary precision (which was not difficult for him, following his excellent apprenticeship with Lardy) the task could be solved elegantly. For the shell under construction it was too late to change but for the future the road lay open. This was the origin of the 'bubble' shells, the form-finding of which is described in detail in the following chapter.

The discovery also changed Isler's life. He saw that nobody had the vision, patience or capability to follow the logical way. However, he could see the potential for the creation of many beautiful objects and so abandoned his idea of studying art at the Academy of Munich. He had the faint feeling that possibly he could express his

Chapter One
Shells, the man, his philosophy and influences

liking of forms, colours and balanced creation in this new domain. So, by the chance observation of the shape of the pillow on his bed, Isler's intention to work in Burgdorf for just a few months has now extended to a stay of over 40 years.

Two years after starting this new avenue of discovery Isler went to see his venerable teacher and mentor, Professor Lardy, to reveal his new ideas. Lardy was amazed with the revelation of his ex-student and assistant and might have pursued academic research in this field with Isler had he not sadly died a short time later.

Isler's first polyester shells
A significant event in the development of Heinz Isler's career occurred when, in 1956, he designed one of his first buildings (with a roof consisting of a series of bubble shells) where he included circular openings of 5 m diameter at the centre of each roof. Once the building was completed the client wanted to order the skylights. At the time there were skylights in Plexiglas, and Isler just phoned the manufacturer and asked for eight skylights. He was asked which size he would like 1·1, 1·3 or 1·4 m diameter but he replied that he wanted them of 5 m diameter. He could hear the laughter at the other end of the telephone line and he was told that such things did not exist. The manufacturer said that he was unable to produce circular skylights any bigger than 1·6 m diameter yet Isler was left with a factory of about 2400 m² with eight holes of 5 m diameter in the roof.

He went to the client, Blaser, and asked what they should do. As an alternative, they considered the possibility of making some conical roofs in glass and steel but Isler did not really like the idea. Then it was suggested to him that he might be able to produce domed skylights of the required size in reinforced polyester. This was a material with which Isler was familiar from his shell models. So he began to think about it, had a test piece made, and showed it to the client. He took a model of a small dome to the meeting but although it had been produced in a factory where they were experienced in working with polyester, the translucence was so poor that he thought that the client would never accept it. When Isler arrived with the sample the client put it on the floor and asked the driver of a forklift truck to run his machine over the dome. He drove over it and the dome did not even have a scratch, let alone collapse. Following that demonstration, the client was very enthusiastic. He gave his approval and even offered the use of his garage for dome production. He had not even looked to see how much light came through! So Isler immediately started to make a mould, then the first piece, then the second, and so on, but instead of production taking the three months that he expected, it took him a whole year to produce them all. Isler can be seen working on these prototypes in *Figs 1.3(a)* and *(b)*.

Subsequently, the idea attracted the interest of a businessman by the name of Eschmann, from Thun, and his company was sold a licence to produce them. This being a highly innovative use of reinforced polyester technology with many applications in building construction, the firm was very successful. The sale of this licence later enabled Isler to develop many novelties in his own design studio, workshop and laboratory at Lyssachschachen, near Burgdorf.

First Congress of the International Association for Shell Structures
The most important event in bringing Isler's innovative method of form-finding of shells to the engineering and architectural establishment came in 1959. In that year, the internationally recognised shell builder Eduardo Torroja presided over the First Congress of the International Association for Shell Structures, in Madrid. Today this same organisation is still thriving, as the International Association for Shell and Spatial Structures (IASS), based in Madrid. Heinz Isler is now a member of its Executive Council. Although Isler had presented his ideas earlier at smaller conferences in Amsterdam 1955[10] and Oslo 1957,[11] this was the occasion when the world of thin concrete shell building was confronted with a new way of finding shell forms.

Because of military service commitments, Isler arrived late for the Madrid congress, just in time to present his paper entitled *New shapes for shells*. Therefore, he did not initially have time to appreciate the eminence of his audience before he started to speak. The paper he presented contained a brief summary of its contents (in

English and in French), little more than one page of text and nine illustrations. And yet, of all the papers given at this congress, this one stimulated the longest discussion. Time for discussion was limited to approximately ten minutes for each paper. However, for Heinz Isler's contribution, Professor Torroja allowed a debate (interrupted by a coffee break) of about 45 minutes in total. Such was the interest generated by this brief description of Isler's form-finding methods for shells.

The text discussed three methods of form-finding, 'the freely shaped hill, the membrane under pressure and the hanging cloth reversed',[12] stating that these led to the generation of a large number of shell forms. In the section on freely shaped hills two examples of their use were discussed and illustrated. The first was a mound of earth (*Fig. 1.4*) on which, in 1955, was cast an atomic bomb shelter of unreinforced concrete that successfully resisted a pressure of 60 tonnes/m². A reinforced plastic free-form swimming pool, only a few millimetres thick and designed as an inverted shell was the second example (*Fig. 1.5*).

Membranes under pressure and soap films were discussed in the second section. Their use as form generators for concrete shells was illustrated by Isler's inflatable rubber membrane model (which is shown in the following chapter, *Fig. 2.3*), two bubble shell projects (one of rectangular shells 20 × 14 m, *Fig. 1.6*, and the other of square shells 20 × 20 m, *Fig. 1.7*) and a project model for an asymmetric shell hangar roof. It was noted that over 11 000 m² of such roofs had been constructed since 1954.

The third section declared that inversion of a hanging cloth or membrane is the best method, stating that it is 'for three-dimensional problems, what the catenary line is for two-dimensional arches'.[13] A model reinforced plastic shell, formed by hanging under its own weight, illustrated this method (*Fig. 1.8*). Also, a corner-supported ice shell, of 3 × 3 m and less than 1 mm in thickness, made in February 1957 by inverting a frozen hanging cloth, was shown (*Fig. 1.9*). The final figure showed drawings of 39 different shell shapes and had the abbreviation 'etc.' in the bottom right-hand corner, suggesting that this was only a selection from an infinite spectrum of possible forms (*Fig. 1.10*).

Despite its brevity, the effect of the paper was dramatic and instantaneous. In an account of the discussion printed together with the paper in the Bulletin of IASS,[14] the discussion amounts to about 300 lines whereas the paper contains approximately 50 lines of text. And yet not all of the debate was reported! The audience for the presentation included many of the most eminent concrete shell designers of the time who were somewhat sceptical of the ideas proposed by the young Isler. Of these, Eduardo Torroja (Spain), Nicolas Esquillan (France) and Ove Arup (UK) dominated the subsequent discussion.

Torroja voiced his concern about the indiscriminate use of models by those who may

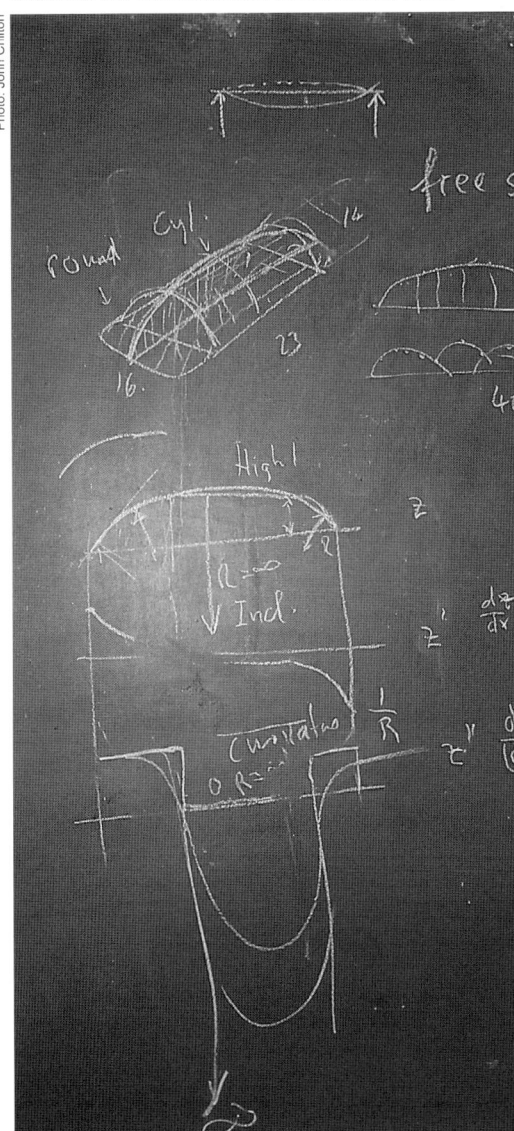

Fig. 1.2. Hotel Kreuz, Langental. Blackboard sketch of the shell roof. Isler's first bubble shell.

Photo: John Chilton

Chapter One
Shells, the man, his philosophy and influences

be inexperienced. For instance, on the subject of hanging membranes he pointed out that woven cloth is not isotropic (as it has threads running in two principal directions) and that by rotating the material by 45° a different hanging form results for the same boundary conditions and loading. Therefore, he said, although making such models was a great aid in understanding the forms that shells might take, great care had to be taken in interpreting the behaviour of physical analogies when compared to that of real structures. Torroja also touched on geometry. Isler had commented that engineers were well versed in the use of mathematics and geometry based on 'straight lines and right angles and then also with symmetry in revolution, spheres etc.' but that these skills were not sufficient when looking for new shapes. However, Torroja, insisted that there were problems in the representation of non-geometrical shapes. He said that shells had to be described by plans drawn on a flat plane and that mathematics were needed to define the points on such surfaces. Cylindrical and polyhedral forms could be modelled in paper but double curved forms required some form of clay or mouldable material and that was not convenient to work with. Finally, he took up a point already raised by Arup, about artistic or architectural expression, in general, in double curved shells. Torroja said that in classical architecture there existed modelling of building façades with planes at right angles to each other (such as cornices, windows etc.), that give expression to the form. However, with double-curved shells there is no such modelling and only the effect of shadows as the sun moves round the building during the day enables the observer to appreciate the three-dimensional form.

Isler replied to Torroja's concerns by, firstly, stressing that his conceptual models (or physical analogies) were only the first stage in the design process and that these were followed by loading tests on small-scale models in the laboratory and long-term monitoring of built examples at full-scale. He said that he was well aware of the differences between the elastic modelling materials and concrete. In reply to Torroja's comment about the problems of defining double-

 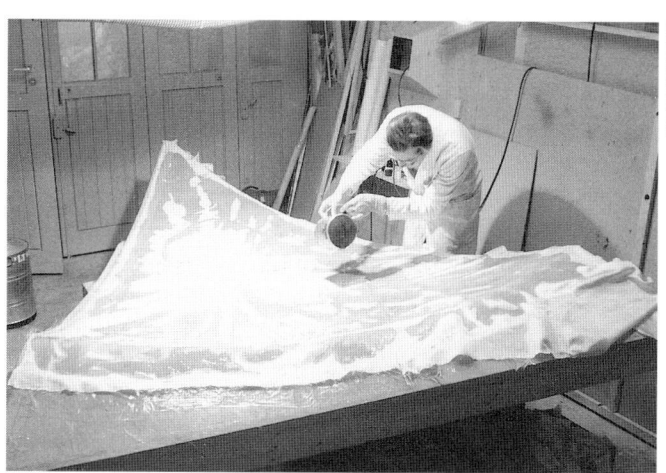

Photos: Heinz Isler

Fig. 1.3. (a) and (b) Heinz Isler working on the prototype reinforced polyester shells, 5 m diameter, built in a garage.

curved surfaces (and a further question on a similar theme, by Mr Hajnal-Konyi) Isler said that the forms were measured with accurate instruments to give a series of curves along section lines. Once plotted as a graph, any error in the curves was easily detectable and could be corrected. He went on to say that it was possible to approximate his forms using a combination of cylindrical, spherical and conical surfaces but that the cylinder and cone were rather weak in resistance to buckling. An improvement in buckling performance, of from 7 to 10% for cylinders and 100% for cones, was achieved by adopting his shapes.[15]

However, Esquillan was more interested in the method of construction and the economics of the non-geometrical forms — particularly the costs for formwork and falsework. He had recently completed, what is still, the world's longest span, thin, double-layer concrete shell structure, the Centre National des Industries et Techniques (CNIT) in Paris,[16] which is a corner-supported structure, triangular in plan with side lengths of 206 m. Esquillan wanted to know how Isler could construct his bubble shells with a shuttering cost of only 20 to 25% when it was more usual for formwork and falsework to represent around 50% of the total cost of a shell, even when the shuttering was reused several times.

This difference in cost was justified by Isler as perhaps being due to the method of construction that was employed. He described

Fig. 1.4. Freely shaped hill for form finding.

how permanent formwork was used (the thermal insulation of the roof) and that this was supported on thin, flexible timber boards, in turn supported on lines of glued-laminated timber beams. As the insulation was a permanent part of the building construction and would have been required anyway, it was not included in the shuttering cost. Also, he commented that the whole system was very lightweight, therefore, the falsework could also be lighter and cheaper.

Arup contributed his opinion about the comparative importance of economy and aesthetics in shell structures and supported Torroja's view that conferences involving architects and engineers would be beneficial. He commented that shells were often used for more

19

Chapter One
Shells, the man, his philosophy and influences

Fig. 1.5. Reinforced plastic free-form swimming pool, only a few millimetres thick and designed as an inverted shell.

Fig. 1.6. Rectangular shells 20 x 14 m, Blaser Hasle-Rüegsau, 1956.

spectacular buildings, where it was the architect who generally decided on the form of the shell and expected the engineer to make it work. This he thought to be 'a most unfortunate state of affairs'.[17] David Billington has suggested[18] that the design of the Sydney Opera House (1957–73) was uppermost in Arup's thoughts at the time. Conceived by architect Jørn Utzon as a thin shell roof, the final solution for the Opera House, obtained by Arup after thousands of man-hours of design, is composed of triangular segments cut from a sphere and constructed from prestressed voluminous concrete ribs[19] (Figs 1.11 and 1.12).

From the general discussion, there appeared to be considerable concern among those present that Isler's paper might give the impression that any natural or model shell could be scaled up by perhaps 1000 times and would still produce a stable structure. For instance, Mr A. R. Flint was concerned that architects would want to construct enlarged versions of snail shells or statues by Henry Moore.[20] Isler accepted these comments, stating that he knew there were limits to the method but that it could lead to 'very nice solution[s]'.

Influences of Torroja, Lardy, Hauri and Candela

Isler's development of shell forms was later influenced by his coming across, in the early 1960s in Zürich, a book cover showing a shell roof designed by Félix Candela, the Manantiales Restaurant in Xochimilco, Mexico, only 40 mm thick. This chance encounter set Isler on an exploration of thinness in his shells. The thinness in itself did not interest Isler, whether it was 8 cm, 4 cm (as Candela) or even 1·2 cm (as Schlaich's mortar shell of 20 years later[21]) was not so important. However, what intrigued Isler was the possibility of showing the slender character of the bearing structure, as extremely beautifully demonstrated in Félix Candela's pavilion in Xochimilco. Isler considers that not only the minimal thickness of this shell but also its unmistakable wave form, with its perfect curves, gives the structure its unique thrill.

Isler returned to the twentieth Anniversary Congress of IASS, in 1979, as a keynote speaker alongside Félix Candela. The theme of Isler's presentation was *New shapes for shells— twenty years after*. By that time, Candela was no longer constructing shells so his presentation was a retrospective review of his previous work, whereas Isler's complementary presentation was that of an inspired designer approaching the peak of his career.

It is an indication of the respect with which Heinz Isler is held within IASS, that he was invited to present a keynote address summarising the achievements of the organisation, at the 40th Anniversary Congress also held in Madrid (where the congress is held every ten years) in September 1999. Concurrently, there was an exhibition of the work of Torroja celebrating the centenary of his birth and during the congress tributes were made to Torroja, as founder of IASS. These included a personal appreciation by Isler who recalled that, in the early 1950s, his mentor Professor Lardy had returned from a trip to Madrid highly enthusiastic about Torroja's laboratory work with models. Lardy, with his assistants Hans Hauri and Jules Jakob, subsequently developed a small laboratory for making Plexiglas models in the attic at ETH in Zürich. These models were loaded and deformations and stresses measured. The new technique of measuring strain with strain gauges was also used. Isler always measured everything 12 times and ignored the worst two results before determining the mean. Here Isler was able to see, from the first experiment, how necessary a careful procedure is to the success of such modelling. He saw that from these models a very useful technical understanding could be acquired.

Patient, accurate and repeated measurement is a philosophy that Isler has since emulated throughout his career. Therefore, through the intermediary Lardy, Torroja influenced Isler's career.

Another very significant individual in the development of Heinz Isler's later career is his wife Maria. They had met while students in Zürich in 1949 but then pursued their own careers (Heinz in Burgdorf, as engineer, and Maria as a medical doctor — paediatrician — in Berlin). Then, in 1968, while attending a Colloquium in Berlin, Heinz went to look for Maria, only to find that she was, by a twist of fate, on holiday in Switzerland. Undaunted, he found her and three years later they were married. So, in 1970, Maria gave up her work

Fig. 1.7. Square shells 20 x 20 m, Ramseier + Jenzer, Biel.

Chapter One
Shells, the man, his philosophy and influences

Fig. 1.8. A model reinforced plastic shell, formed by hanging under its own weight.

as a paediatrician to help the smooth running of Heinz Isler's design office. A task which she still carries out highly efficiently to this day allowing her husband to concentrate almost entirely on his work and numerous hobbies.

Munich Olympic Stadium

It was around the same time that, together with Jürgen Joedicke, Heinz Isler was involved in the engineering development for the prize-winning design for the Olympic Facilities for the Games in Munich in 1972 (architects Günter Behnisch and Partners). At that time Isler had about 30 engineers working at his office in Burgdorf and another 30 working for the big Olympic Stadium in Munich. However, the detailed development of the winning roof design (once approval for its construction had been granted), was mainly supervised by Fritz Leonhardt who employed the young Jörg Schlaich to do the work in collaboration with Isler. A discussion of the debate surrounding the roof design of the winning competition entry is given in a recent book by Alan Holgate, in which he reports comments by Jörg Schlaich that without Heinz Isler's involvement the present roof would probably not exist.[22]

Design philosophy

Heinz Isler's guidelines for design may be summarised as follows
- simplicity and modesty of means
- purity of the concept
- precision and purity of physical experiments.

In accordance with the first guiding principle on this list, undoubtedly, his main concern is respect of the natural world. He continually asks what are the consequences for the environment, the world about us. To that end, he searches for structures of high efficiency with the lowest environmental impact.

This means that Isler, in his concrete shells, adopts the attitude of always using the minimum everywhere to fulfil a given task. It starts with the enclosure, by using the minimum volume — no more space than necessary. It continues by providing the minimum surface for that enclosure, which equates to the minimum use of energy. Then he uses the minimum quantity of building material, reducing weight and keeping dimensions small. Low stresses lead to low maintenance structures and maximum life.

Isler believes that one should also strive to reduce the number of building components. A good shell roof is weather-resistant and impermeable. Therefore no coating is needed and there are no joints with all their problems. Also, concrete under compression is one of the most durable materials. A good shell surface loses about 3 mm of its thickness in the first ten years but then it becomes stable and can endure many decades. Minimising the number of elements is probably driven to the limit in a shell building. Instead of having many beams, purlins, plates and slabs under many coats of weather protection, the monolithic shell is the one and only element fulfilling all needs. Therefore it has

Fig. 1.9. A corner-supported ice shell, of 3 x 3 m and less than 1 mm in thickness, made in Feb 1957.

intriguing unsurpassed simplicity and modesty. And that Isler likes.

The design methods that Isler has developed over several decades are a way of leading to an infinite spectrum of applications. He is very shy of what he has discovered considering it to be almost something holy and of a very high beauty. When, after several years, others were able to get very close to Isler's free forms by using powerful computers running structural shape optimisation software and giving three-dimensional representations, he says that at first he was very angry.[23] Isler described his feelings about this in a conversation with the author in August 1999. He said that it was as if he had been climbing a wall, a high wall in the mountains, a very dangerous and very lonely path but he climbed it, and when he finally reached the top he found a valley which nobody had ever seen before. There was a paradise full of flowers, rare or unknown and in there he lived and could make his forms. He thought that there might well be others who would follow him, climbing up by the same or similar way. A few started but nobody arrived. Then suddenly one morning there was a loud noise and out of the valley side there came a tunnel with a road, a motorway, where others could come to his valley in complete comfort and with little effort. He felt robbed and that everything had been taken away from him.

Now he is more realistic, understanding that others can emulate reasonably closely the forms that he has painstakingly found by decades of experiment and development.[24] He points out that although others may have emulated his forms on computer screens no one has yet used their programs to design and manufacture any real shell. Some have made models in plaster or with micro-concrete and have tested them to compare their computer analyses with the behaviour of a real physical object. That he recognises as valid because he considers that all the investigations by computers may be useful but they are dangerous, as nobody has seen if the programs or results are real. The numerical accuracy is very high but only in the calculations. If, at the beginning, erroneous assumptions were made or data input incorrectly it is almost impossible to determine whether the output from the computer is correct without testing it against a real structure.

Isler considers that even the best computer calculation is no better than his formula by hand. Why? Because all the material constants, the properties of the section etc., are based on the same inaccurate but practical hypotheses as his hand calculation. The numerical accuracy gives, in his opinion, a false sense of safety. For him, where concrete shells are concerned, practically everything is in doubt. Even if he were to have the most elaborate computations, model, or model tests, he knows that all have very little to do with his building. The building itself is something absolutely different, new and unique. He considers that its behaviour depends on the quality of design and the quality of the concrete; it depends on the temperature when poured; it

Chapter One
Shells, the man, his philosophy and influences

Fig. 1.10. The 39 'etc.' different shell shapes showing only a selection from an infinite spectrum of possible forms.

depends on the construction sequence; it depends on the age; it depends on everything and the life of the structure really begins at the moment when he removes the scaffolding. Then the shell is free.

For Isler, the design of an integral shell building will always remain the result of careful pondering of all influences by an expert designer. Computerised optimisation for a limited number of criteria will not do the job. Although an optimised form can be achieved, most of the time this is far removed from a good, balanced design!

Isler's only real motive from the start has been to create beauty and he recoils from the act of construction as he equates this to some extent with the destruction of the nature that he loves. This wish to intervene gently in nature is abundantly demonstrated by his offices, which were built in 1964. Approaching the building at Lyssachschachen, near Burgdorf, visitors would not think that they were about to arrive at the workplace of the designer of nearly 1000 thin shell concrete structures. Without suitable directions it would be difficult to encounter by chance, as there is no sign directing the casual visitor and, once there, no large polished brass plate announcing its function. Taking the path from Kirchberg along the south side of the River Emme, which gives its name to the region and the Emmental cheese for which it is famous, one first passes a dilapidated timber building. Then following the route through the trees lining the riverbank a large industrial building topped with Isler bubble shells appears between the trees.

Although close by, this is not the office, being one of Isler's projects, a factory for the former Moser Company, also constructed in 1964. One has to continue further along the rough shale track, with a small wood and the sound of the fast flowing river to the left and an open field stretching towards the Burgdorf–Solothurn railway line to the right. After about 300 m one sees a fantastic structural graveyard hidden among young trees and shrubs and, at its heart, a two-storey concrete building half-buried in the ground. *Figure 1.13* shows the Isler office, soon after it was constructed, and *Fig. 1.14* shows it as it is today, blending into the surrounding woodland.

When Heinz Isler first decided to construct his own offices for his engineering consultancy firm, he originally proposed a building made of lightweight glass-reinforced polyester boxes that could be fabricated off site and transported to the final location by truck, railway or helicopter. At the time he was experimenting with this material and developing many interesting structures with it. However, his bank was not prepared to finance such a scheme but would if he redesigned the building in reinforced concrete, a more traditional material that was understood better.

The present two-storey building is made of reinforced concrete and is 'Y' shaped in plan, with 120° between each of the equal length wings. It houses a laboratory (or 'Feinlabor'), a workshop, archives, a model storage and exhibition area, a lecture space for 50 people and

Fig. 1.11. Sydney Opera House 1957-73 (Architect: Jørn Utzon, Engineers: Ove Arup and Partners) is made from triangular segments of a sphere.

private rooms in the basement, while the design offices, administration offices, meeting room and Heinz Isler's own study are housed on the upper level. Each floor is 400 m² in area. The three, 10 m long wings stretch out from the hexagonal entrance foyer, which is full of large plants thriving under the subdued light filtering through the 4·5 m diameter polyester shell dome at its centre. Inside it is much like most design offices save for the large number of shell models that are on display. However, outside it is striking for the apparent neglect, which is in fact deliberate, giving it back to nature.

Heinz Isler has experienced the impermeability of good quality concrete, if it is in compression to avoid the development of tensile cracks. He applied this conviction to the design of the flat roof of his office. His reasoning was thus. A simple-span beam or slab in bending exhibits compressive stresses in the upper portion and tension in the lower. Concrete in compression is generally uncracked. Good quality concrete is impermeable. Therefore, the top surface of a simple-span slab made from good quality concrete should be impermeable. If the slab is also lightly prestressed then there is even less

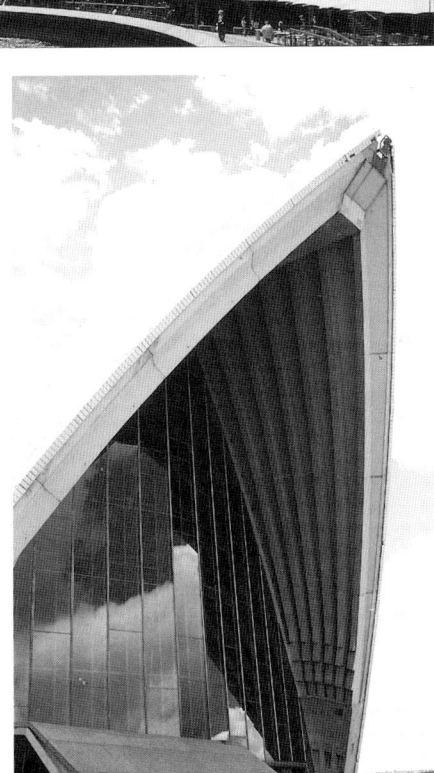

Fig. 1.12. The concrete ribs used to form the curved segments of the Sydney Opera House.

Chapter One
Shells, the man, his philosophy and influences

Fig. 1.13. Heinz Isler's office, soon after it was constructed in 1964.

possibility of cracking and water penetration. Following this rationale he decided to construct the roof of his office using an unprotected prestressed concrete slab supported on flexible columns that would allow the slab to move and bend freely and even sag in a shallow catenary.

Despite the slab being cast on wood-wool slabs when it was first constructed the offices were found to get very hot on summer afternoons when the ambient temperature in the region can sometimes reach well over 30°C. The roof was behaving as a massive radiator heated by the sun. In an effort to reduce this effect, the roof drainage was blocked in order to maintain a thin layer of water on the surface to reflect the heat of the sun and absorb energy by evaporation. However, it was found that once all the rainwater had been warmed up the thin layer of red algae made the surface darker and more solar energy was absorbed. Nevertheless, slowly the algal layer built up, turned green and transformed the energy into biomass. Plants started to grow on the roof surface, first lichens, mosses and grasses, then small bushes and finally small trees, until today the office is practically hidden below a small thicket. The roof, now 35 years after its construction, remains damp throughout the year and the overheating problem has disappeared. It is host to wild flowers, some not seen in the area for 50 years, and trees up to 10 m high. And the roof has remained watertight, without the least maintenance or repair.

The domed roof light mentioned above is yellow/brown in colour. This is one of the disadvantages of using polyester. It slowly turns brown from the light, so an ultraviolet (UV) absorber must be incorporated in the material. This absorber prevents the polyester from turning red or brown but the UV light consumes it within seven years. Then the discoloration process starts. To continue to protect it, one must apply a coat of UV filter on top, which will last approximately another seven years before it needs to be renewed once more. If one does not renew the coating after seven years, the polyester begins to yellow. The dome in the Isler offices is now over 30 years old and it has never been recoated or even cleaned. However, he likes the pleasant filtered light and mellow atmosphere that this produces and the plants obviously thrive on it. The external surface has never been cleaned, so the dirt takes about 50% of the light. Inside the dome is stained brown because of condensation, which encourages the growth of algae. It could be cleaned but Heinz Isler prefers to let nature take its course.

The incorporation of a teaching area in the offices is also very important to Isler as he enjoys telling all that are willing to listen and learn about the exciting things one can do with structures. Nearly every month he is host to individuals, groups of university students or other interested groups (even school children) that come to visit him. He can then show them experiments and make explanations in the lecture room and around the exhibitions.

Besides the frequent courses, lectures and seminars held by Isler himself, others have also taken the subject of modern shells into their teaching. One of the first was Prof. Tsuboi of Tokyo University, who immediately following Isler's presentation in Madrid, in 1959, included Isler's methods in the teachings of his school. Another was Prof. David Billington who created an exhibition of Isler's work that travelled around the main universities in the USA and some in Japan. Since 1974, Prof. Billington, when lecturing about structures, technology and the history of engineering, all over the United States, in summer sessions for teachers as well as for undergraduate students, has included in his dozens of classes a lecture about Heinz Isler's shells.

Fig. 1.14. Heinz Isler's office, as it is today, August 1999, blending into the surrounding woodland.

Professors Ramm and Schunck created a very successful exhibition 'Isler shells' which so far has been presented at 27 universities in Europe. More recently, the late Prof. Hangai of Tokyo University and Mr Y. Isono created a book containing details of hundreds of interesting structures including several Isler shells. Their locations are given and instructions on how one can find them, including even bus and train timetables.[25]

The story of the office roof confirms one of the greatest influences in Heinz Isler's work, his love of the natural world. This is where he gains inspiration and stimulation and he believes that

Chapter One
Shells, the man, his philosophy and influences

the human race should make the minimum intervention in the environment. i.e. the minimum of new construction using the minimum of material at the least cost in terms of energy and destruction of the beauty that surrounds us.

At his private house, a large Swiss farmhouse at the end of a winding lane, he continues to apply this philosophy. He has left the immediately surrounding land (previously devoted to intensive agriculture) to mature into a small natural wood, which provides shelter for deer and foxes. Interspersed within this wood are small structures and disintegrating trees, some of which have been taken over by wild animals for their homes. Adjacent land that he owns is rented to local farmers on the agreement that they use no fertilisers or poisons. To improve the quality of the water running through the site, which had been over fertilised from agricultural activities, he diverted the drainage water out of it's pipes into the open air. The water now passes through the young woodland where he has had dug a series of linked ponds to allow a natural self-creating purification system to develop. It is something like a reed bed but one established by the biosphere itself.

Isler likes the wilderness with its richness of content and picturesque aspects. He says that two other similar biotopes are growing just half an hour's bicycle or ski-walking distance away and comments that he gives back to nature what has been taken from it.

Creative play

It is sometimes said that children are born creative and that their creativity is then educated out of them: that creative play is the mother of invention and innovation. Heinz Isler has not forgotten how to play and this is, perhaps, one of the reasons he is so innovative. To reveal something of the playfulness of Isler, one might tell of his love of model trains. When growing up in the 1930s, like many young boys at that time, he had a train set. But he was told to sell it when he was 12 and the whole set was disposed of for 100 Swiss Francs. On his way to school he daily passed by the house where the set had been purchased, hoping to see someone playing with it or to be invited in to play. But no such thing ever happened. Many years later, while already in Burgdorf, he passed down the same street and saw a model locomotive for sale in a shop window. The price was exactly the same as he had sold his entire set for, 100 Swiss Francs. Undeterred by the price, he returned to buy it and made a small circuit to run it in his lodgings. Later, he constructed a short straight track in the grounds of his office but realised that the grass would grow too high and that the track would sink into the soil. Experiments making raised track with plastic sleepers cut from old watering cans and rails made from galvanised iron band were unsuccessful due to corrosion problems. Therefore, finally, he had fabricated 30 m rolls of special metal alloy to make his own rails and plastic supports to elevate the track. With this he laid a circuit of one third of a kilometre and ran seven trains. Sadly, the system is now falling into disrepair through lack of use, time and maintenance.

Another aspect of this playfulness is exhibited in Isler's passion for producing delicate ice structures in the depths of the cold Swiss winters. These magical forms are lit at night and visitors, school classes and television companies come to see them. Although this might at first appear rather childish, it definitely is not. This is serious play, the results of which provide statical insight, stimulation and inspiration for Isler's design of concrete structures. His experiments in this field are described in detail in chapter seven.

A final example of Isler's continual playful experimentation is his use of exotic materials for modelling of structural behaviour.[26] He cites the local Emmental cheese as being an excellent material for investigating concrete structures, as it is an elastic material with very limited tensile strength — just like concrete. Isler says that it is perfect for seeing, within seconds, where reinforcement is required around prestressing anchorages. He describes how when he presses into the cheese with his thumb it first goes in and then the cheese begins to crack. So he can see directly the disposition of the tension forces, which he will have to reinforce against to avoid bursting of his structures.

The future of the practice

There is no doubt that Heinz Isler is the inspiration behind the work of his practice. Over the previous decades, he says that there have been perhaps six possible successors from the engineers that have worked for him. However, none have stayed, as all have realised that Isler was the creator of this structural art form and that they never would be able to live up to that. Once an engineer with another practice did approach Isler with the suggestion that they should form a partnership. The potential partner was perhaps more entrepreneur than engineer and Isler felt that his own passion for the shells was not fully shared. Consequently, the deal was never signed. So as Isler puts it, he is 'continuing to work with his crew'.[27]

Chapter Two
Finding the form and proving its strength

Chapter Two
Finding the form and proving its strength

Given the number and complexity of the shell structures that Heinz Isler has constructed since the 1950s, his design methods may surprise many readers. On entering his office one would expect to see several powerful computer workstations running sophisticated finite elements modelling software. But there are none. Isler's methods are based on finding the correct form and then conducting small-scale model tests to verify the performance of the shell. Models from many past projects are proudly displayed around the offices. In this chapter it is proposed to take the reader through the design processes that Isler's shells undergo, from their conception in his highly inventive mind to the monitoring of full-scale structures on site, sometimes for decades after their construction.

Why shells?

Before explaining the form-finding processes that Heinz Isler uses it might be helpful to show the efficiency of thin shell structures in order to understand why he has devoted most of his professional life to their design and construction. In the corner of the office basement where Isler lectures and demonstrates to visiting students of all ages (from school children to postgraduates), to architects and to engineers, there is a simple physical model (*Fig. 2.1*), which consists of two sheets of thin plastic. One sheet is flat and the other formed into a double-curved shell arch. Putting the flat sheet across two supports, Isler places a small weight at its mid-span and immediately the sheet deflects and rests on the baseboard. The shell arch sits on the base and has a thin tie connecting its end supports to resist any outward thrust. Upon this Isler places a weight 30 times heavier than that on the flat sheet and only slight movement takes place. The ties become a little straighter but any deflection of the shell is hardly detectable by eye. He explains that, although the same volume of material is used in both cases, in the latter case the loadbearing capacity and resistance to deformation have been greatly enhanced by the addition of curvature. A simple bending element has been transformed into a thin shell. Despite the arch shape not being ideal to resist the centrally applied point load (as this results in bending as well as pure compression in the arch) the structure is still very much more efficient than the flat plate acting as a simple beam. This is what Isler is searching for, structural forms where the least material is disposed in the best way to resist the applied forces with the minimum of stress and deformation.

The process of form-finding

The majority of building structures consist of a framework of horizontal beams or trusses supported by vertical columns. Therefore, to some engineers and architects it comes as a surprise that one might have to determine the form of one's structure before being able to calculate its load carrying capacity and stiffness. This process is necessary for all form active structures including tension membranes and thin concrete compression shells. The skill in the design of such structures is the determination of the most efficient form, such that for the most common load condition the surface is in pure tension or compression respectively. For tension membranes the most commonly applied load is usually the prestress, which greatly exceeds the loading due to the material's own weight. However, for thin concrete shell structures the main load is their own weight, which is usually higher than any wind load, temporary snow load or other imposed load. Therefore, the most desirable form for a thin concrete shell is that where the surface is in pure compression over the whole surface under its own weight.

Form-finding, as the process is known, can be approached from many different starting points and Heinz Isler uses various methods to determine the appropriate shape for his shells. Observation of the natural world, where most structures have organic shapes with double curvature is very important to him,[28] however, he mainly uses physical models to search for efficient structural forms. Some of the modelling techniques are founded on the principle that a loaded structure in pure tension, when inverted, will be the perfect form for a similarly loaded pure compression structure.[29] This is appropriate as most, but not all, of Isler's shells are made from reinforced concrete, the major component of which is a material strong in compression but weak in tension.[30] Several ways of achieving such tension forms are described in detail below in relation to the types of shell for which they are used.

'Bubble' shells

As related in the previous chapter, the origin of Heinz Isler's bubble shells[31] was his observation of the shape of the plumped-up pillow on his bed. This form makes itself automatically due to the outward pressure exerted on the pillowcase by the feathers or other stuffing material inside (*Fig. 2.2*). Isler's problem was how to make an artificial pillow of a form suitable for use as a structure and accurate enough to be measured and scaled up to 50 or 100 times its original dimensions. His solution was simple. He constructed a rectangular wooden frame and placed it on a wooden baseboard, which had a small central hole drilled in it with a sealed connection to a flexible pipe and hand pump. With a sheet of pliable rubber sandwiched between the frame and the baseboard and the two wooden sections clamped firmly together to restrain the perimeter of the sheet, he was then able to gently inflate the rubber membrane into a double-curved synclastic[32] surface. This generally domed shape is in pure tension and, therefore, when inverted would be suitable for a compression shell under the same or similar loading.

The original rectangular wooden frame[33] exists still in the basement of Isler's offices (*Fig.*

Fig. 2.1. Model demonstrating the efficiency of a double-curved shell made from thin plastic compared to a similar plastic sheet acting as a wide flat beam over the same span. The load on the shell is 30 times the load on the flat sheet.

2.3), where it is stored with a cover to prevent deterioration of the rubber membrane, which becomes brittle with ultraviolet light. Another, square demonstration model (*Fig. 2.4*), with a square grid marked on the surface so that the effect of inflation is easily discernible, also resides in the corner of the teaching area of the basement.

However, with the basic form, *Fig. 2.3*, there is a drawback. At the corners of the rectangular frame, the curvature of the membrane becomes negative, that is, in the opposite sense to the rest of the surface, and this is undesirable as it results in a reversal of the line of thrust[34] in the shell. To avoid this phenomenon, Isler has to make a correction to the form. The solution he adopts is to round off the corners of the

Chapter Two
Finding the form and proving its strength

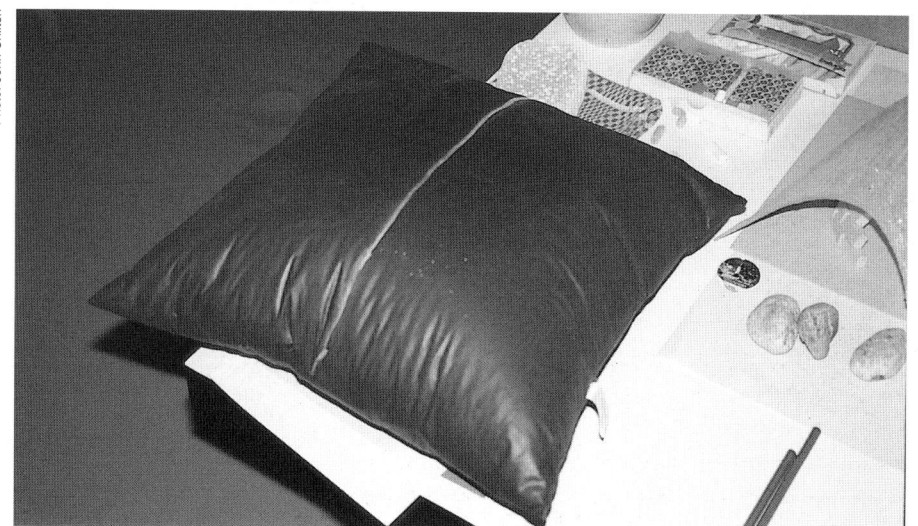

Fig. 2.2. Plumped up pillow - the inspiration for Isler's bubble shells.

rectangle,[35] giving a slight curve in plan. With this correction the membrane adopts a form where the whole surface has positive curvature, *Fig. 2.4*. A permanent record of the inflated shape can be made by covering the rubber with a quick setting material such as plaster (*Fig. 2.5*).

Inflated by air pressure, the rubber membrane is formed by load acting perpendicular to its surface whereas the weight of the concrete shell, which is the predominant loading, acts vertically under the force of gravity. Hence, the majority of the concrete shell's strength is used to resist the effects of gravity on the material from which it is made. If the shells are reasonably flat and not too large this difference in loading direction may be ignored.[36] Further, the clamped perimeter of the membrane resists horizontal as well as vertical forces. However, as Isler was to discover later, from laboratory tests where he measured the stress distribution on physical models, such forms span mainly from corner to corner with only a small proportion of the applied load being carried along the sides.

These loading tests were carried out because Isler wished to determine the distribution of stresses in the shell and to calculate the required strength of supporting walls beneath the shell perimeter. In order to do that he had to know what the force was, that was coming down onto the wall. He measured the forces on the scale model and, because he did not get the results that he was expecting, thought that there was some mistake; so he measured them again with the same result. Then he measured them for a third time in a different way, again with the same result. At first he could not understand what was happening. The total weight of the shell was 100% but the strange thing was that the walls, in total, received only 10% of that load. That is to say 10 times less than he thought they should.[37] However a total of 90% of the roof load was arriving directly at the four corners. That meant 22·5 % of the roof load to each corner and only 2·5% distributed along each side wall. Isler was struggling to explain this until he realised that different areas of the shell had different forms, some stiffer than others — some parts more conical, some more spherical and other parts more cylindrical.[38] The load was being attracted to the stiffer areas of the shell, which in

Fig. 2.3. The original rectangular wooden frame inflated membrane model used by Isler to investigate his bubble shells.

Fig. 2.4. Square demonstration inflated membrane model, with a square grid marked on the surface so that the effect of inflation is easily discernible.

this case were the four corners.

From these experiments Isler realised that it was possible to support the bubble shells only at the corners and on light edge beams and still retain a stable and efficient structure.[39] Any small percentage of roof load attracted to the edge beams is carried by prestressing cables running slightly deviated between the corner columns. These are the same prestressing cables that pre-compress the shell surface to ensure that tension is never present, not even due to local bending effects. The architect, therefore, has almost complete freedom in the design of the façade of these structures, which are able to span up to 60 m without intermediate perimeter supports.

Expansion forms

Another form that Heinz Isler has studied is that of 'expansion', 'flow' or 'growth' forms. These can be seen when, for instance, a loaf of bread rises in the baking tin or plastic foam bursts forth from the mouth of a tube. In the natural world the growth of certain fungi (*Fig. 2.6*) or fruit provide similar examples. The varied rate of advance causes the expanding material to form a double curved surface. Such forms came to Isler's attention when he was visiting a factory where he noticed an 'organic hill form' being generated by polyurethane foam oozing from a square cup. There at the top was a rounded form produced by the expanding foam. The shells inspired by this observation are described in chapter four.

Free-form shells from hanging membranes

A further method of form-finding used by Heinz Isler is to suspend a membrane between supports disposed in the same relative positions as in the real structure and leave it to deform under its own uniform load. Under this load the membrane takes up a shape such that, within it, only tensile forces are present, as a cloth (wet or dry) affords no resistance to bending or compression. By inverting the form so obtained the resulting structure will be in pure compression when subjected to similar vertical loading. This idea came to Isler in the early summer of 1955 when he observed a piece of jute cloth, soaked by overnight rain, suspended across a square mesh of steel reinforcing bars — the cloth was forming a tension surface purely under its own weight.[40]

Chapter Two
Finding the form and proving its strength

Fig. 2.5. Acquiring the form by inflation of the membrane just as the plaster mixture is setting.

Fig. 2.6. 'Expansion' or 'growth' form - for example, some fungi.

Such hanging forms have been used for projects such as the service station roof at Deitingen (1968), Sicli Building, Geneva (1969/70), the outdoor theatre and dance studios at Stetten (1976/9), an outdoor theatre at Grötzingen (1977), near Stuttgart and a large number of tennis and sports halls. These structures are described in detail in chapter five.

Perhaps one of the simplest ways to generate these shapes was demonstrated by Heinz Isler at an international seminar of the Structural Morphology Group of IASS,[41] which was held in Stuttgart in 1994. Fittingly, this demonstration took place on the stage of the rehearsal theatre at Stetten auf den Fildern, under a shell roof designed by Isler with the architect Michael Balz. Initially Isler showed, with only limited success due to problems with the plaster, the technique with the inflated membrane. Then he showed a small cloth suspended between four short dowels attached to a baseboard. After carefully pouring a quantity of self-setting polyester resin[42] into a shallow dish, he immersed the cloth in the liquid resin and gently withdrew it. Under the weight of the resin the cloth took up a hanging form, which was then bathed in ultraviolet light to speed up the setting process. The resulting form is shown in *Fig. 2.7*. This method of form-finding obviously has huge potential for the development of many exciting new structural types.

Using this method Isler discovered an aesthetically pleasing manner of stiffening the edges of his free-form shells. Initially, he was suspending pieces of cloth between the supports by their corners and striving to achieve a straight edge. This gave very interesting shell forms but the free edges remained susceptible to buckling (*Fig. 2.8*). However, one day he did not remove the excess cloth that lay outside the lines between supports, so the cloth was suspended inward of the corners. The result surprised him. Instead of hanging limp and vertical, the area of material outside the direct line between the supports took up a double-curved form, which made the edges more rigid (*Fig. 2.9*).

This is the difference between Isler's early free-form shells, described in chapter four and those derived from hanging forms, described in chapter five. The former have an approximately spherical central area of shell that has its edges stiffened by cantilevered shells that spring at an angle normal to the main shell. There is a distinct change of direction and sometimes prestressing is required along the edge of the cantilevered shells to compensate for traction. In the latter, there is no abrupt change of direction at the edge but a smooth transition, and the stiffening element requires no additional prestress. Because the shape is derived from the hanging form, where all is in tension, when the standard prestressing is applied between the corner supports the whole surface, including the upturned edges, is stressed in compression. In the first case, with a lot of effort, Isler made a counter curvature along the edge with the cantilevering roof but in the second case it came automatically.[43]

Isler has commented that it was a sort of 'not-correctness' in his idea at first, a mistake. He was unhappy that this experiment did not succeed but finally he realised that it was giving him the solution for three problems that he had not thought of. He believes that so many things have come to him through his experiments. He has done something, wanted a specific result and yet only later did he see that the model is much cleverer than he, giving him answers for problems that he did not know he had! Taking this process even further one finds that if there is too much material the edge again becomes flexible with reduced buckling resistance.

Other hanging forms that Isler has explored are even easier to produce. Very attractive gently folded surfaces, almost like a flower, may be generated by simply saturating a cloth with the resin and then lifting one point at the centre of the surface (*Fig. 2.10*). This generates the form of a compression structure directly as in this case, instead of inverting the structure the load is

Fig. 2.7. Hanging membrane model generated by self-setting polyester resin.

Photo: Heinz Isler

Chapter Two
Finding the form and proving its strength

applied in the reverse direction. Although Isler sees these mainly as playful experiments, theoretically, such structures would be ideal for supporting large single point loads. Similar forms can also be produced on cold winter nights by simply leaving outside a suitably draped wet cloth to freeze overnight. Many such hanging forms have started life in Heinz Isler's winter playground, the magical world of ice structures that he creates in the garden at his house each year. These beautiful and enchanting creations are shown in chapter seven.

The finding of an appropriate form for a shell is not a simple process. Many factors have to be considered, not least the aesthetic appearance and structural performance of the shell.

Therefore, in Heinz Isler's offices one may see the many and various development models that have been used to refine the form, to get it looking just right while efficiently carrying the loads using the minimum of material. Form-finding is the first step in the design process. The other equally important steps are the determination of the forces within the shell, the reinforcing, its stability, the way of measuring the double-curved form, its construction and long-term monitoring of the shell's behaviour.

Forces in the shell

At the beginning of this chapter, Heinz Isler's minimal use of computers was mentioned. This lack of computing facilities can perhaps be explained by his description of how easy it is to estimate the forces and stresses in many of his shell surfaces by simple hand calculation or even in one's head.

Isler says that he has a different attitude to statics. He considers that, where traditional statics ends, with loads, moments, shear forces, torsion, reinforcement, stresses (positive, negative and combined) etc., where a normal calculation ends, there the calculation of a shell starts. He is confident that he can analyse many of his shells approximately, by hand, in a few seconds. He can tell you roughly what the stresses are and they are so small that he does not really need to prove it. In the majority of the shell surface they are not even 15% of what is allowed, so even quite large

Fig. 2.8. Hanging membrane model with unstiffened free edges.

Fig. 2.9. Hanging membrane model with upturned stiffened free edges.

errors in the approximations are insignificant.[44] Sketches made by Isler during the following explanation are shown in *Fig. 2.11*.

Take, for example, a typical shell on four corner supports.[45] The predominant load is self-weight and one can say that the load on one corner is a quarter of the total load. Hence, knowing the area of the roof, the uniform imposed load and taking a typical shell thickness of 100 mm, it is very straightforward to calculate the total vertical load and, hence, the vertical reaction at each support. Assuming that there are no moments in the shell and given the angle that the shell makes with the ground at the supports, the horizontal reactions and the axial force in the leg can easily be determined — by resolution of forces i.e. simple statics. Then knowing the cross-section of the leg the mean stress within it can be found.

Once the forces at the supports have been found it is then straightforward to determine the stresses at the mid-span of the shell. With uniform loading on a symmetrical compression shell there are only horizontal forces acting at mid-span and these are the same as the horizontal reactions at the supports. Therefore, given, for instance, a length of 20 m across a shell profile and taking 100 mm as the thickness, the stressed area is 2 m². Assuming a horizontal reaction of say 100 tonnes, the stress in the shell at mid-span is then 50 t/m², or 0·5 N/mm². Compare that with the 28-day crushing strength of good quality concrete, say 40 N/mm², and one can see that even large errors in the assumptions are unlikely to mean that actual stresses even approach the strength of the material. The mean stress at mid-span is a little over 1% of the crushing strength, or perhaps 4% of the design strength. Although the stress distribution in the shell is not uniform, even if the maximum is three times higher than the mean, then the working stress due to the loads will still only be 1·5 N/mm², around 10 to 12% of the design strength.

If the shell is thin enough there are practically no moments. All of Isler's shells have only small moments but they are not considered significant. Isler says that he can calculate the stresses in a typical shell while walking from his study to the tearoom. He knows the answer from experience and from his experiments with the

Fig. 2.10. 'Flower' form generated by lifting one point of a draped cloth.

Chapter Two
Finding the form and proving its strength

physical models. In a shell of 20 or 30 m span he would expect the stresses to vary from about 1·5 to 3·0 N/mm², including the effect of the prestressing. However, Isler considers this to be simple statics with the real problems starting later. What he is most anxious and careful about is the shell's resistance to buckling instability and the long-term behaviour.

Only at the point supports does Isler have to calculate a moment, and for that moment the stresses, because the foot of the shell is the only point where the stresses go above 50% of the allowable concrete strength. A great reserve of strength has been shown by full-scale tests (discussed in the next chapter) carried out on some of Isler's bubble shells before they were demolished to make way for another building.

Model tests

Isler determines the forces in his model shells using electronic strain gauges and the buckling behaviour from load tests. A typical model testing arrangement is shown in *Fig. 2.12*. The polyester model is set within a timber framework and load is applied through small wooden pads distributed evenly across the surface to simulate the uniform loading. Isler makes many frameworks from wood but this means that he has to continually monitor the temperature and humidity in his north-facing basement laboratory to ensure that measurements are only taken when the wood is in a stable state.

A single load is applied at one location, by hydraulic jack or dead weight, and distributed to

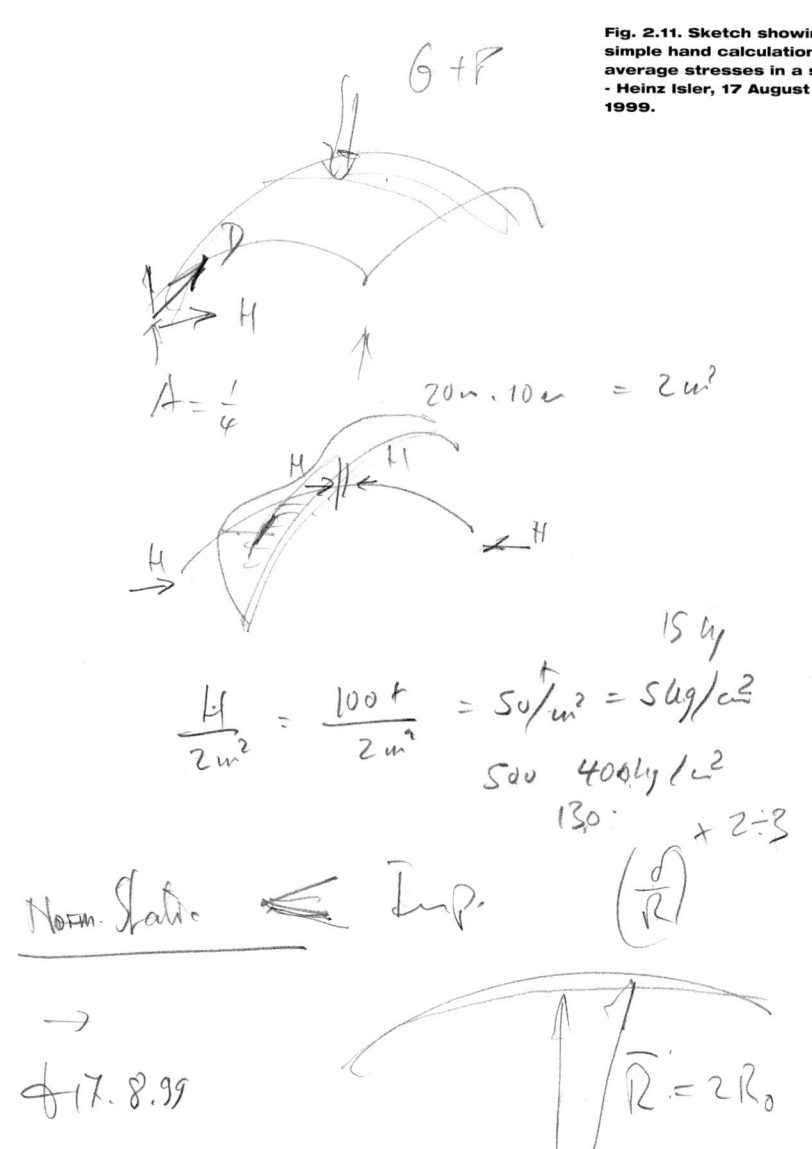

Fig. 2.11. Sketch showing simple hand calculation of average stresses in a shell - Heinz Isler, 17 August 1999.

40

the individual patch loading points by a system of small wooden beams connected in the appropriate manner. This enables Isler to apply full uniform load, half- or quarter-uniform load or even point loads if he wishes. By means of movable supports he is also able to apply prestress forces to the model shells or determine the effect of subsidence of the supports. The former can be applied using pulley systems and the latter by adjustable screws to change the position of the support. *Figure 2.13* shows the model used to check the effects of re-stressing a shell that was affected by a severe fire, in order to return it to its original form (described in detail in chapter four). All the models are preserved for further investigations to be carried out if necessary. At least one model has been loaded to assess its long-term behaviour over several years. Today, the systematic testing of scale models that was previously carried out in Isler's office to determine statically behaviour has mainly been replaced by computer calculations, as they are quicker and give more information. However, in important cases, accompanying models are still used to verify the computer results.

Instability

As Isler describes it, the different possible instabilities of the shells are first at the supports, second due to general buckling, third due to local buckling of the free edge (for which the counter curvature is so important) and finally other modes. It is possible to study all these different kinds of buckling with Isler's models, which are deliberately made too weak.[46] He discovered more than a dozen different buckling modes with his models.

In a paper presented at a colloquium in 1982, Isler gave his general equation for shell buckling which he described as his 'private "compass"…'[47]

$$P_k = c \cdot E \cdot (t/r)^x \geq s \cdot P_{eff}$$

Where

P_k is the critical buckling load

c is a modification factor, the product of alpha — a number between 0·2 and 1·2, beta — a practical reduction factor for inaccuracies etc. (about 0·3), and gamma — a form specific factor for every shape

E is the modulus of elasticity (short- and long-term)

t is the shell thickness

r is the local radius of curvature

x is a power between about 2 and 3 dependent on the form (2·5 to 3 for a cylinder and 2 for a sphere)

s is the safety factor

P_{eff} is the actual load.

According to this equation, the critical load in the shell is a function of the radius of the element in compression, its thickness and its elastic modulus with modifying factors that depend on the form of the shell and an assessment of how well it is constructed. As he

Fig. 2.12. Typical model testing arrangement in Isler's basement laboratory.

Chapter Two
Finding the form and proving its strength

points out in the paper a long cylindrical shell has only about one thirtieth (approximately 3%) of the buckling resistance of a spherical shell of the same thickness and radius. The form of a shell is therefore highly important.

The elastic modulus of the polyester or Plexiglas that Isler uses for models to investigate the buckling of his shells is 6000 N/mm². This is much lower than that of concrete, which is about 30 000 N/mm², and very much lower than steel, which is around 200 000 N/mm². When a more elastic and thinner polyester material is used, buckling occurs at the same location and in the same manner, but at a much lower load. Therefore, the buckling behaviour can be studied more easily and the critical buckling load established by experiment for the weak model. The actual buckling load can then be calculated for the real shell by multiplying this load by the appropriate ratios of elasticity, radius and thickness etc.

The initial cast form and the subsequent deformation under load are both very relevant to the buckling behaviour of shells because the structures rely on curvature to resist buckling. Therefore, the flatter they are the more likely they are to fail. This is because the radius of curvature reduces, so (t/r) becomes smaller and that parameter is taken to the power 2 or 3 in the buckling equation. There is reasonable management of the original shape by the use of a pure compression form for self-weight loading, accurate positioning of the formwork, use of good quality concrete and well controlled post-tensioning. However, with time the shell may deform with consequent reduction in buckling resistance. Similarly the initial thickness is very important as, for example, in a spherical shell with the parameter $(t/r)^2$ in the buckling equation, a reduction in thickness of 20 mm in a shell of 100 mm reduces the buckling resistance of the thinner shell to just 64% of the thicker.

Usually, Isler sees only small deformations in his shells, even over 15 years. If it is more than 50 mm it effectively increases the radius of curvature slightly and reduces its resistance to buckling. Taken to the extreme, if the original radius were to double, then the safety factor goes down to a quarter or one eighth depending on the shape of the shell. So instead of a safety factor of three one would have 0·75 or 0·375, and that means the shell would collapse. So the deformation of a shell is critical for its stability, for its load carrying capacity and for its life. Therefore, Isler insists that he has to be very careful to keep deformations to the minimum. This cautious attitude has meant that right from the beginning of his career as a designer of thin concrete shells, Isler has diligently recorded the long-term movements of many of his structures.

He considers that there are many processes and phenomena that affect the movement of his shells, such as creep and shrinkage, but in some cases these well-known phenomena do not seem to explain what is occurring and one cannot predict the behaviour. Particular problems occur when the radius of the shell surface becomes bigger, when it becomes flatter, especially in areas that are initially quite flat. In fact there was one shell that Isler became very anxious about as it was deforming in a way that he thought might endanger its stability. First he looked for mistakes in his calculations then, on finding none, he had the same shell analysed independently by different organisations (as a new project) using the latest finite element computer methods. All the results were positive, indicating that there was no stability problem with the shell. He still does not totally believe the results but thinks that he was fortunate to have designed the original form with a more than sufficient factor of safety.

Measuring the form

To reduce the possibility of buckling failure of the shell it is essential that the initial surface be of the correct form. Therefore the measurement of the physical model, which is the result of a special experiment, is certainly one of the most important processes in the design of an Isler shell. Unless the shell is small or of a previously constructed form Heinz Isler carries out most of these measurements himself, sometimes working late into the night to do so. He also conducts all of the experiments to determine stresses in the shell surface and buckling loads. He declares that to create such models is a sort of art. To achieve such accuracy with every point precise to a fraction of a millimetre can be done only with great experience, great skill and much patience.

The device where Isler measures the three-dimensional form of the model shells (*Fig. 2.14*) is a simple wooden box frame with calibrated metal bars fixed along two opposite sides. A metal tubular section, with a third calibrated rod attached to one side, spans between these and carries a clamp holding a small diameter metal rod that is free to slide and equilibrated vertically. This arrangement allows him to move the pointed rod along predetermined lines in the 'x–y' plane and to measure the 'z' co-ordinate to an accuracy of one fiftieth of a millimetre. Vertical profiles are determined along lines specified by the contractor and these are usually along the lines where the main supporting beams for the formwork will be placed. This simplifies the measuring procedure, as measurements are taken directly from the models and only where needed, without frequent changes to the position of the beam spanning across the box. The readings are entered into tables, then the values are plotted onto a drawing as a series of large-scale sections. Here in the tables and the plotted sections any inaccuracies in the measurements are immediately apparent and the curves may be smoothed manually to correct any inconsistencies. The adjusted profile is finally scaled up appropriately to give manufacturing dimensions for the glued-laminated timber beams. Final, small adjustments to the profile may be made on site, when the beams are positioned vertically on lightweight scaffolding to give the closest possible agreement with the shape obtained in the model.

As they are measured to an accuracy of one fiftieth of a millimetre one might perhaps have expected the models to be made to a scale of 1 to 50, to give millimetre accuracy in the real structure. However, this is not the case. The same equipment is used for all models, no matter what is the size of the final structure. Its size is determined by the length of Heinz Isler's arms, as he finds it better to always measure the whole model from one position. He is to able move around the model to measure but has found that when he has tried this, more inconsistencies appear in the measurements. For instance, the small diameter rod used to gauge the 'z' co-ordinate is assumed to be straight but in reality it is not quite; it is slightly curved. Therefore, if used carelessly, it might lead to erroneous readings. For this reason, Heinz Isler always uses the rod in the same position, for which he has a mark that is always kept in sight when he takes a reading. He must be very careful to always do the same thing, repeating the same movements and looking in the same direction, to avoid errors due to parallax. This requires absolute concentration, so he carries out the measurements at night or on Sundays while his wife Maria holds phone calls at bay. If he does receive an urgent telephone call, he says that afterwards he can see the evidence in his readings. To check the readings, which are taken at regular intervals along the spanning rod, he records the differences between them and the second order differences, recording the curvature.

Fig. 2.13. Model used to check the effects of re-stressing a shell that was affected by a severe fire.

Chapter Two
Finding the form and proving its strength

If this does not change smoothly there is a problem.[48] Therefore, the measurement of the model shell surface has to be concentrated work of many hours duration, where Isler has to be very calm and quiet (not tired). Then he says, only then, does he get the precision he needs.

Construction

As under most loading conditions there is only compression in the shells it would theoretically be possible to use no reinforcement. Of course, although conceivable, Isler has never built any shell without reinforcement, because if something unexpected occurred then the unreinforced shell would be vulnerable to breakage. The reinforcement, therefore, is provided mainly for resistance to impact and/or local bending and a primary property of concrete, strength in compression, can be utilised to the full. In fact two layers of reinforcement are provided in Isler's shells, although this is not necessarily normal practice for all shell builders. However, he considers that two layers of reinforcement reduce deformations due to local bending[49] and therefore diminish the likelihood of instability due to buckling of the shell.

A desirable consequence of designing a concrete structure subject only to compression is that cracks are completely eliminated (at least in theory), which greatly reduces the possibility of corrosion of the steel reinforcement. To ensure that the shell form is in compression under all possible loading conditions, not just uniform load, it can be prestressed by pulling the support points slightly inwards using pre-tensioning cables within a foundation ring beam or across the diagonals. By prestressing as soon as the concrete has sufficient strength Isler ensures that there is never tension in his shells thus avoiding cracks and maintaining their impermeability. However, the ties have to be protected carefully from corrosion by full injection grouting of the cable ducts and prestressing the tie-beam to avoid cracks.

Monitoring of lifetime performance

As Heinz Isler observed in his paper presented at the International Association for Shell and Spatial Structures 30th Anniversary Congress,[50] 'good shells last for centuries'. He commented that his shells undergo a process of natural erosion, losing about 1 or 2 mm from their surface in the first ten years. The weaker surface layer of cement and fine sand is washed away leaving a lightly textured surface with the aggregate slightly exposed. He states that, over 35 years, this erosion does not usually exceed 2 to 4 mm and this may be reduced by coating the concrete surface. Where no coating is applied, Isler states that with time a harmless natural protective coating of lichens takes over the surface, providing the best and cheapest protection. Isler goes on to complain that there have been clients who thought that the lichens were harming the shells. He says that they used various means including scrubbing, chemicals and high-pressure water jets to remove the offending growth but at the same time often eroded the surface far more than would occur naturally in perhaps 200 years of normal service. After the brutal cleaning the shell was leaking at several points.

During a similar period of about 35 years the concrete (if initially of good quality) will suffer carbonation[51] to a depth of less than 10 mm — less than the cover to the reinforcing bars. In his paper Isler also describes certain surface defects where points of rust occur on the surface (at a rate of about one per 40 m^2, over a period of 20 years) but these are usually due to corrosion of reinforcement tying wires protruding slightly from the shell. These cosmetic blemishes can be repaired by cutting out the offending area then filling the small hole with mortar. Isler considers all of these effects to be highly important to the efficient performance of his shells. He also monitors their movements in order to understand better their 'state of health'.

At first, Heinz Isler says he was very proud when he found out that the maximum displacements of his shells were so small that instead of the 1/300 or 1/200 of the span accepted for most structures he was achieving 1/1000 or even as little as 1/5000. This made him think that it was not exceptional, firstly because he knew that his shells are very strong and secondly, because he believed that it confirmed how accurate his laboratory models were and how good his form-finding and measuring techniques. Then, because he was monitoring the

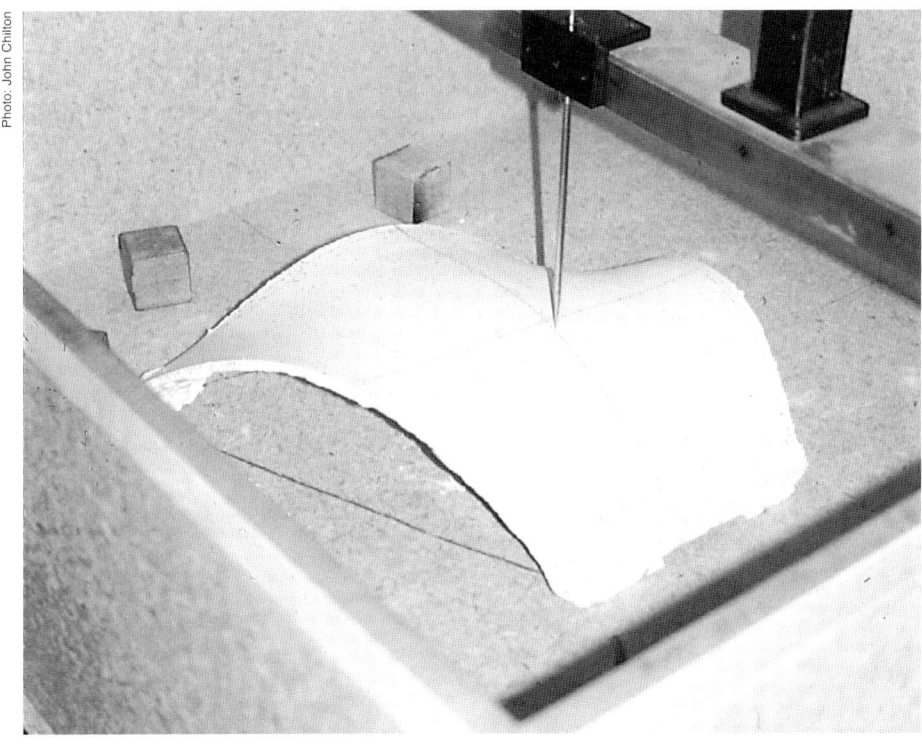

Fig. 2.14. The device with which Isler measures the three-dimensional form of the model shells.

long-term shape of his structures, he began to puzzle when he saw how his shells moved after one year, two years, five years, and even ten years after construction. He noted how they changed their shape from the original, so-called ideal shape. The shape became different and he became very cautious, circumspect and very modest. No longer did he proclaim his good initial small deformations but continued to watch the behaviour of his protégés. In his laboratory he has diagrams recording the long-term behaviour of model tests, over more than seven years, in which the shells deflect down and down until after five years their deformation stabilises. As Isler points out, few engineers even measure the deformation of the structures they design on the first day, or at all.

Heinz Isler not only measures the deformation of his shells on the first day but some of the shells also after the first week, the first month, the first year, the first decade, the third decade, for as long as he feels it is necessary. Then he can appreciate their long-term behaviour from his diagrams. Fortunately, most of the deformation curves have been asymptotic. When they are asymptotic he says 'that is a sound child now. I can stop, it's adult now'. But there have been cases which were not so, where he had to study the development of the whole circumstance very carefully. He comments that there is little published about the long-term behaviour of structures.[52] In his studies at the ETH, where the behaviour of large dams was covered, he learnt about the need for monitoring, about responsibility for one's creations and about the lifetime behaviour of a structure. He acknowledges that a dam is a very terrifying thing when it fails — it may take hundreds, even thousands of lives and that it is extremely important that they are safe, whereas his structures are relatively small. However, he adopted similar techniques to the dam

Chapter Two
Finding the form and proving its strength

Fig. 2.15. Scale model of the falsework and formwork for one of Isler's early shells.

monitoring in order to acquire his knowledge. He concludes that all calculations which are made in advance, be they very simple in one's head or on one page of paper, or with a formula, or with a sophisticated computer program, or with a model test, are just hypotheses that attempt to describe reality. For him the real life of a structure starts later and about that he thinks we know practically nothing (or at best very little).

Is the physical model dead?

At the IASS Structural Morphology Colloquium in Nottingham, in August 1997, Heinz Isler presented a paper with the above title.[53] His question concerned the ever-increasing use of computers in architectural and engineering design. Although he considers computers to be useful, in fact indispensable in modern life,[54] he considers that they are better left to routine work and repetitive activity for which they are admirably suited.

He is particularly concerned that within the

creative world of 'non-cubic' architecture it is invaluable if not essential to work with the human imagination and physical (and/or natural) models. As he pointed out, building actually takes place in three-dimensional space therefore design problems are also best studied in three-dimensions. To do this adequately requires the making of a physical model, as in its construction one has to confront many of the same problems that occur in the building itself.

For Isler the physical model is very important and the question of shape is best studied by modelling it, in a three-dimensional structure not just as a picture on a screen. A model is made of a certain material, which has its own physical properties, thickness, strength and elasticity. As Isler points out in his paper, the model requires joints, where different elements meet in space, either on a line or at a point. Everything has a thickness and is not an abstract dimensionless point. In model structures, elements that are too thin buckle just like real elements in buildings. He feels strongly that during the modelling process all of one's senses are involved.[55]

Apart from the models that Isler uses directly to find the form of his shells or the forces within them, he also has a multitude of exploratory and construction models. For instance, a foldable hyperbolic paraboloid, hinged at two opposing corners of the square frame. Points at equal distance along opposing edges are connected with elastic threads so that as the frame is folded out of plane, the threads form a double-curved saddle surface. In a corner he has a scale model of the falsework and formwork for one of his early shells (*Fig. 2.15*). A square frame supported by a net of radial and circumferencial cords hangs from a central support. A flat sheet of Mylar, stamped in the centre with a spherical die, forms a square based tented shape, a prototype for 12 m^2 structures never built. Altogether, there is a multitude of models and from this, it is obvious that for Heinz Isler the physical model is not dead and neither is shell building! To those who aspire to create efficient structures of beauty he may be an excellent example to follow.

Chapter Three
'Bubble' shells

Chapter Three
'Bubble' shells

The inspiration behind the development of the bubble shell, which is the most commonly constructed of all Isler's shell types, was, as described in chapter one, Isler's observation of the plumped-up pillow on the bed at his lodgings in 1954. Returning early one morning from the design office where he had been struggling with the geometry of a shell roof to cover a slightly tapering rectangular plan, he realised that here was a possible form to solve his problem. Subsequently, the inflated membrane model 'technical' pillow, described in the previous chapter, gave him the opportunity to determine various aesthetically pleasing forms and with cast models to ascertain the load paths within them. As noted previously, at first Isler expected that, when loaded in plan, the shells would give approximately equal load all around to the supporting walls. However, from his laboratory tests, he found this not to be true. With walls under each side of the shell the total reaction along the sides was only 10% of the total load (or

Fig. 3.2. Slightly rounded corners of the shell to avoid curvature reversal.

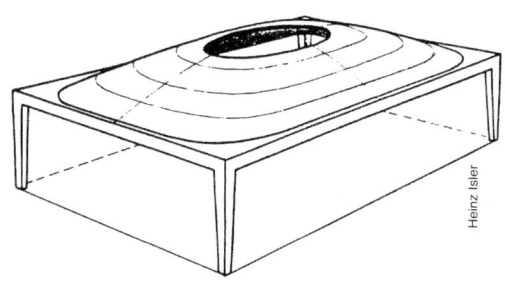

Fig. 3.1. Standard bubble shell type with only corner supports.

only 2·5% of the total to each side) and about 22·5% to each corner. As the load was already directing itself mainly to the more rigid corners, this enabled him to develop a standard shell type with only corner supports (*Fig. 3.1*). Within the rectangular plan between the columns, the thin shell was a smaller rectangle, framed by the edge beams. The shell had slightly rounded corners (*Fig. 3.2*) to avoid the curvature reversal, described earlier, which occurs at those locations if the corners are square. This enabled Isler to slightly taper the width of the edge beams, enlarging them near the columns to accommodate the prestressing cable anchorages,[56] as seen in the plan and section of *Fig. 3.3*. The edge beams also incorporate an integral gutter, which discharges rainwater into a downpipe concealed within each column. As a three-dimensionally stiff frame is formed between the edge beams, shell and columns, the cross-section of the legs can be tapered down towards their base — essentially, they can be pin-jointed at the lower end. The pleasing form of the gentle taper and corner curve of the edge beams and tapering of the column are shown in *Fig. 3.4* for the internal support of a multi-bay building for Eschmann, Thun.

Architectural considerations
Planning

These standard shells, which are mainly used for small industrial units, garages, warehouses and the like, can be assembled in groups to produce large open volumes with a very limited number of

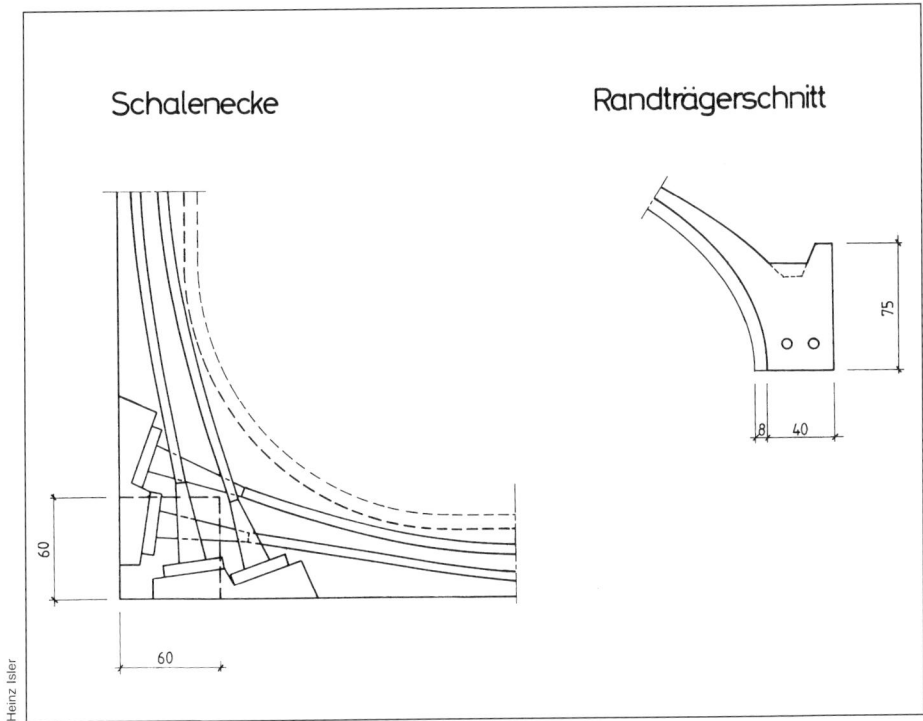

Fig. 3.3. Plan and section of typical prestressing cable anchorages in the bubble shells.

Fig. 3.4. The pleasing forms of the edge beams and column for the internal support of a multi-bay building for Eschmann, Thun.

internal supports (*Fig. 3.5*). For example, with four shells of 30 x 30 m, a floor area of 3600 m² would have only one internal column. Architecturally, the shells give great freedom for the design of the building elevations, as there are no intermediate supports for the roof. The only structure required on the elevations is that necessary to frame glazing and cladding in order to transmit wind forces to the ground floor and roof. If a large enough and strong enough pane of glass were available one would be able to have a completely clear façade.

Once Isler had set out on his own, between 1955 and 1959 a total of 33 shells of this type were constructed, ranging in size from 14 x 20 m up to a maximum size of 22 x 22 m. Rather than constructing individual shells, they were

Chapter Three
'Bubble' shells

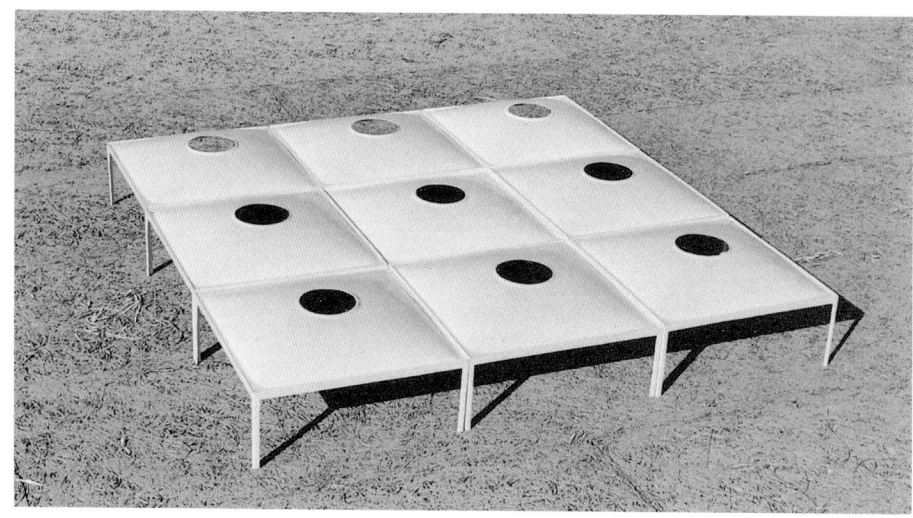

Fig. 3.5. Assembly of bubble shells into groups to produce large open volumes with a very limited number of internal support.

generally arranged in groups of various configurations. Standard sizes were developed in order to economise on the costs of formwork and falsework.

Shell thickness

It is rather difficult to appreciate fully how very thin the bubble shells are. At the edges there are beams, even though they are much lighter than one might expect for the distances they span (approximately 1/25 of the span including an upstand to form a gutter). At the rim of the openings for the skylights the true thickness of the shell is not seen either. This is because there is always a thickness of insulation, the permanent shuttering, and also because of the upstand around the opening that is necessary to prevent rainwater from entering. The total apparent thickness around the skylight is in the region of 250 to 300 mm, which still appears very thin. Yet only 80 to 100 mm of this is the structural shell! *Figure 3.4* shows an opening with practically no upstand.

Façades

One of the challenges to architects is that it is difficult for them to impose their personality on one of Isler's bubble shells. The form is so elegantly simple that the only place that remains for them to make their mark is in the façades. But because the shells generally span between corner supports at least 20 m apart, the façades are completely open canvases where they only have to span the short distance from ground to shell.

Isler finds, therefore, that architects (contrary to their normal habit) wish to emphasise the elevation whereas he himself usually tries to play it down, using small section mullions that are dark in colour.

Daylight and ventilation

A distinctive feature of all the standard bubble shells is the use of domed roof lights. For the smaller shells, up to 25 x 25 m, there is usually just one central dome but for bubble shells of 30 x 30 m four are generally used, one at the centre of each quadrant (*Fig. 3.6*). From the architectural point of view these roof lights have several advantages. Firstly, the intensity of light from above is greater than that entering through windows in the perimeter walls and this light is delivered to the centre of the large clear span where it reduces the need for artificial lighting during the day. Secondly, the roof lights can be opened to provide ventilation. As, in the smaller shells, these openings are at the highest point in the roof, the natural airflow is encouraged. Stale warm air collects at the high point of the shell where it is then vented while fresh air is drawn in at low level. The opening of the roof lights is achieved by the provision of hydraulic or electric lifting devices that raise the whole dome by up to 100 mm. On a typical 5 m diameter dome this provides a maximum ventilation opening of over 1·5 m² at the most advantageous location. The lifting devices on the roof of the Bösiger offices in Langenthal are shown in *Fig. 3.7*, in which the apparent thickness of the shell may also be noted.

As Isler points out, very good ventilation is achieved without any fan, without using any energy, and almost without noise. When ventilation is not required the skylight can be closed by releasing the oil pressure in the hydraulic system or by reversing the drive of the electric device. The form of the shells themselves and the domed skylights aid the ventilation due to the Venturi action. As the wind passes over the curved surfaces the pressure slightly decreases because of its increase in speed. This means that there is a small difference in air pressure at the perimeter of the skylight so air is sucked out by the motion of the wind. However, this causes no vibrations, because there is no turbulence due to

Fig. 3.7. The lifting devices on the roof of the Bösiger offices in Langenthal.

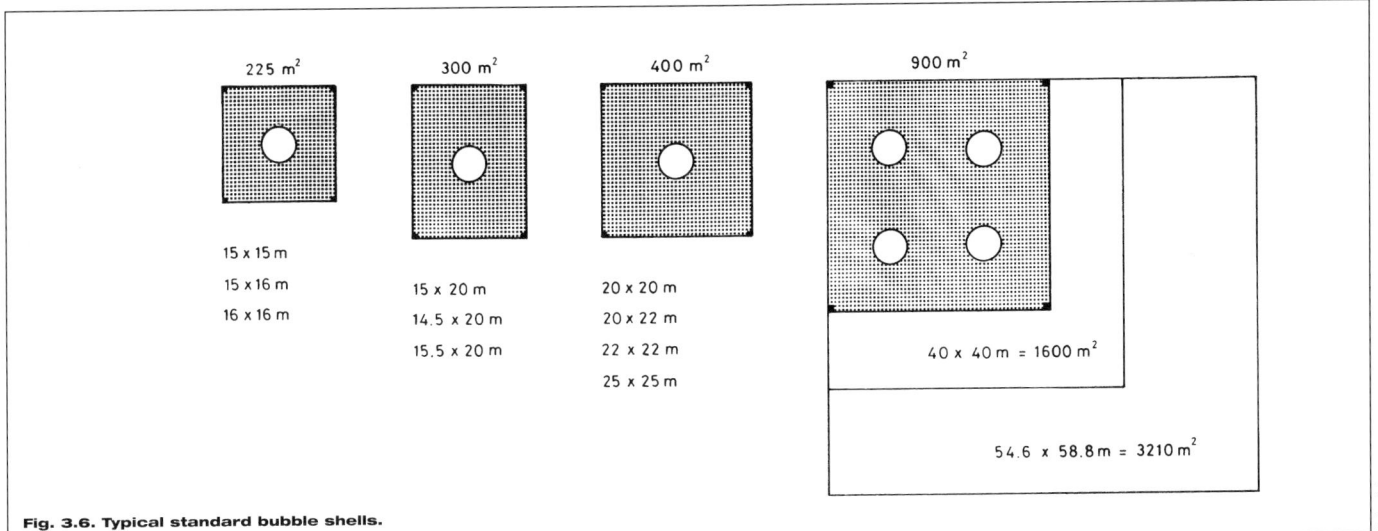

Fig. 3.6. Typical standard bubble shells.

Chapter Three
'Bubble' shells

Fig. 3.8. Lighting fixtures disposed in a star pattern radiating from the centre of the shell at the Avag Garage, Solothurn.

Fig. 3.9. Vehicle works of Moser AG, of Lyssach.

the overall aerodynamic shape.

Artificial lighting

Isler thinks that it is also important, from the architectural and functional points of view, to carefully consider the disposition of artificial light within the bubble shells. He dislikes the use of parallel lines of fluorescent tubes that bear no relation to the form of either the shell or the circular domed roof light. His preferred solutions are to place the lighting fixtures in a ring at some appropriate distance around the central skylight or in a star pattern radiating from the centre of the shell (*Fig. 3.8*).

Because of the form of the surface it is also eminently suitable for the projection of light from below so that the internal space is bathed in reflected light of reasonably uniform intensity. This solution has been adopted in some of the garden centre shells described in the next chapter.

Moser, Lyssach, 1964

A later development of the bubble shell type included an integral crane beam. By making the edge beams slightly deeper and adding a small nib at the bottom of their cross-section a crane rail could be incorporated with no additional intermediate supports. An example of this is the vehicle works of Moser AG, of Lyssach, (*Fig. 3.9*) built in 1964, near to and in the same year as Isler's office. This building consists of ten, 22 x 22 m bubble shells, arranged in two rows of five, as seen in *Fig. 3.10*. The crane beams, seen in section in *Fig. 3.11*, are 1·45 m deep, 750 mm wide at the perimeter and 950 mm wide along the long central axis of the building. This allowed the installation of 5 tonne capacity cranes capable of covering the whole floor area of the building. This was achieved with only a small increase in the overall cost of the structure. There are only four internal columns in the building, which covers almost 5000 m^2 and the crane beams span the full 22 m between them, as can be seen in the interior view of *Fig. 3.12*.

COOP, Wangen bei Olten, 1960

The largest of Isler's early bubble shells was constructed in 1960, as a distribution facility for the COOP in Wangen bei Olten. This building of 54·6 x 58·8 m had a shell rising at the centre to 9 m above the supports and containing 17

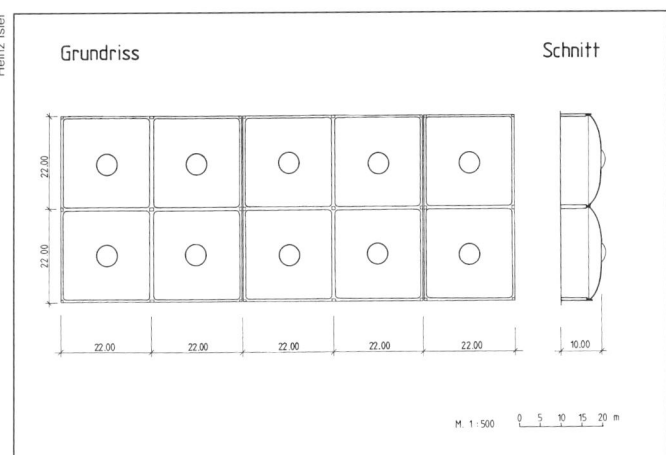

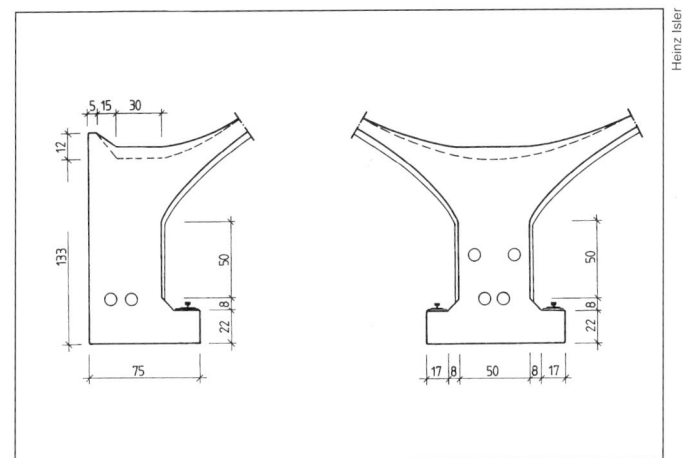

Fig. 3.11. Sections through crane beams.

Fig. 3.10. Plan and section of the vehicle works of Moser AG.

Fig. 3.12. Interior view of the Moser AG vehicle works, showing the inconspicuous crane beam.

circular roof light domes, as shown in the plan and section of *Fig. 3.13*. In this case six intermediate supports were provided along each edge of the shell giving a column-free area of over 3200 m² with the highest point of the shell at over 15 m above ground level. The large and flexible free space allowed railway wagons to enter the building for ease of loading.

Given the size of this shell, compared to the previous examples, Heinz Isler was very concerned about its buckling behaviour and constructed a 1:50 scale model in polyester to test in his laboratory (*Fig. 3.14*). His concern was due to the fact that the parts of the large-span shell were close to cylindrical in form, a shape that has a much lower buckling resistance than Isler's normal double-curved surfaces. The model looks rather primitive being held together with plastic clothes pegs but was appropriate for the purpose of determining the buckling failure mode and critical load.

Isler had constructed many similar forms before on a smaller scale and therefore knew very well how the forces were distributed through the surface. Predominantly the loads are carried in arch-like sections of the shell, from corner to corner along the diagonals and these arches lean against each other. However, the buckling behaviour was less certain. He expected local buckling to occur in the surface underneath the arches near the edge beam, because that was nearly cylindrical, and not in the double-curved arch sections. But when buckling finally occurred it was where he did not expect it, he did not

Chapter Three
'Bubble' shells

understand why and did not believe it. Fortunately, the model did not break so he was able to repeat the experiment. The second time the loading was applied more slowly when nearing the critical buckling load. When closely observed it was possible to see that the buckling actually started in the weaker cylindrical section and travelled to the location first observed in a split second. When talking about this model Isler commented that it was very important that engineers understand the qualitative behaviour of their structures so that they can detect when unexpected things happen.[57] To get the model shell to buckle Isler had to hang more than 1·5 tonnes distributed over the surface. Following the test he was then able to dimension the shell appropriately thickening it to 150 mm in the critical areas, assuming that all factors were unfavourable for the shell construction — i.e. that the weather was not good, the concrete not good, the scaffolding not good etc. In the event, when the shell was constructed everything was in favour — the weather was good, the concrete was good, the scaffolding was good — so instead of having a safety factor of about three, this was increased to approximately five. Of course, both Isler and the client were pleased with this outcome.

Supporting beams for this shell were of glued laminated timber radiating from the centre of the roof (*Fig. 3.15*). The binders each had a different shape (with mirror symmetry about the two axes perpendicular to the sides of the shell). Prestressing was provided by span-length cables

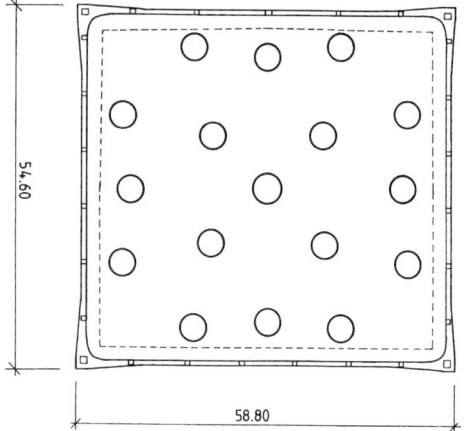
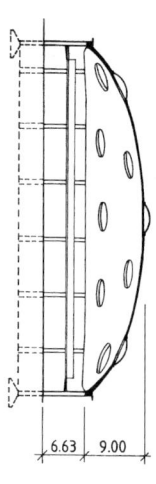

Fig. 3.13. Plan and section of the COOP in Wangen bei Olten.

Fig. 3.15. Supporting falsework beams for the COOP shell in Wangen bei Olten were of glued laminated timber radiating from the centre of the roof.

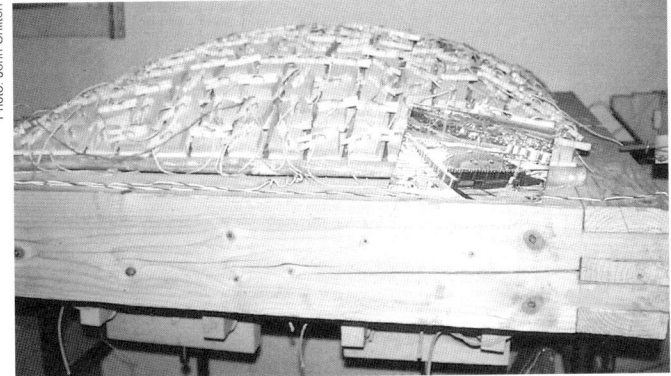

Fig. 3.14. Buckling investigation model scale 1:50 in polyester of the 54.6 x 58.8 m roof of the COOP in Wangen bei Olten.

Fig. 3.16. The prestressing cables are crossed over and under each other at the corners.

in the edge beams, anchored at the corner supports, with total prestressing forces of 1300 tonnes in the long sides and 1200 tonnes in the shorter sides. However, the prestressing cables are crossed over and under each other at the corners (Fig. 3.16). The initial cable forces were sufficient to counter any relaxation in the cables or the imposition of any reasonable additional loading.

The roof pour was large and complicated (Fig. 3.17), therefore concreting took place in a continuous process over three days and three nights, using around 1000 m³ of concrete in total. A major problem on a pour of this size and duration is that of 'cold joints' between different sub-pours. To avoid this, as concreting began on a front 220 m long, heavily retarded concrete was used. The specially designed concrete mix, as

Chapter Three
'Bubble' shells

Fig. 3.17. Concreting took place in a continuous process over three days and three nights using 1000 m³ of concrete.

Fig. 3.18. Small circular concrete upstand, to prevent the ingress of rainwater round the openings.

well as being retarded had, on the one hand, a lot of plasticiser to ease compaction around the prestressing cable ducts and, on the other hand, sufficient stiffness to prevent it slipping down the slope of the shell, particularly at the more steeply angled corners.

In this shell there are 17 domed roof lights that represent 4% of the total roof area. These are arranged so that they bring adequate and reasonably even daylight into the whole warehouse space below. The pattern of 4·0 and 4·5 m diameter openings is so organised that the corner to corner arching of the shell is not interrupted. Each dome sits on a small circular concrete upstand, formed on the shell as concreting progressed, to prevent the ingress of rainwater round the openings (*Fig. 3.18*).

A total of 749 bubble shells were constructed between 1956 and 1985. Of these, the majority received no surface protection to prevent the usual problems of permeability and carbonation of the concrete. The concrete used in the shells is of high quality with double-layer reinforcement. As it is thin in section the concrete is also well compacted and, as the shell is post-tensioned, the surface is always in compression so that cracks are avoided. Therefore, up to 40 years after their construction, these shells present none of the usual difficulties associated with unprotected concrete. They acquire a surface coating of naturally growing lichens, which means that the colour of the concrete blends better into natural surroundings.

In architecture there is a current move towards sustainable construction and for earth covered structures that do not overly intrude into their environment. Isler's bubble shells would provide excellent long-span structures for such developments as they have the loadbearing capacity to resist the weight of imposed soil, use little energy-rich material, are well-insulated and would need little or no applied waterproofing.

Recent applications of the bubble shells

More recent applications of the bubble shells have included a warehouse for Formex AG at Bubendorf, Switzerland, built in 1994, and a bus depot at Müllheim in the Schwarzwald, Germany, built in 1996/7, as well as an office building under a bubble shell 25 x 25 m, for the Bösiger Company in 1997/8.

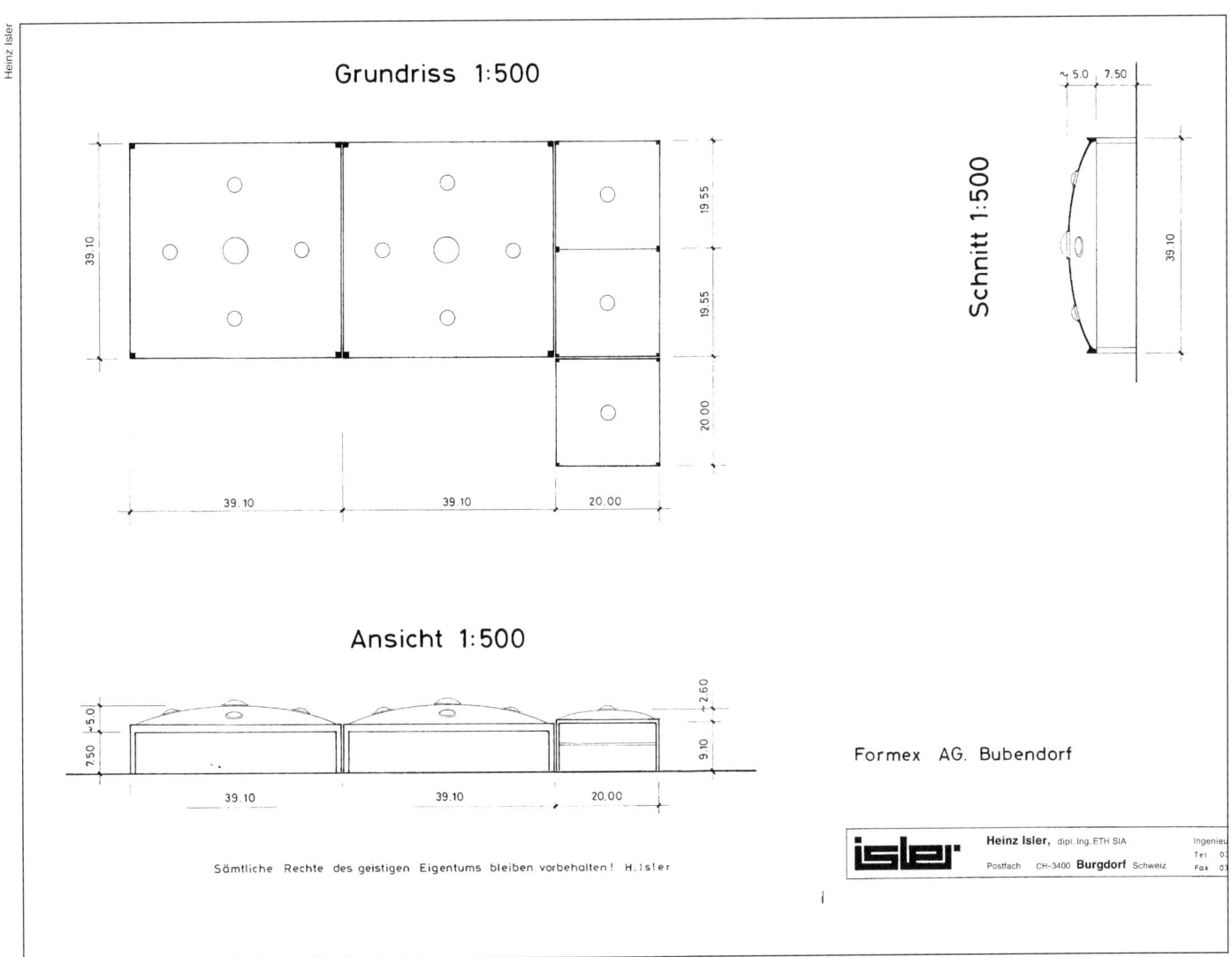

Fig. 3.19. Plan, elevation and section of the timber warehouse for Formex AG, Bubendorf.

Chapter Three
'Bubble' shells

Fig. 3.20. Two 40 x 40 m shells for a timber warehouse for Formex AG of Bubendorf under construction in 1994.

Fig. 3.21. The completed Formex AG complex with 20 x 20 m shells adjacent to the larger 80 x 40 m warehouse.

Fig. 3.25. Elevation showing the heavy edge beams used to conceal the automatic door mechanism for the bus garage at Müllheim.

Warehouse Formex, Bubendorf, 1994[58]

In 1994, Formex AG of Bubendorf planned to construct a new warehouse for timber products. The client specified that the space of 3200 m² should be without interior pillars, to allow flexibility in use (*Fig. 3.19*). They also specified that the structure should be fireproof, needing no sprinklers, which, if triggered, might ruin the timber goods stored in the warehouse. Two Isler bubble shells were chosen with the knowledge that the building floor area could be doubled and still have only one internal column. The square shells each span 40 x 40m and were constructed within four months (*Fig. 3.20*). As they needed no waterproofing or plumbing they were immediately ready for use after the prefabricated façades were mounted. To one side a group of 20

Fig. 3.22. The interior of the Formex AG warehouse gives some idea of the size of column-free space that can be covered by just two 40 m square Isler bubble shells.

Fig. 3.23. Aerial view of the bus garage at Müllheim in the Schwarzwald, constructed in 1996/7.

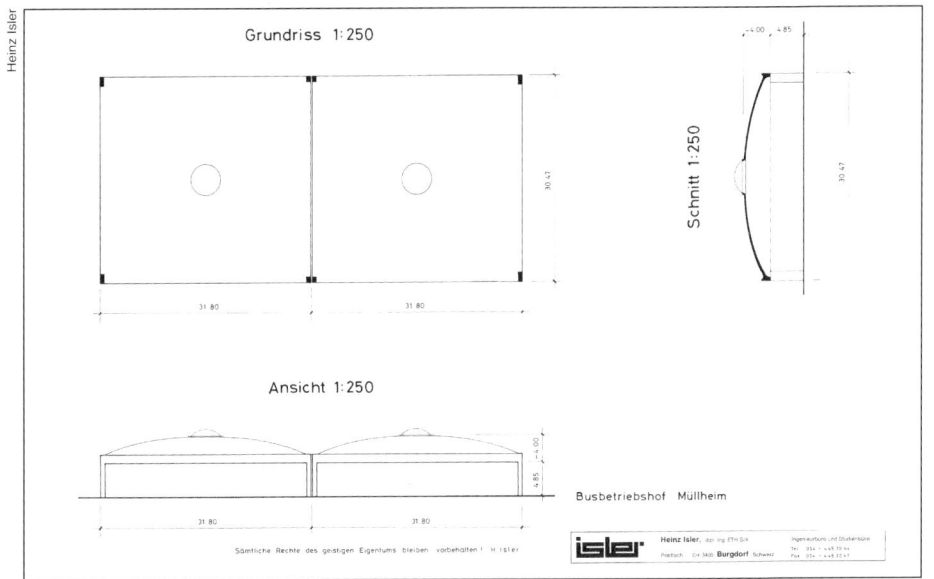

m shells completes the halls, and to the north a large office building adjoins the warehouses (*Fig. 3.21*). *Figure 3.22* gives some idea of the size of column-free space that can be covered by just two 40 m² Isler bubble shells.

Bus depot, Müllheim, 1996/7

The bus depot at Müllheim (*Fig. 3.23*) consists of two corner-supported shells each 30·47 x 31·80 m (*Fig. 3.24*). Isler is pleased by the architect's[59] treatment of the glazed façade, as it is light and inconspicuous, but he is not so pleased with two other aspects of this building. Firstly, because along one side there must be a deep downstand

Fig. 3.24. Plan, elevation and section of bus garage, Müllheim, in the Schwarzwald.

Chapter Three
'Bubble' shells

Fig. 3.26. Interior view of the bus garage at Müllheim showing the size of column-free space that can be covered by just two (medium-sized) Isler bubble shells.

Fig. 3.27. Office of Bösiger AG, main contractor for Isler's shells.

below the edge beam to accommodate the mechanism to open the automatic doors the architect required a similar downstand on the other elevations, giving them a heavier appearance (*Fig. 3.25*). His second criticism is of the artificial lighting, which is placed in regimented rows at low level. This is said to be necessary to provide sufficient light for washing and maintaining the vehicles but Isler is convinced that a more sympathetic system of illumination might have been found with the necessary function. As it is, glare from the lights detracts from the appreciation of the 30 x 30 m shell. Again, *Fig. 3.26* gives some idea of the size of column-free space that can be covered by just two, medium-sized Isler bubble shells.

New office building, W. Bösiger AG, Langenthal, 1998

In 1998, the company W. Bösiger AG erected a three-storey office building for themselves under a bubble shell of 25 x 25 m (*Fig. 3.27*). The upper floor of this building is a large mezzanine level, which is used for an office space and gallery for coffee shop and exhibition area, under the 625 m² clear span roof. Situated under a dome-like shell, with a central roof light that introduces pleasant natural daylight to the workplace, this is an appropriate and a well regarded solution for modern offices. The new offices are adjacent to a large building, used for workshops and storage of materials, plant, equipment and vehicles, which is covered with eight bubble shells and was built in 1985. At the entrance there are two smaller shells a hyperbolic paraboloid 'hypar' (*Fig. 3.28*) and a carport designed by Michael Balz (*Fig. 3.29*).

Co-operation with contractors

When the wooden formwork and falsework were removed from the first real bubble shell (Trösch Bützberg, 1955) to be burnt, Isler had the definite feeling that this was not the best practice. For the next building Isler made agreements with the contractors that the falsework beams would become his property after use (free of charge, instead of being destroyed). Alternatively, they would go to the client for later reuse, in case of extension of the building, while Isler retained the right to use them elsewhere if necessary.
This policy set the basis for a continuous

Fig. 3.28. Hyperbolic paraboloid 'hypar' shell entrance canopy designed by Michael Balz, at the Bösiger office.

Chapter Three
'Bubble' shells

Fig. 3.29. A small shell carport designed by Michael Balz at the Bösiger office.

Fig. 3.30. Heavy iron ball being dropped onto a shell during demolition. Although holes were punched in the thin surface, the load carrying performance was not adversely affected.

production of Isler shells at moderate prices. At the beginning, in most cases, a new contractor was chosen by each new client, which resulted in a lot of tedious work for Isler. He was confident and skilled about his drawings, calculations and designs. However, the practical details — how to place the beams of the falsework with the necessary precision, how to mount the insulation boards, how to install the steel reinforcement and prestressing cables, all also to high precision — had to be transmitted to the building contractor, from the chief to every workman. Isler conducted instruction courses with practical exercises. At first, he even placed the ten different kinds of stirrups around the prestressing anchors in person. If these stirrups are placed in the wrong order, the corner of the shell becomes one centimetre higher with each mistake. The rainwater would never have found its way to the downpipe in such a gutter.

Fortunately, in the course of time, the number of new contractors diminished and some could offer experienced crews. However, when the shell applications switched to other countries the problem arose anew. Finally, the situation began to improve due to co-ordinated co-operation relating to the falsework beams, plant and machinery, construction crews and know-how. The exchange of falsework beams or binders, for instance, was organised in Isler's office. Sometimes the wooden binders went directly from Germany to France or Austria without passing through Switzerland.

Isler was assisted by a number of friends — top experts in their own field. Hans Schmid was the expert for all questions relating to concrete, Kurt Herzog, from Gipsunion, for insulation boards, Max Birkenmaier for prestressing, Emil Roth for curved laminated timber binders etc. The specialists for the building process were Max and Heinz Bösiger, from the company W. Bösiger.

The co-operation was free, without a contract and distinct for every new operation. Sometimes one of the collaborators could apply one of his products but the team also functioned without that. Isler believes that one thing is certain: he would never have been able to realise so many of his built shells, in so many varieties of innovative form and in so many countries and

Fig. 3.31. Pulling down one corner of the shell to simulate possible differential settlement of the support.

Fig. 3.32. After complete removal of the column the shell cracked across the diagonal between the adjacent columns.

locations, without this great and sometimes idealistic team. Even today, after so many years, so many successes and so many economic crises in the different countries, the team still partially exists, although it may consist of other people.

The company Bösiger has emerged as main contractor. During all periods they were able to keep their personnel and resources and were able to execute Isler shells with the necessary quality, speed and at a competitive price. Therefore, it was natural that Isler should grant a general licence to the company W. Bösiger to construct certain shells of the types that present the smallest technical risk.

Currently Bösiger holds a licence to construct three types of standard shell — the bubble shells that are mainly used for factories and industrial buildings (in spans up to 50 x 50 m), the tennis hall shells (18·6 x 48·0 m) and the swimming pool enclosures (up to 35 x 35 m). However, they are only permitted to construct these in certain countries and where there are no exceptional loading or environmental factors that might affect the performance of the shell. Other types of shell are only allowed when individually permitted by Isler. As an interesting example, there was a proposal to construct a shell of the swimming enclosure type in a desert location. But Isler was concerned that wind-blown sand would potentially build up unevenly on the shell surface and, as sand is much denser than snow,[60] (for which the shells are normally designed) the shell might fail. Following wind tunnel tests to see how sand might be deposited, Isler insisted that the shell could only be built if a wide and deep ditch, covered with a grid, was built round the corners to intercept the sand. This ditch had to be emptied at regular six-monthly intervals.

Bösiger have built most of Isler's shells and this has enabled them to construct them with great economy. This economy has resulted from the initial training of the construction team, by Isler, in the accurate methods and quality control needed for the erection of the shells. Further economy has resulted from the savings that have been possible through the reuse of the falsework, initially owned by Isler, employed to support the wet concrete. It is an excellent example of what can be achieved through co-operation between engineer and contractor rather than the sadly more common conflict.

Chapter Three
'Bubble' shells

Fig. 3.33. With two supports removed the shell still would have protected the occupants.

Fig. 3.34. With all supports removed and the shell on the ground it is still basically intact.

A detailed account of how the shells are actually constructed is provided in chapter five, in the section on The Norwich Sports Village — a report of the author's first hand experiences.

Demolition of bubble shells

It is difficult for a structural engineer to accept the destruction of their work and most hope that this will not occur during their lifetime. However, it does occasionally happen and for someone like Heinz Isler who is the designer of almost 500 structures there is a higher probability that it might. In fact, some have been demolished, some modified in ways that Isler finds inappropriate and one of his most dramatic works (the triangular roofs over the motorway service station at Deitingen) has recently been under threat.

Isler considers that it is still not safe from the demolition man's steel ball but others have already succumbed.

The first time Heinz Isler had to confront the fact that his work was perishable was when a small factory, HABA Uster, built in 1972, had to be demolished. In 1980, the bubble shells had to give way for the construction of a warehouse with a high level racking system. It was really a shock for Isler when this group of shells had to go. He says that he was agonising over it for weeks. At first he could not come to terms with their destruction but then he eventually accepted that such things are not eternal and turned the situation to his gain. His client did not want to demolish the shells but had no alternative, as he was required to at the end of his lease of the site.

So Isler asked if he could, at least, have the chance to carry out some tests. The client agreed, so Isler took advantage of the opportunity and, in co-operation with ETH Zurich and the Research Institute EMPA Dübendorf, he conducted a programme of investigation, from which he learnt much about concrete and the behaviour of his shells under extreme loading conditions.

During the demolition of the bubble shells they were gradually loaded to see how they would eventually fail. Isler says that the consequences of the tests, for him, were enormous, as he made several really important discoveries concerning the safety of his shells. Since seeing the great reserves of strength that the shells have he has become less circumspect.

Previous to the tests, for instance, he always

provided three alternative means of resisting the high shear force at the corner of a bubble shell. Isler had always considered it to be a little ambitious to have such a big surface (sometimes 1000 m^2) resting on one single point. He was concerned about what was happening at the corner and was afraid of a shear failure there, because if a crack were to form in the shell around the support, then the roof would collapse — the column would be intact and the shell on the floor. So he did everything that he could to prevent this from occurring. He provided stirrups and bent-up bar reinforcement, both capable of resisting the full shear load, and a third method, the prestressing in the edge beams. Each one of these would be capable of carrying the total shear load, because he was not certain how the shells behaved.

Fortunately there was rock underneath the structure to be demolished, so it was possible to drill to form anchorages and to pull down on the shell against the mass of the ground, otherwise it would have been extremely difficult to apply sufficient load. On application of the load initially nothing happened and no crack appeared at all. Isler had always expected a diagonal crack to appear across the corner but no such crack manifested itself. The loading jacks were pulling down with the highest force that they could apply until eventually the operator cried that he had to stop. Isler thought that this was because the roof was failing but it was because the jack was bursting. It would have been impossible to apply the failure load, which is estimated to have been thousands of tonnes. Subsequently, the prestress anchorage blocks could be dismantled which provided more useful information. Isler was conscious that they might explode during the loading test but again nothing happened. The grout injection around the prestressing wires was so dense that it was possible cut it in one location and after about 100 mm the full prestress was available in the concrete. When, eventually the prestressing cables were removed the wires were in almost perfect condition, as on the day of installation almost ten years before.

In a preliminary test a heavy iron ball was dropped onto the roof at various locations, thereby punching holes in the thin surface but the load-carrying performance was in no way adversely affected (*Fig. 3.30*). However, the most spectacular part of the investigations was the gradual pulling down of one corner of the shell first by 100 mm then 500 mm and then 1000 mm, simulating possible differential settlement of the support (*Fig. 3.31*). Finally, the whole 4 m high column was removed, this total removal of a corner support corresponding to the column being rammed and demolished by impact from a heavy vehicle. At this juncture the shell did indeed have several cracks across the diagonal between the columns adjacent to that which was removed (*Fig. 3.32*). However, the two main sections remained intact and it would even have been possible to lift up the corner again.

The remaining supports were then removed one after another until the shell fell down completely (*Figs 3.33* and *3.34*). However, the two main sections of the shell remained essentially intact, retaining some load-carrying capacity, so that anyone trapped under the fallen shell would have been able to survive. Following this, the remains of the fallen shell were finally broken up piece by piece with the steel ball. Demolition had lasted just two and a half hours and complete removal of the shells took less than one day. The speed of this demolition process demonstrated the problem-free dismantling of this relatively large-scale and non-conventional reinforced concrete structure.

Following this episode Isler understood that all things are perishable. Although saddened by the loss of one of his shells he realises and accepts that nothing lasts forever.

Chapter Four
Free-form shells

Chapter Four
Free-form shells

Before Isler began to construct his free-form shells, practically all previous shells, constructed by other shell builders, had been based on forms that could be described by simple geometry, so that equations could be derived to calculate the forces and stresses within them. The forms were mainly, cylinders, cones, spheres and hyperbolic paraboloid (or saddle) surfaces and combinations of them. With his bubble shells Isler had moved away from this emphasis on geometrical description and developed a method of form-finding based on physical models. However, following his development of the bubble shells, Isler's earliest 'free-form' shells, are not quite what they seem. These shells are free form in the sense that they do not have a regular geometry, however, they are essentially based on combinations of circular curves.

The development of these forms is best shown by a series of built examples starting with the Wyss Garden Centre of 1962 and terminating with the Bürgi Garden Centre of 1973. The Chamonix shells of rigid spherical form that Isler built in collaboration with the architect R. Taillibert are also included here.

Wyss Garden Centre, Solothurn, 1962

Wyss Garden Centre in Solothurn, built in 1962, was Heinz Isler's first free-shaped shell. Having convinced the clients that a shell would be the best solution for their requirement for a garden centre showroom, Isler then needed to get

Fig. 4.1. The Wyss Garden Centre built in 1962.

permission to construct from the local authorities. This was very easy and quick (taking just eight days!) despite this being a little known type of construction in Switzerland at the time.[61] Although apparently free form, the shell is actually geometric, with the 650 m² of surfaces being entirely generated by circles — but a blend of circles, which are so in balance that one does not notice that it is a geometric shell. This shell was Isler's entry into the exciting realm of construction of free forms. Commenting about the fact that the shell looks free form but is actually not he says, 'you see it could also be done with geometric tools but you must have the feeling for it.'

Although the majority of Isler's shells are exposed, unprotected concrete, in this case the exterior of the shell was painted white. There are two reasons for this. Firstly, the client wanted to have an advertisement for the company, so it was decided to paint the shell white to provide a dramatic contrast with the landscape behind, the beautiful dark slopes of the nearby Jura Mountains. This dramatic contrast can clearly be seen in *Fig. 4.1*, which shows the structure shortly after completion. Secondly, Heinz Isler wanted it to be painted from the beginning, because it was not a pure compression shell. From his numerous laboratory experiments on physical models, he knew that there were small areas of tension within the surface, because the form was not derived from a hanging shape. Where there is tension the reinforced concrete will crack, thus the paint provided additional protection against corrosion of the reinforcement and reduced the possibly of rainwater penetration of the building envelope.

Formwork for the shell was provided by curved trusses sitting on three curved glued-laminated timber beams. Supported on scaffolding towers, the beams ran along three parallel lines (two facing sides and the centre line in one direction), as seen in *Fig. 4.2*. One of the problems encountered by Isler and his contractors is that standard commercially available scaffolding is usually designed to carry heavy loads. In Isler's thin shells the total load, including insulation, shuttering and the supporting beams of the falsework, is only around 300 kg/m² so the typical scaffolding, seen in *Fig. 4.2*, is more than strong enough. To form the curved profile of the shell, thin timber boards are placed at regular intervals across the beams or trusses. On top of these the insulation (usually wood-wool slabs) is placed and this acts as permanent shuttering.

Fig. 4.2. Falsework for the Wyss Garden Centre shell.

Photo: Heinz Isler

Chapter Four
Free-form shells

Fig. 4.3. With wire enclosed in small plastic tubes, Isler was able to shape the functional and aesthetically pleasing form that he desired for the foot of the Wyss Garden Centre shell.

At the time of construction of the Wyss shell, three-dimensional solid modelling computer software was not available and it would have been extremely difficult to convey, using only normal engineering drawings, the required form of the concrete at the feet of the shell (in the corners). The foot of an Isler shell is a complex three-dimensional object where two adjacent edges meet at the ground beam and the shell itself thickens to accommodate the forces concentrated at the support. It is also the point where rainwater comes to the ground, as there are no gutters. There is nothing except the concrete shell itself to channel the rainwater into the corners, therefore, the shape at the corner must also form a suitable channel taking the water to a gully underneath. Within this complex three-dimensional form the prestressing cables and anchorages also have to be accommodated. To overcome the problems of somehow describing this complex solid, Heinz Isler proposed that, rather than make sketches, drawings, or even a model of the detail, they should resort to modelling it at full-scale on site.[62]

As well as the structural and constructional considerations, because the rainwater would be concentrated into the corners, Isler wanted to have a beautiful shape to lead it down into the surrounding meadow. Once the majority of the shell formwork was on site, with wires enclosed in small plastic tubes, Isler was able to shape the functional and aesthetically pleasing form that he desired (Fig. 4.3). The shape of the foot could be physically modelled and seen in three-dimensional space. He considers that that was by far the easiest way to shape such a complex detail — to design it in situ. Subsequently, the contractor just took thin timber boards and cut them to fit the profile described by the wires to make the necessary formwork. In the opinion of Isler, despite the current availability of excellent three-dimensional solid modelling programs, this would have still been his preferred method of determining the correct aesthetic and functional shape.[63] He considers that designing on site is the most rational and simple way to design such a shape because one can look at it from every side at full scale. On the drawing board one cannot do that and on a computer screen one still has a two-dimensional representation of a three-dimensional object. Even a scale model does not give a true representation of the situation.

The corner detail was very important because the maximum stresses of the whole shell occur there. Generally, the stresses throughout this shell are relatively low except in the corners and in the stiffening cantilevers along each edge. To provide the necessary edge stiffness, Isler says that he could have incorporated large perimeter arches, perhaps three or even ten times the actual 70 mm thickness of the main shell. But then the structure would have looked heavy and ugly, or as Isler put it, 'it would just kill the whole view'. In the shell, as built, there is a stiffening cantilever, normal to the shell surface at the edge and with a thickness of only 60 mm. This cantilever has a maximum width of 3·5 m and spans 24 m. At the point where the main shell and cantilever meet the shell was thickened to 120 mm. This form anticipates to some degree the upturned lip of Isler's later forms derived from inverted hanging membranes but here the shape is defined in a more rigid geometrical manner.

Given the non-conventional form of such a shell, fenestration has to be reconsidered. How does one put windows into the elevations below the curved surface? In a typical building elevation the glazing is vertical and spans between a horizontal roof and/or floors but here the edges of the shell are curved in plan and the height of glazing varies from about 5 m at the middle of each side to nothing in the corners. Ideally, Isler

would have liked to have a single piece of glass 24 m long rising to 5 m high. At the time that did not exist (and does not yet) although it will come one day, Isler believes.

This necessitated the use of glazing mullions — although here they are designed in a very different way. Seeing the purity and poise of a 'naked' Isler shell just after the formwork and falsework have been removed, it is difficult to see how glazing can be installed without detracting from the elegance of the form. The conventional solution would be to take a uniform mullion profile thick enough to resist the pressure of the wind and carry that pressure in bending over the longest span between the shell at the top and the ground slab or ground beam at the bottom. However, Heinz Isler considers this to be

Fig. 4.4. Lightweight glazed façade of the Wyss Garden Centre, with tensioned mullions.

Chapter Four
Free-form shells

inelegant or even wrong, because at the top there is no moment, at the bottom there is no moment and in between there is just the wind pressure. So, in order to have the mullions as light as possible, Isler devised the following system of support.

Instead of allowing the base to rest directly on the ground, the concrete was not placed on bedrock nor on soil but on a bed of straw. Isler reasoned that as the straw became damp, it would rot and disintegrate after a few months. Then there would be a void under the foundations and they would not be bearing on the earth below. Why would they not? Because the mullion posts were welded at the top to the steel reinforcing bars of the stiff shell. The shell was extremely rigid and capable of carrying hundreds of tonnes, therefore, the whole façade could easily be suspended from it. In fact, not only was the façade suspended, it was even prestressed by the weight of the concrete blocks hanging underneath it. Consequently, the mullions were not subject solely to bending, nor to a combination of bending and compression (as are most traditional mullions) but a combination of bending with tension. As compression and, therefore, buckling was avoided the elements could be made very thin. To further reduce the visual impact of the glazing supports, the steel profile was cut to a taper. At the top the profile is only 10 mm tapering out to the full section at the base where it was, in fact, considered to be partially fixed rather than pinned. This is an elegant example of a post-tensioned glazing system (*Fig. 4.4*).

Another common feature of most Isler shells is that they do not have plane or straight façades. In this case the façade was curved in plan, not by much but sufficiently, so that it made a cylindrical shell of glass. Additional horizontal bending stiffness was therefore gained, so the profiles could be made even lighter. With such a slender façade Isler was concerned about possible vibration. Because the window was so light certain wind conditions might incite the façade to oscillate. His simple solution was to provide a system of small bolts and screw fixings so that if such vibration was ever detected light cables could be installed to damp the system. However, the vibration has never appeared and the cables have never been installed.

The structural art and expertise of the engineer was used here to make the mullions as slender as possible but, to enhance this effect even further, colour was also employed to minimise the impact of the sections when seen

Fig. 4.5. The Wyss Garden Centre as it was in Aug. 1999.

Photo: John Chilton

Photo: Heinz Isler

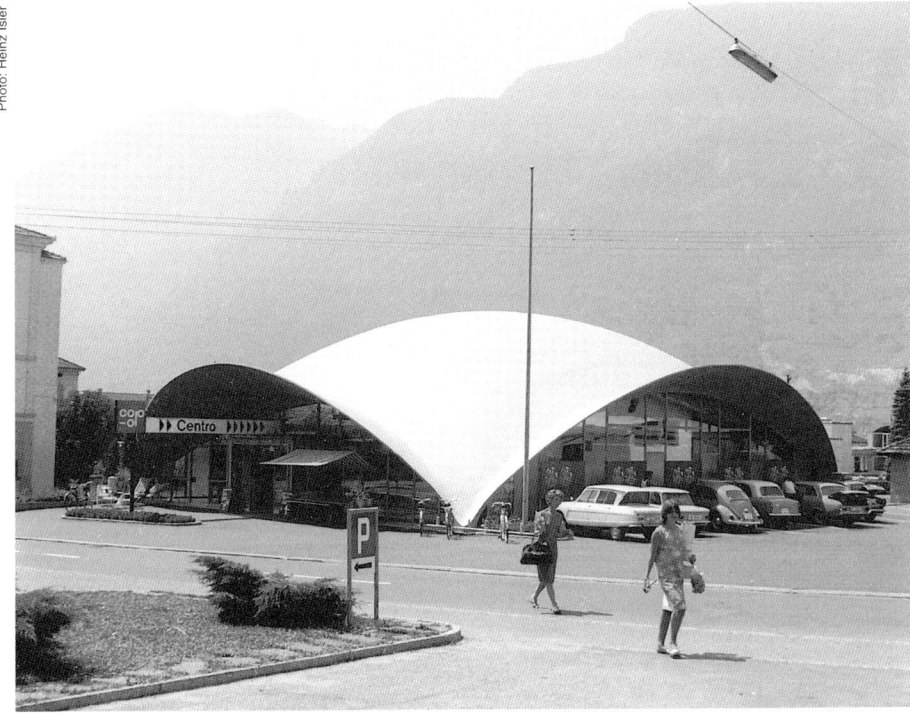

Fig. 4.6. Small supermarket, with a ground plan of 440 m^2, in Biasca, south-east Switzerland, 1963.

Fig. 4.7. Heinz Isler's sketch of proposed supermarket, Bellinzona, 1964.

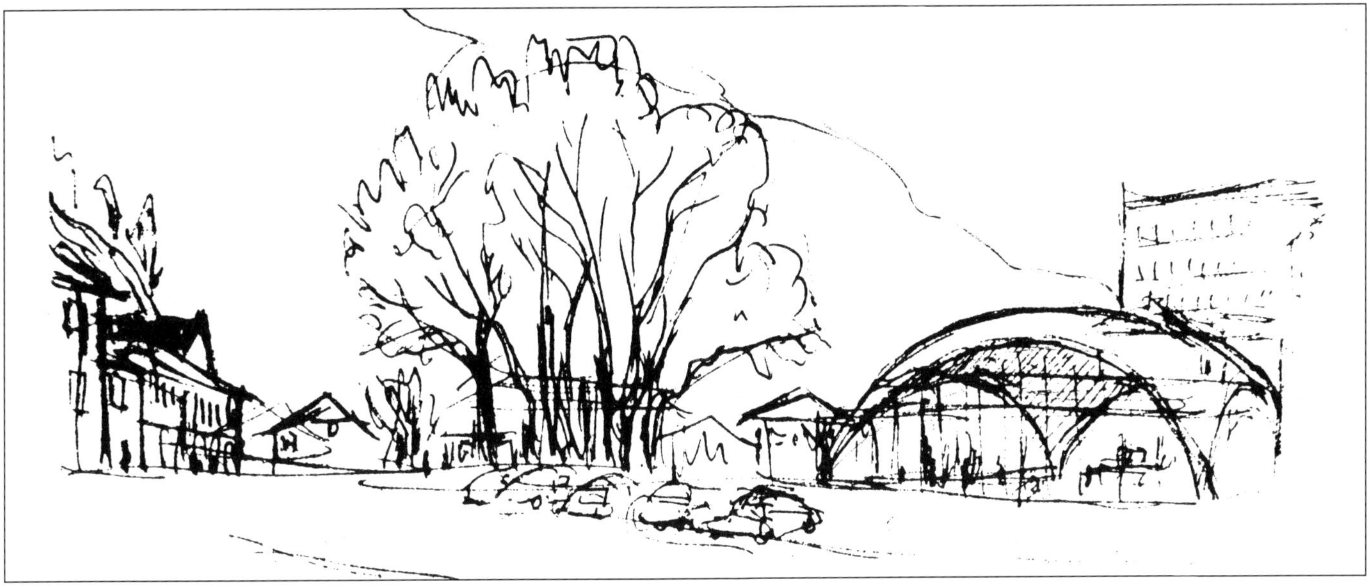

Chapter Four
Free-form shells

Fig. 4.8. The completed Bellinzona supermarket and adjacent office building.

Fig. 4.9. One tenth scale micro-concrete model of the Bellinzona shell roof, actual size 3.2 x 3.2 m, just 8 mm thick.

from within or without the building. Inside, the sections were painted white so that they did not contrast unduly with the light of the sky and outside they were originally painted a dark shade (although they are now painted a vivid green), because the reflection of a window is generally dark grey or green. Thus, one did not really see the windows when the building was finished, so that the pure form of the shell could be appreciated.

Heinz Isler is justifiably proud of the fact that one practically could not see the windows, just a darkness below the shell, unless the sun was shining directly on the façade. Equally he is very proud of the following detail. At the top of the glazed walls there is a junction between a cone (the edge cantilever shell), a spherical surface (the main shell roof) and a cylindrical shell of glass. And yet these three curved surfaces come together along a single line, that almost does not have a thickness. There is just a pane of glass coming into a small recess in the concrete at the intersection of the two concrete surfaces.[64] There is no profile just the mullions, which are hanging, very slim and prestressed off the shell. Heinz Isler thinks that is the way one should progress in structural engineering and architecture, by, as he puts it, 'dematerialising structure to the least possible'[65] and he considers that shells could all be that way. He feels that this building was his proof of how architecture and engineering could be elegantly combined in one object. Here he believes that he demonstrated how it could be done but does not think that his example has been followed.[66]

When newly built, the Wyss Garden Centre shell appeared extremely light, poised and refined. It was set in a park, which presented it beautifully. Today, (*Fig. 4.5*) the shell is surrounded by the paraphernalia and outbuildings of the garden centre and the mullions are painted bright green but the clarity and fineness of the original conception is still there for those with eyes to see it.[67]

In the following year, 1963, working with the architect Sigg of Basel, Isler designed a shell to house a new supermarket at Biasca, in south-east Switzerland (*Fig. 4.6*). The form was based on the Wyss shell so that the same formwork and falsework could be used. However, the smaller ground plan of 440 m², meant that this shell appeared more squat and less elegant than that of the Wyss Garden Centre, an impression aggravated by its urban location. Here the aerodynamic shape of the shell was used to assist air movement in the underfloor, ducted-air heating and ventilation system. It is interesting to note that the temperature within the supermarket decreased by several degrees when the shell exterior was painted with a white Hypalon coating, making the surface more reflective of solar radiation. Later followed the construction of a shell to house a supermarket more than twice the size in Bellinzona.

Soc. Migros, Bellinzona, 1964
Architect: Chiesa, Bellinzona and Büchler
Engineer: Heinz Isler

The larger project was for a supermarket, covering 961 m², for the Soc. Migros, to be constructed adjacent to a new office block in the centre of Bellinzona, a medieval town in the south of Switzerland. After considerable deliberation the clients and architects, Chiesa, Bellinzona and Büchler, were convinced that a shell structure was the best solution and of the various possible forms a simple dome on four supports was preferred. Of all the shell forms considered, this was felt to be the most appropriate for the situation, which was surrounded by historic houses and churches and overlooked by an ancient castle on a nearby hill. Despite considerable local opposition the authorities finally gave their permission after

receiving the drawings and being shown previously built examples. Isler's sketch of the proposal is shown in *Fig. 4.7*. A view of the completed supermarket and adjacent office building, taken from the nearby castle (*Fig. 4.8*), shows the slender profile attained by Isler for the shell.

Before the construction of the much larger Bellinzona shell, a 1:10 scale micro-concrete model (actual size 3·2 x 3·2 m) was built in the grounds surrounding Heinz Isler's offices. Reinforced with two-layers of fine steel wires to represent the two layers of steel reinforcement in the real structure, the model shell is only 8 mm thick. Despite its slenderness, it is still there today, over 35 years later (*Fig. 4.9*) and in very good condition bearing in mind that it has been completely exposed to the elements for that time and is coated in a layer of lichens and mosses. The model shell is elevated and there are steps that lead down to a small space below so that one can enter and view the structure at the level of a

Fig. 4.10. Eero Saarinen's Kresge Auditorium, Massachusetts Institute of Technology (MIT), a point supported triangular segment of a sphere with lenghts of 48m.

Photo: Neil Jackson

Chapter Four
Free-form shells

Fig. 4.11. Slender free edge of the Bellinzona shell.

Fig. 4.12. Sketch by Heinz Isler illustrating the method of vertical prestressing for the Bellinzona shell - Heinz Isler, Aug. 1999.

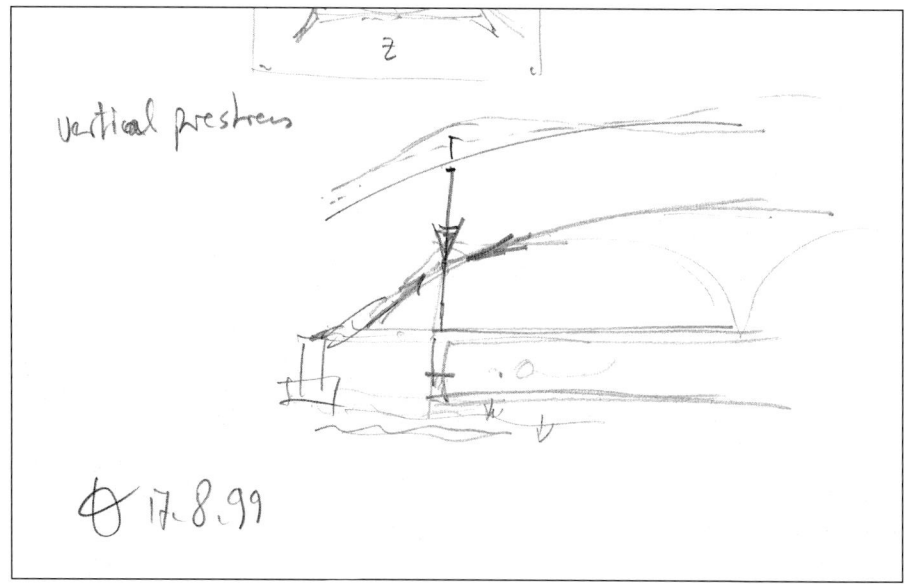

person actually in the supermarket hall. This model was made to show the clients how the shell would look inside. In making the model, Isler experimented with the placing of the wood-wool slabs used as insulation and formwork in order to determine the best pattern with the least cuts. Notwithstanding the slabs being rectangular and the shell in a way spherical, he found that it was possible to install the insulation slabs almost without cutting. There are just a few slabs that have to be trimmed near the corners. The rest of the surface is quasi-developed. For him that was a really valuable discovery because if the layout had been wrong the contractor would have had to cut the slabs everywhere, with consequent waste of material and extra cost.

The Bellinzona shell roof is approximately elliptical, on a square plan of 32 x 32 m and rising to a maximum height of 10 m. Until this time most shells of this form and size had required an edge beam in order to stiffen the boundary and such beams make the shell appear much heavier than it actually is. One particularly infamous example of a shell of this type is the Kresge Auditorium at (MIT), Massachusetts Institute of Technology, (*Fig. 4.10*), which is a point supported triangular segment of a sphere with side lengths of 48 m. The shape of the shell was chosen purely for its pure spherical geometry and is not really the most appropriate in terms of structural efficiency.[68] Despite having heavy edge beams, up to 0·93 m deep, the structure has had problems since shortly after it was built and has required strengthening. Commenting purely on the aesthetics of the MIT shell, the architect Eero Saarinen is reported in Joedicke (1963)[69] to have said

'The building has generated a good deal of discussion, pro and con. I think some of the criticisms have a certain amount of justification.'

However, Isler did not wish to have edge beams; he wanted free edges and did, in fact, achieve them (*Fig. 4.11*). The ideal form to accomplish this is as near as possible a catenary surface with sufficient double curvature at the free edge to prevent it from buckling. But, due to certain design constraints, this ideal was not possible. The shell had to be made flatter at the top and rise more steeply from the corner supports in order to remain within the restricted site area. This meant that in certain areas of the shell the line of thrust would have passed outside its surface causing bending and buckling problems. The thickness of the shell, its radius of curvature and the compression force expected in the free edge also had to be carefully considered, as well as any potential deformation of the edge.

To overcome the problem of the steep slope at the corners, the 80 mm thick shell was prestressed vertically. This was achieved by pulling down on the shell against the dead weight of the building's basement with six tensioned bars near each corner (three on each side). Thus prestressing had the effect of diverting the thrust line in the shell, making it more vertical. Pinnacles topping the buttresses of Gothic cathedrals serve a similar purpose, helping to divert the horizontal thrust of the vaulting down into the column. A sketch by Heinz Isler illustrating the method of vertical prestressing is shown in *Fig. 4.12* and the bars can just be discerned near the corner in the internal view of the unclad shell in *Fig. 4.13*. It is interesting to note that during construction of the shell sprayed concrete was used at the corners and conventional skipped concrete over the centre portion (*Fig. 4.14*).

Fig. 4.13. Internal view of the unclad Bellinzona shell, in which the prestressing bars can just be discerned near the corner.

Fig. 4.14. During construction of the Bellinzona shell, sprayed concrete was used at the corners and conventional skipped concrete over the centre portion.

Chapter Four
Free-form shells

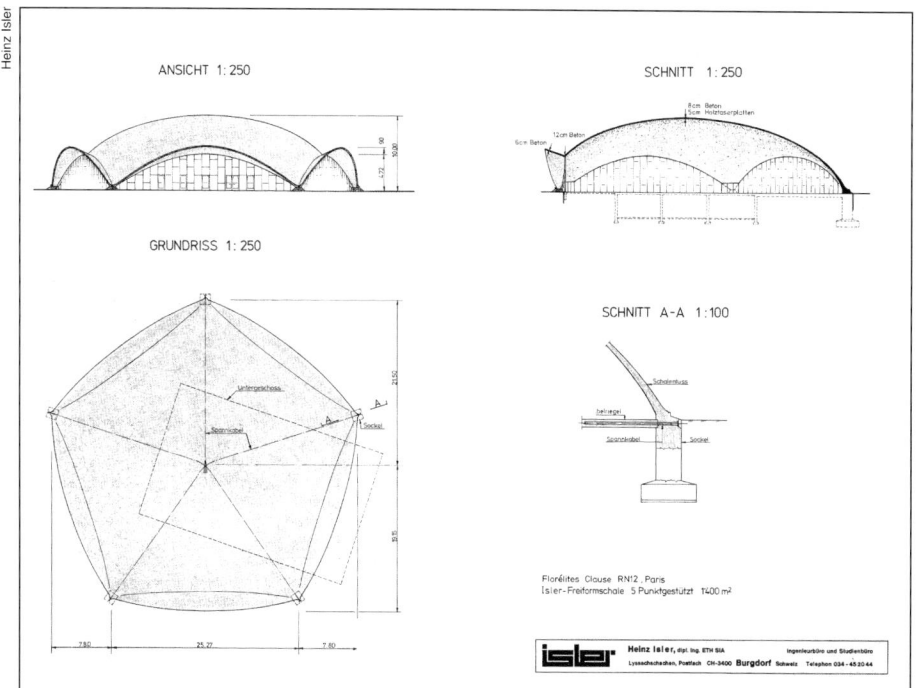

Fig. 4.15. Plan, elevation and sections of the Garden Centre Florélites Clause SA, St. Appoline, Paris with detail of the prestressing cable location at the foot of the shell.

Garden Centre Florélites Clause SA, St. Appoline, Paris, 1965

Design: Heinz Isler
Collaborating Architect: Dresse, Paris
Collaborating Engineer: Summer, Paris

The French seed company, Clause SA, wished to construct a large garden centre, adjacent to a motorway, near Paris. For the prominent site they wanted a striking building, out of the ordinary, that would be seen from some distance. The directors had seen the Wyss Garden Centre, in Solothurn, designed by Isler a couple of years earlier and commissioned a similar building but of 1400 m^2 floor area. Here, Isler proposed a pentagonal shell 80 mm thick (*Fig. 4.15*), with side lengths of 25·27 m and a diagonal span length of almost 41 m (measured across two-sides of the pentagon). The maximum height of the shell above floor level was approximately 10 m with a basement 3 m deep over part of the floor plan. As at the garden centre in Solothurn, this shell had a surface generated from curved profiles and edge stiffening cantilever shells that also served to shade the glazed walls. It was also painted white to add to its visibility (*Fig. 4.16*) and did, as the clients required, create a stunning addition to the skyline.

Isler derived the aesthetics of the shell using models and then used the final model to determine the flow of forces within the structure and its buckling resistance. He did, however, encounter some resistance to his design from the French authorities, as they usually require full

Isler monitored the deformations of this shell closely over the early stages of its life because the shell was subject to tensile stresses. It was reported[70] by Isler that cracks appeared in the shell, when the weather conditions changed, about one month after prestressing was completed and the falsework was removed. Initial elastic deformation of the shell had remained constant but, when the full cracking pattern appeared, deformations increased rapidly before halting at about another 100% of their initial values. He feels that this was a great opportunity to observe the effect of the formation of tension cracks on the deformation of shells.

Fig. 4.16. Garden Centre Florélites Clause SA, St. Appoline, Paris, 1965.

Fig. 4.17. Load test model of the shell for the Garden Centre Florélites Clause SA, St. Appoline, Paris.

calculations to be supplied to justify the strength and stability of a building. Because the form could not be described mathematically, Isler had to persuade them to accept the results of his model tests to prove the adequacy of his shell. Load tests on the model (*Fig. 4.17*) had shown practically no measurable movement.

In 1969, the second Garden Centre, of 2000 m² in size, at Ville du Bois, RN 20, suffered a severe fire that started in the basement. The fire lasted for seven hours during which time the whole structure expanded by approximately 150 mm and the maximum height of the shell roof dropped by about 200 mm. The ferocity of the fire can be judged by the fact that the building was still hot when Isler arrived on site after being summoned urgently from his office in Switzerland. As the temperature of the structure gradually returned to normal there was some recovery of the deformation and the shell rose 100 mm from its lowest position.

On examining the shell roof the concrete seemed untouched by the fire. However, although there was apparently no damage to the shell Isler was concerned that its future performance should not be prejudiced. He immediately set about conducting tests on the shell model in his office (*Fig. 4.17*), to determine whether it would be possible to induce additional prestress in the shell in the hope that it would return to somewhere near its original shape. His tests proved that this was possible and so new stressed tendons were installed across the floor slab. New tendons were used because it was uncertain to what degree the

Chapter Four
Free-form shells

old tendons in the slab of the basement had suffered in the fire.

An interesting discovery that came out of Isler's reassessment of this shell type was its flexibility. When the model was placed on the floor it was very stiff and, with the restraints provided by the supports in the real building, the shell was very strong. However, Isler noticed that if one of the supports was lowered the shell was highly flexible and accommodated easily to the settlement. In fact, he found that the thin shell could accommodate up to 1 m of settlement. This led him into some preliminary studies, which he sadly has not continued, into shell forms that are so flexible that they can be rolled up like a carpet but with appropriate supports become stable enclosures.

This was a highly successful shell type for Isler, as the same company commissioned many further shells of similar configuration. All have a pentagonal plan and similar aspects but they are generally one of three standard sizes between 31·0 m and 46·6 m span on the diagonal respectively. These were built at the following locations in France — La Ville du Bois (1969), Rennes, Toulouse, (1972), Bordeaux, (1974), Moisselles (1975), Ponthierry and Laval (1976), Villeparisis (1977) and Sevron (1980).

Fig. 4.18. Factory for F. Kilcher, at Recherswil near Solothurn constructed in 1965.

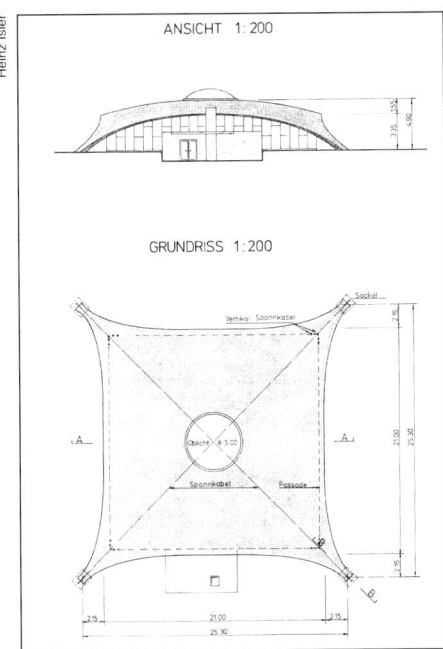

Fig. 4.19. Plan and elevation of the factory for F. Kilcher, at Recherswil near Solothurn.

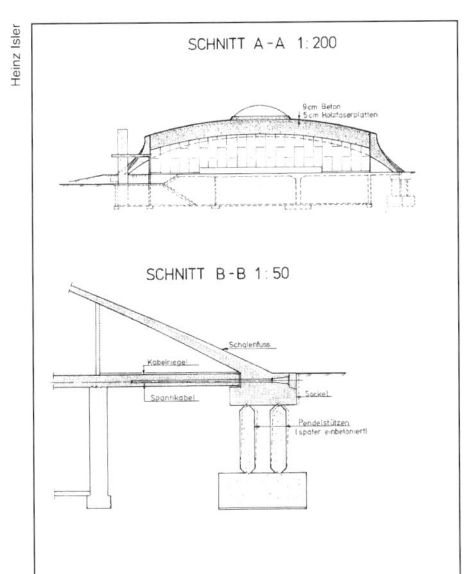

Fig. 4.20. Sections of the factory for F. Kilcher, at Recherswil near Solothurn.

Kilcher Factory, Recherswil, Solothurn, 1965

A factory for the building insulation company F. Kilcher was also constructed in 1965, at Recherswil near Solothurn (*Fig. 4.18*). Isler was responsible for the engineering and overall design in collaboration with the local architect, Paul Wirz of Solothurn. As the proposed factory was to be located adjacent to a recently opened motorway, the client's brief called for an eye-catching building showing the latest developments in thin shell construction.

Square in plan, the 20 x 20 m factory is accommodated below a slender, 90 mm thick shell of 25·3 x 25·3 m span between the four corner springing points, as can be seen in the plan and sections, *Figs 4.19* and *4.20*. Rising to 4·9 m above floor level, at its centre there is a 5 m diameter domed skylight. The central portion of this shell is similar in form to that of Bellinzona, described previously, but in this case there were not the same geometrical design constraints and the profile of the supports was able to follow the line of thrust more closely. In fact, the shell is based on a flow form but is also a modified form of both the shells at Bellinzona and St. Appoline, Paris. By basing the shape on these

Fig. 4.21. Plexiglas model of the Kilcher shell, Recherswil, used to determine the force distribution in the shell and its buckling behaviour.

Chapter Four
Free-form shells

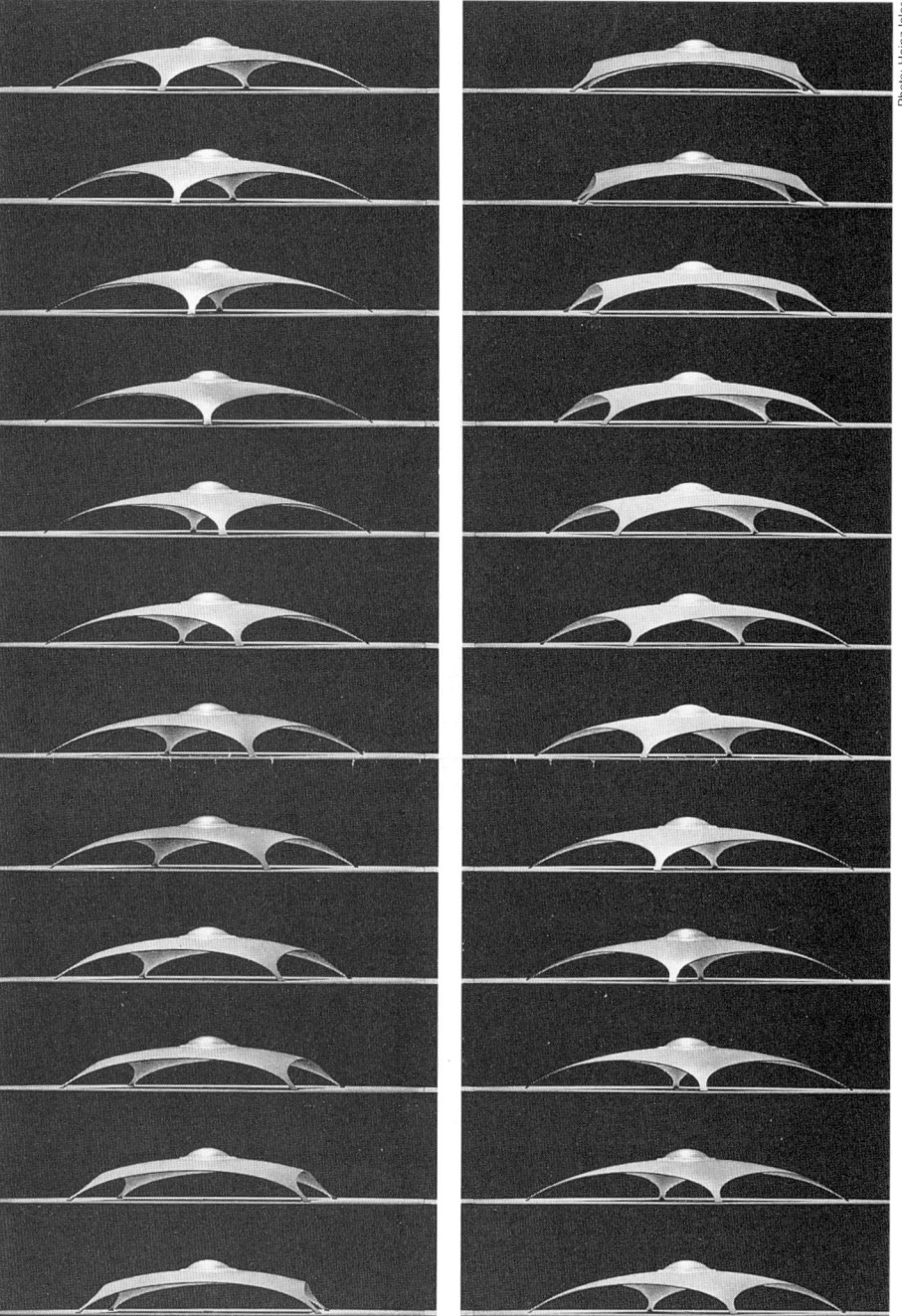

Fig. 4.22. Multiple sequential views of the Kilcher shell as would be seen by a passing motorist.

previous shells, it was possible to reuse the same falsework, once more, which meant that this project could be built more economically.

Prestressing of the surface is achieved by tensioning cables in the tie beams connecting the feet of the shell across the diagonal of the plan. Thereby the supports are pulled towards the centre of the building, making the shell lift off the formwork. To accommodate this movement the shell was initially sustained on pivoting supports, which were later encased in concrete blocks. In order to confirm the stability of this daring shell, particularly with respect to its buckling behaviour, Isler carried out laboratory tests on a scale model made of Plexiglas (*Fig. 4.21*). Various loading conditions were examined with electric strain gauges used to assess the distribution of forces in the surface.

It was possible to move the feet of the shell back by a small amount due to the vertical stressing hidden in the façade near the corners. The weight of the basement structure was used to pre-load the slender buttressing sections of the shell in order to prevent them from buckling upward and outward near the supports. There was a potential problem here that the groundwater might in future rise and cause the basement to float so reducing the available resistance to uplift. The main shell prestressing was introduced by the tensioning of cables linking opposite corners across the diagonals.

As can be seen in *Fig. 4.18*, the free-edges and supporting legs appear exceedingly slender, right from where they spring from the ground. To demonstrate how the finished shell would be seen by motorists passing by on the motorway, the scale model was rotated and photographed at different angles. This allowed varied aspects of the same shell to be seen in order to simulate this progression (*Fig. 4.22*). The fact that this work has been featured in many periodicals and also on the cover of the catalogue[71] of a highly successful

Fig. 4.23. The Bürgi Garden Centre, Camorino, built in 1973.

Photo: Heinz Isler

Chapter Four
Free-form shells

touring exhibition of Isler's work, held in 1986, shows the extreme elegance and poise of the shell which 'touches the earth lightly'.

Bürgi Garden Centre, Camorino, 1973

The Bürgi Garden Centre, Camorino (Fig. 4.23), built in 1973, is very similar to the Kilcher factory in Recherswil but in this case the shell is of slightly greater span, thereby avoiding the need for the vertical prestress. Again the shell is square and has a free form with an unstiffened edge, spanning 27·2 x 27·2 m between the springings, or 38·4 metres across the diagonal. In this case, the rise is approximately 4·7 m, so the form is slightly flatter, giving larger horizontal forces at the mid-span of the shell (see plan and elevation of Fig. 4.24). This shape, Isler considers, is getting 'close to the limit' for a shell of this type with unstiffened edges. The extremely slender appearance of the shell, which is only 80 mm thick, can be seen in Fig. 4.25, which was taken before the glazing and central skylight were installed. This lightness is still evident in the interior view of the completed building (Fig. 4.26).

Fig. 4.25. The Bürgi Garden Centre, Camorino, bare shell before the addition of glazing.

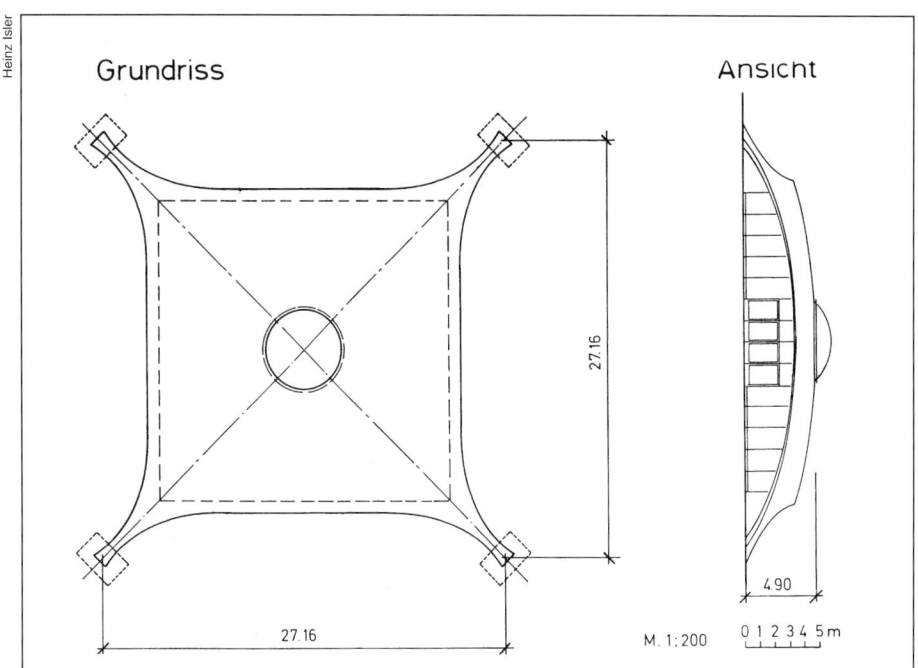

Fig. 4.24. Plan and elevation of the Bürgi Garden Centre, Camorino.

Sports and Ski Centre, Chamonix, 1970–75

Architects: Roger Taillibert, Paris; BET Europé Etude, Paris
Engineer (shells): Heinz Isler

The 28 shells at Chamonix cannot really be described as free form. But, this is a situation where, with a little more collaboration between architect and engineer, they might well have been.[72] This is one occasion in which the architect, Roger Taillibert, dictated to Isler what form the shells should take. In consequence, Isler is not so pleased with the results of his labours, dramatic though they may be.

All of these shells are of simple geometric

Heinz Isler

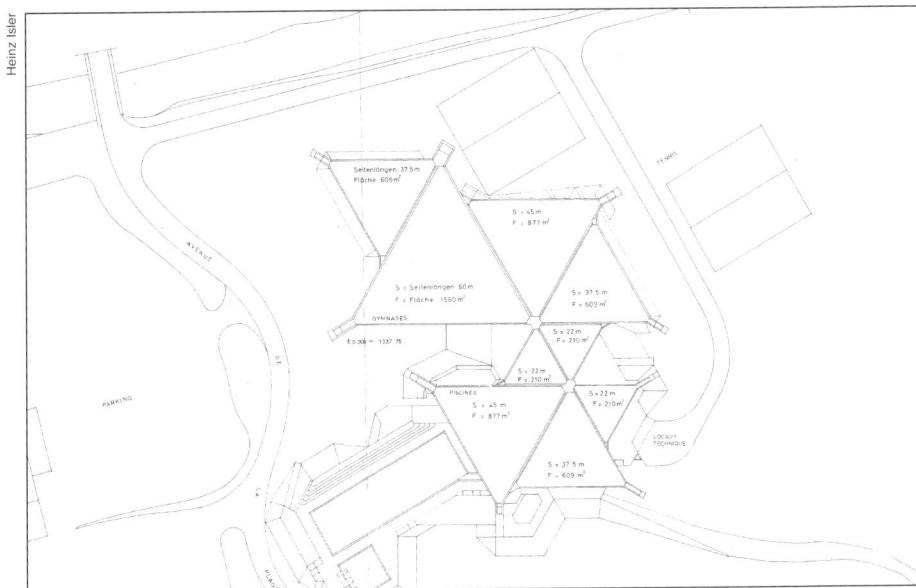

Fig. 4.27. Layout of a group of nine geometric, equilateral, triangular segment shells for the sports and ski facilities, Chamonix, France, 1970-75.

Fig. 4.26. Lightweight appearance of interior and façade, Bürgi Garden Centre, Camorino.

Photo: Heinz Isler

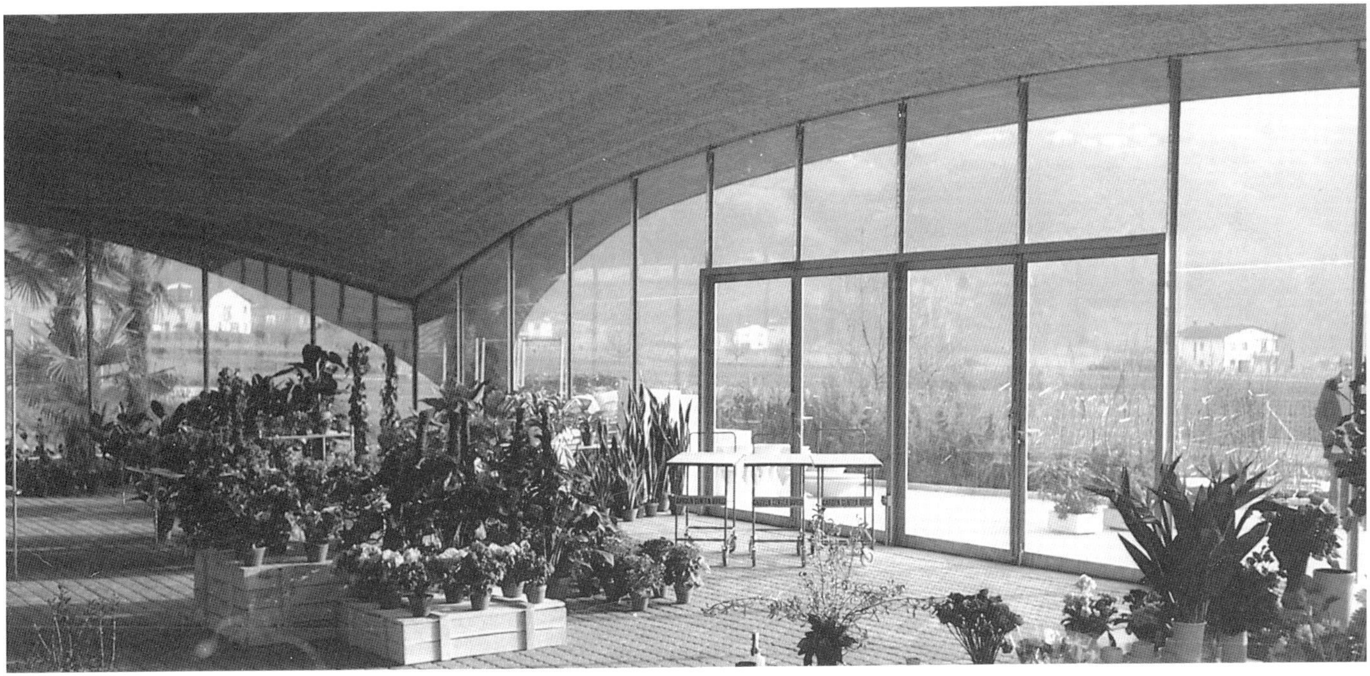

Chapter Four
Free-form shells

form, namely equilateral triangular segments (*Fig. 4.27*) taken from the surface of a sphere, and this form was rigidly ordained by the architect. The spherical segments, of various sizes, are all supported on points at their corners (*Fig. 4.28*). As in terms of statics this is an inefficient structural configuration, cumbersome and rather unsightly edge beams had to be introduced. In certain areas of the complex the permitted rise of the shells was also rather mean. This flattened their curvature and consequently meant that the edge beams had to be even thicker. Furthermore, being located at the foot of Mont Blanc a design snow load of 833 kg/m^2, which is extremely high, had to be imposed. Because of these various factors the shells look rather heavy, nowhere near as slender as those normally created by Isler. This is rather sad as the location is dramatic and the project of international acclaim (*Fig. 4.29*).

The development took place over six years,

Fig. 4.29. View of a group of Chamonix shells below Mont Blanc.

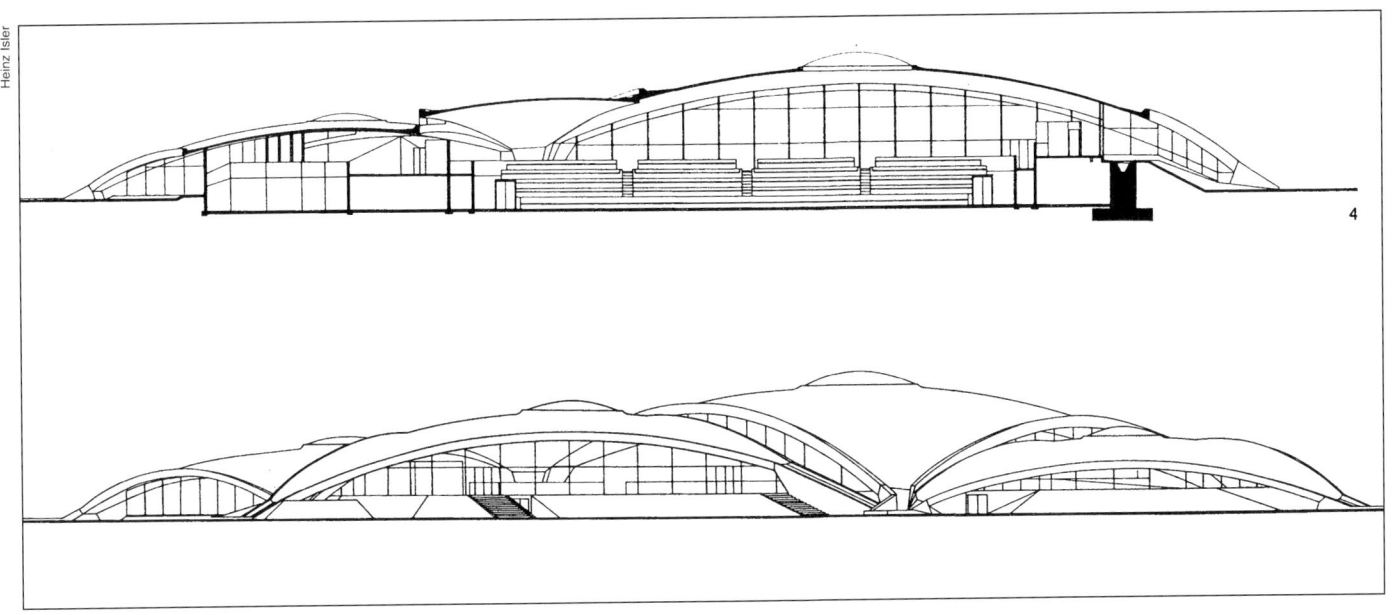

Fig. 4.28. Section and southwest elevation of the swimming arena shells at Chamonix.

commencing in 1970–71 with the construction of the swimming and sports facilities. This first phase consisted of nine triangular shells with side lengths of 22, 37.5, 45 and 60 m which covered a total area of about 6000 m². The spherical surface segments were of different radius and thickness, ranging from 26 m radius and 80 mm thick for the smallest 22 m side length roofs up to 70 m radius and 150 mm thick for the 60 m roofs. There was up to 3 m difference in level between the supports of any individual shell and these were isolated or common as appropriate in the overall layout. Prestressing of the shells was by tie beams between the corner supports, parallel to the edges, and involved forces varying from 150 to 1200 tonnes with steel cables of 12 x 5 mm diameter. Some of the prestressing cables are set very deep in the basement and Isler says that this needed huge masses of concrete to equilibrate the forces.

In several locations the edge beam of one shell was located directly above the adjacent shell (at lower level). The gap between the two shells was clad with Sécurit glazing mounted on tubular mullions set radially on the arched edge beams. These mullions were fixed only at the lower end and allowed to slide at the top, transmitting only horizontal wind forces to the upper shell. Thus the predicted differential movement between the adjacent shells, of 50 to 120 mm vertically and 50 to 80 mm horizontally, was accommodated.[73]

Between 1972 and 1974 the school centre was developed and this involved the building of ten triangular shell roofs with side lengths varying from 22.5 m to 45.0 m. At the same time the l'Ecole Nationale de Ski et d'Alpinisme (ENSA) was under construction, having five triangular shells of 22.5 m to 30.0 m side length. Finally, in 1975 the Community Centre and Library, incorporating four triangular shells of 22.5 to 37.0 m side length, were built. Altogether, the development housed swimming pools, sports halls, training rooms and changing rooms as well as meeting/lecture rooms, workshops, offices and a library. In this building phase the proportion of height to span of the shells was better, therefore the forces within them and the size of the edge stiffener were smaller.

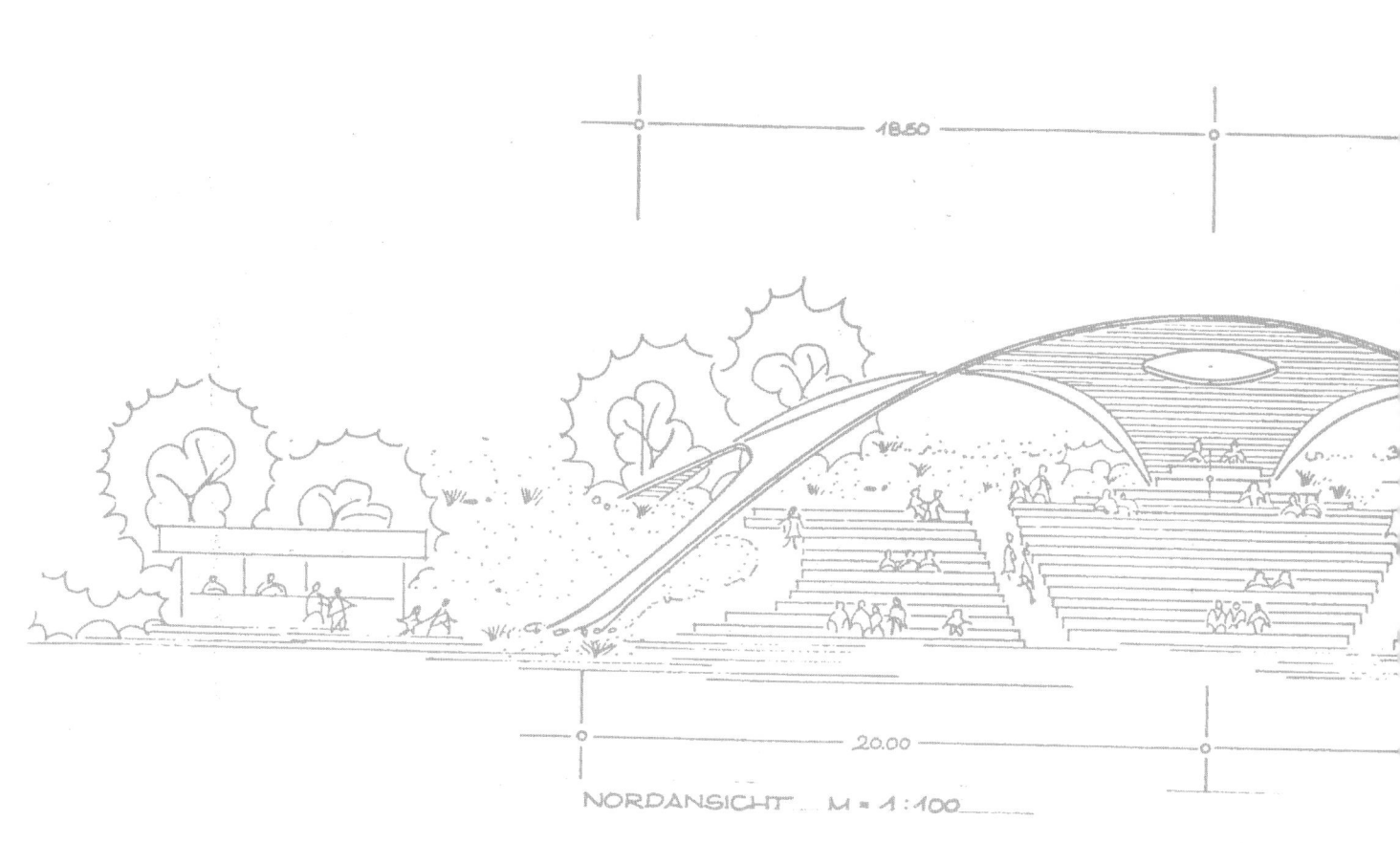

NORDANSICHT M = 1:100

Chapter Five
Inverted membrane shells

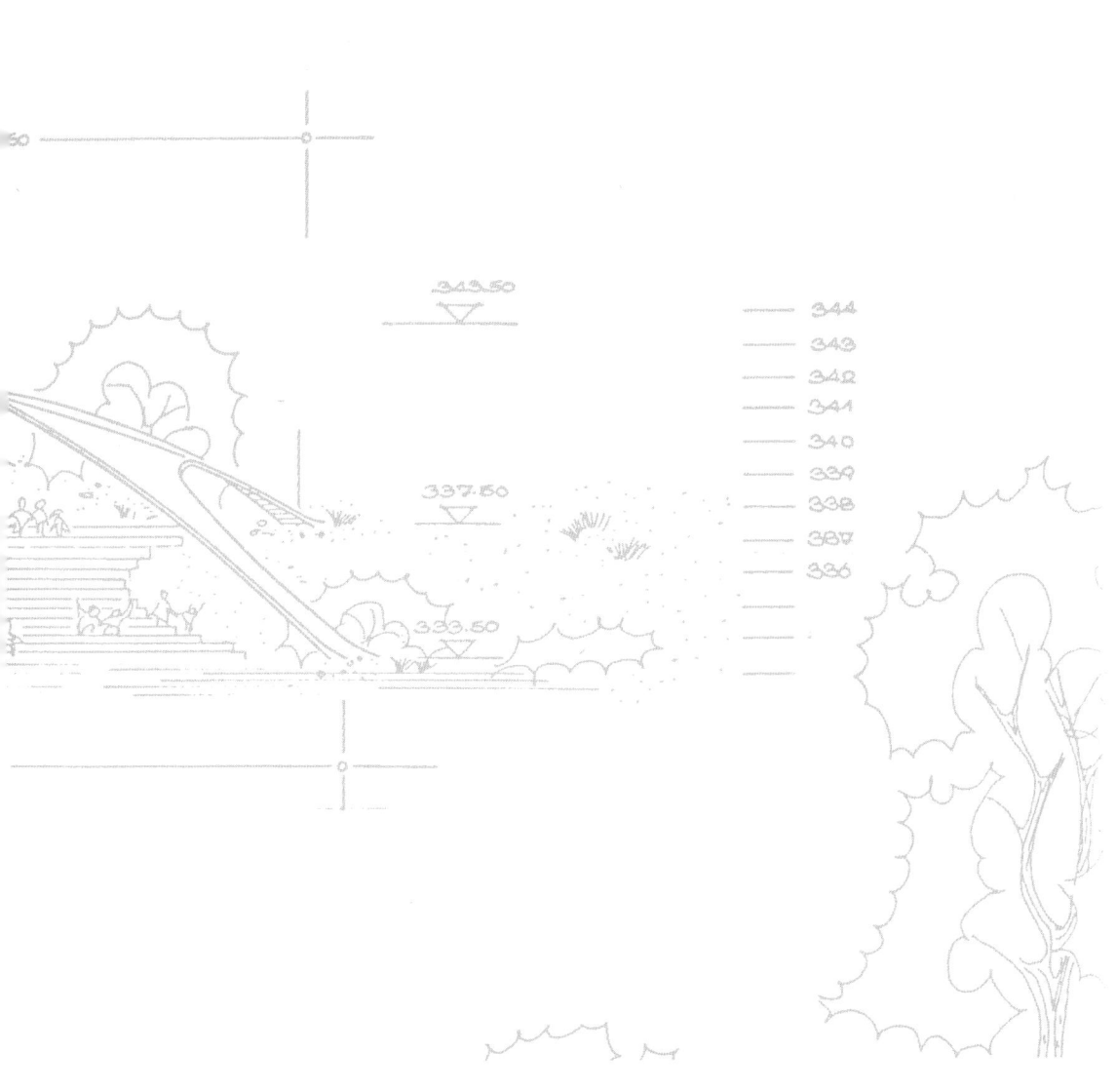

Chapter Five
Inverted membrane shells

Fig. 5.1. Pair of elongated triangular shells at the Deitingen Süd Service Station on the N1 motorway between Bern and Zürich, soon after construction.

Perhaps the most dramatic of Heinz Isler's structures are the free-form shells derived from his lifetime observation of shapes in nature and experimental studies with small-scale structural models. In particular, as discussed in chapter two above, the free-form shells are mainly generated from the inverted shape of hanging membranes, with supports disposed as in the actual structure. Using this method an efficient form can be found for almost any applied loading and ground plan. It is Isler's opinion[74] that the shell shapes found by the inversion of hanging membrane models, because they are almost pure compression structures, are the best.

Motorway Service Station, Deitingen Süd, 1968
Engineer and General Architecture: Heinz Isler
Situated on the N1 Motorway between Bern and Zürich this pair of visually exciting elongated triangular forms, almost sculptural in nature (*Fig. 5.1*), was one of Isler's first excursions into shells generated by hanging membrane models. The two shells lie symmetrically each side of the amenity building, which houses a shop, restaurant and toilet facilities of the service station. Compared to the shells that sit above and rest on it, the amenity building is mundane and of little architectural merit. Unlike the triangular shells of Chamonix, described at the end of the previous chapter, where the architect Taillibert dictated the form to Isler, these triangular shells are shapes that have been designed for structural economy. Isler was in charge of the form-finding here.

It is uplifting to come upon these two, three-point supported, prestressed concrete shells, in the Swiss countryside. Each is 31·6 m long and up to 26·0 m wide (*Fig. 5.2*). They face each other like two giant duelling crustaceans across some man-made rock or, when seen in elevation, like the wings of a bird in flight (*Fig. 5.3*). In plan the two shells are spaced just over 7 m apart each with two feet resting on the structure of the amenity block, giving an overall distance of 68·24 m between the outer supports. Each shell rises to a maximum height of 11·5 m above ground level.

As the shape of the surfaces was derived from that of a scale model produced by hanging a

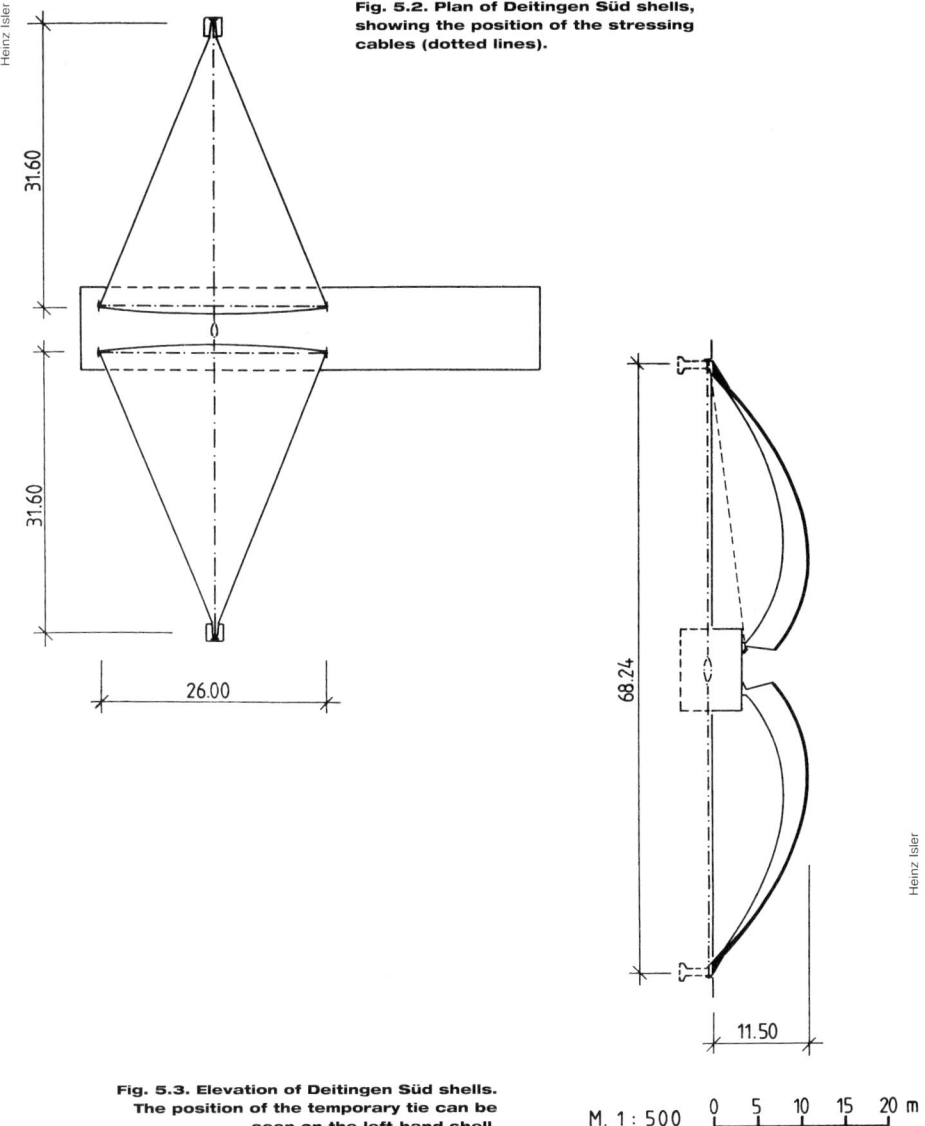

Fig. 5.2. Plan of Deitingen Süd shells, showing the position of the stressing cables (dotted lines).

Fig. 5.3. Elevation of Deitingen Süd shells. The position of the temporary tie can be seen on the left-hand shell.

suitably weighted membrane from three supports at the appropriate spacing, a statically ideal configuration was found. By inverting the hanging membrane model, which cannot do other than be in pure tension, the structure will be in pure compression under its self-weight (which is the dominant load). The 90 mm thick concrete forms are synclastic, with the principal curvatures running parallel and perpendicular to a line between the outer supports. Double curvature ensures the stability of the free edges without requiring stiffening edge beams. Prestressing of the surfaces by drawing the outer supports towards the centre of the building ensures that the shells are always in compression and uncracked. To examine the behaviour of the shells under load, including the prestressing forces, tests were carried out on the model shown in *Fig. 5.4*.

The combined structural system of the two shells is rather interesting, as they are mutually supporting, relying on the presence of the amenity block to maintain their equilibrium. As the shells are arched in both directions (*Fig. 5.5*), it is necessary to resist an outward horizontal thrust at each foot. For the shorter spans of each shell the two feet resting on the amenity block are connected by prestressed ties so that the outward thrusts parallel to the line between these supports is balanced. In the other direction an underground tie with prestressing cables connects the two single point supports (through the base of the amenity block). However, the shells are not directly connected to each other at the centre, so

Chapter Five
Inverted membrane shells

there is also an inward horizontal thrust at each of the inner supports. These horizontal forces are transmitted between the shells by the slab of the amenity block. Two shear walls are also contiguous with the base slab. Thereby, a closed structural system is produced and static equilibrium is preserved, also for unsymmetrical and wind forces.

This rather elegant structural solution required temporary restraints during the construction process. To stress the system as a whole requires both shells to be in place but it would obviously be uneconomic to cast both simultaneously, as two sets of formwork and falsework would be needed. Therefore, the solution was, with the structure of the amenity

Fig. 5.5. View of shell from one of the outer supports, showing the synclastic double curvature.

Fig. 5.4. Model used to examine the behaviour under load of the Deitingen Süd shells.

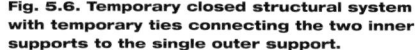
Fig. 5.6. Temporary closed structural system with temporary ties connecting the two inner supports to the single outer support.

building in place, to cast one shell and to install temporary ties connecting the two inner supports with the single outer support, so forming a temporary closed structural system (Fig. 5.6). Moving the shuttering to the other side, the second shell was then cast and when the concrete had gained sufficient strength the full system was stressed. To introduce compressive stresses into the whole surface the two outer supports, which were at this stage free to slide, were each pulled in by approximately 12 mm towards the central services building. Once stressing was complete the ducts in the tie beams were grouted. With this structural system mainly vertical load is transmitted to the bases, the only lateral forces being due to wind action on the shells.

At the outer supports the upper shell

surface is moulded to form an edge lip to direct rainwater towards the stone filled drainage trough. The concrete has a white external protection with slight surface discoloration because of dirt. However the shells appear still to be in perfect condition after 31 years of service. They still form a striking contrast with the dark slopes of the nearby Jura Mountains (*Fig. 5.7*).

There is a very interesting story to relate about these shells. In 1999, the petroleum company BP (in Great Britain), the current owners of the service station, decided that they wanted to remove the concrete shell roofs and replace them with their standard steel framed canopies in order to maintain their corporate identity in the fiercely competitive market of vehicle fuel sales. Isler was at first shocked by the intention to demolish the shells but then began to deal with their destruction in his mind, although regretting their demise. However, word of BP's intentions got out and, without any intervention from Heinz Isler, a campaign was started to resist the demolition of what had by now become a well-known and loved national monument.[75] In fact, in Switzerland there had previously been some suggestion that several of Isler's more sculptural shells should be protected as listed structures. Once word was out, Isler was contacted by newspapers, radio and television companies seeking his opinion on the subject of the demolition.

Much to Isler's amazement on the 18th July 1999, when he opened his Sunday newspaper,

Fig. 5.7. Deitingen Süd shells as they were in Aug. 1999.

Chapter Five
Inverted membrane shells

Sonntagszeitung, in the culture section on page 45, he came across an article in which five Swiss architects had written in support of the campaign to keep the shells and decrying the vandalism that BP were about to commit. Of the five[76] who were offering their support, the best known outside Switzerland is perhaps Mario Botta who in his letter said 'Wegen ihrer Schönheit muss die Konstruktion unbedingt bewahrt werden'.[77] The tremendous reaction to the threat of demolition and the wide popular support for the retention of the shells was completely unexpected by the oil company. Since then, they have (for the time being, at least) decided not to proceed with their proposed 'upgrading' of the service area.

Fig. 5.8. Site model of the Sicli SA factory, Geneva, 1969.

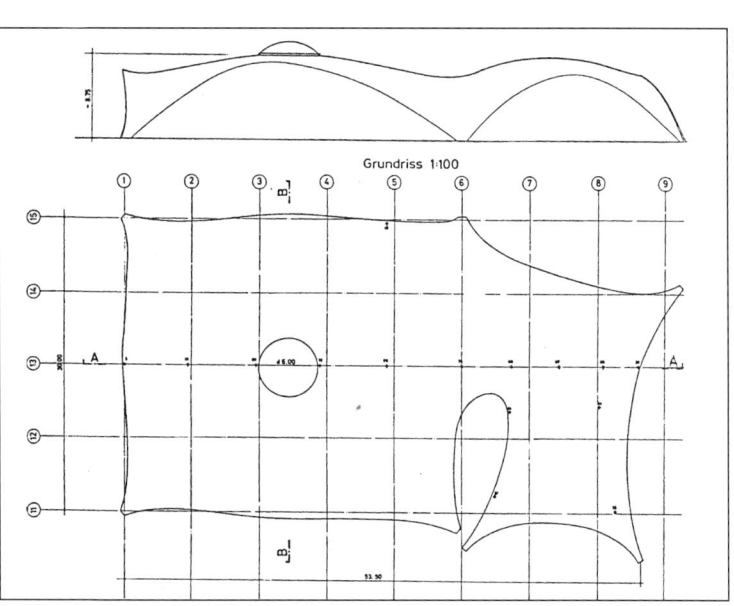

Fig. 5.9. Plan and elevation of the Sicli SA factory, Geneva.

Fig. 5.10. Elevated view of the Sicli SA factory, Geneva.

Fig. 5.11. The two-storey administration building in the smaller section of the Sicli shell.

Fig. 5.12. A shallow valley connects the halls of the Sicli factory.

However, Isler thinks that this is only a reprieve and not an acquittal. When visiting the shells with Isler in August 1999, it could be seen that concrete cores had been taken near each of the shell supports, presumably to assess the current state of the structure and perhaps in an effort to produce evidence that the shells are no longer sound.[78] Let us hope that this is not just a reprieve, for the destruction of these shells would be a considerable loss to the history of structural engineering and architecture.

Factory for Sicli SA, Geneva, 1969

Architect: C. Hilberer, Geneva

Engineer: Heinz Isler (form and statics)

As a single shell surface of irregular plan form on seven supports, this is perhaps the most complex of Heinz Isler's hanging free-form prestressed concrete shells. It was built in 1969 as a factory for the fire extinguisher manufacturer, Sicli SA, in Geneva.

As can be seen from the model (*Fig. 5.8*) the form could perhaps be perceived as two separate free-form shells that share one support. However, when viewed in plan (*Fig. 5.9*) or from the elevated position of *Fig. 5.10* it can be seen that the apparently separate surfaces are, in fact, connected by a gently moulded valley for about half the distance between the intermediate support. The shells, therefore, interact structurally. One portion of the shell, the larger, is roughly square in plan, varying in width from approximately 30 to 32 m while on the slightly longer axis it is about 35 m long. This form is

Chapter Five
Inverted membrane shells

perhaps a precursor of similar sized swimming pool shells, which Isler was to develop later. Housing the production area, the main volume has a diagonal span of 58 m and at its centre there is a 6 m diameter polyester shell dome skylight.

Beside the main hall, the two-storey administration building (*Fig. 5.11*) is accommodated within the smaller section of the shell. This portion is rotated clockwise in the horizontal plane, by an angle of about 10 degrees relative to the larger portion, and shifted forward by about 2 m. It has an approximately rhomboidal form tapering from a maximum of approximately 34 m long on the side adjacent to the main hall, down to 28 m on the opposite side. The width varies from 23 m, where there is a shared support with the larger hall, down to 18 m across the two independent supports. A large teardrop shaped opening, intended for use as a winter garden, is formed as part of the boundary between the two surfaces. Where the halls are connected by the shallow valley adjacent to the shared support (*Fig. 5.12*), they are pierced by a series of small diameter circular openings (*Fig. 5.13*). An interior view during construction is shown in *Fig. 5.14*.

The final shape of the building with the double shell was developed after a series of model studies with roofs of differing configuration. Remarkable in concept, the final integrated shell form, which includes the opening for the winter garden, was the result of numerous experiments

Fig. 5.13. The Sicli shell is pierced by a series of small diameter circular openings.

Fig. 5.14. Interior view during construction of the Sicli factory.

Fig. 5.15. Small-scale model of the Sicli factory, used to determine forces within the surface and its buckling behaviour experimentally.

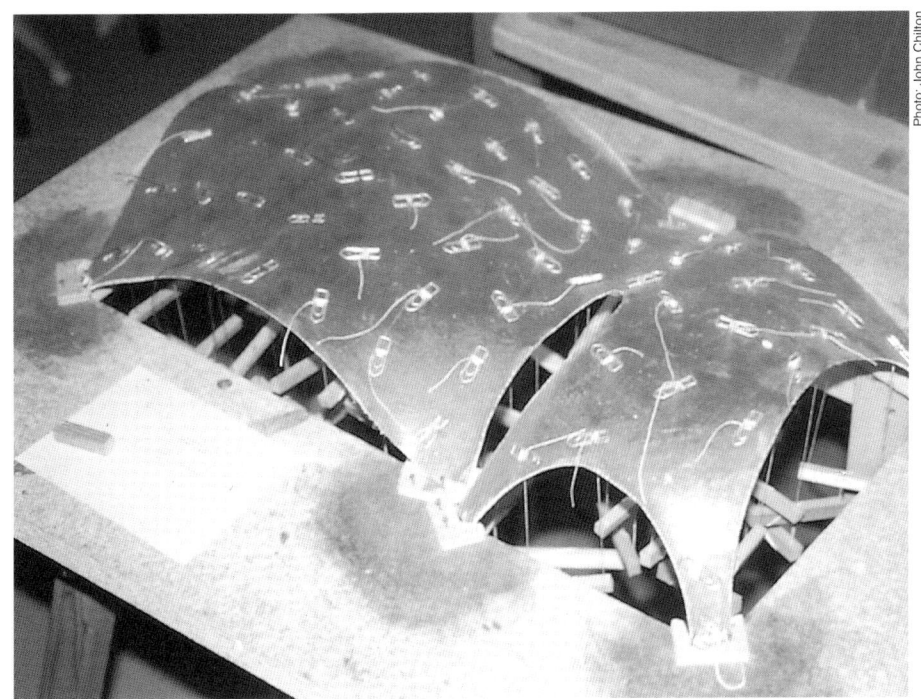

with hanging models. The seven-point supported completely irregular surface encloses the entire production and administration accommodation of the firm under one roof. It was chosen to make maximum use of the irregular boundaries of the property.

The shell has no edge beams and a general thickness of only 100 mm. Because of the total asymmetry and complex geometry the forces within the surface and its buckling behaviour were determined by the use of experiments on small-scale models (*Fig. 5.15*). Finite element computer calculation of such structures was, at that time, not available. Even today it would be difficult because of total absence of any symmetry.

Due to the complexity of this surface with its seven-point support, Isler has taken a great interest in its long-term behaviour since construction. The deformation of the structure was monitored over almost 20 years at a regular grid of points across the shell. The results of his study were included in a conference paper that he presented in Tokyo in 1993.[79] Here a plan showing the principle monitoring points on a section through the long axis of the shell was shown together with a plot of the deformations along that line. Deformed shapes were plotted, for occasions when the ambient conditions were similar, over a period of 19 years, from the day the prestressing force was first introduced into the surface (*Fig. 5.16*). This revealed some very interesting details about the long-term behaviour of this thin shell.

5.16. Deformation along the long section (see Fig. 5.9).

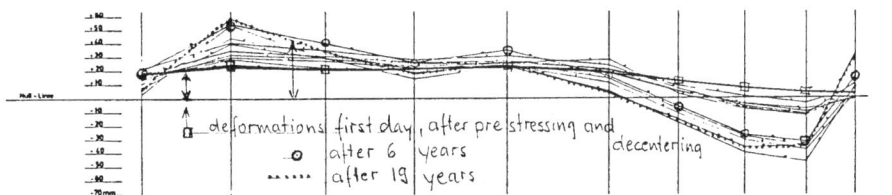

Pict. 3 Concrete Shell, Plan, Section, Deformationlines on Main Axes.

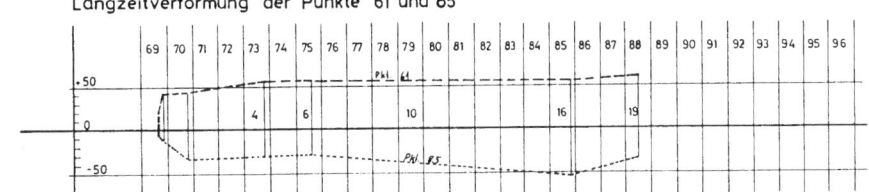

Pict. 4 Simplified Longterm Diagrams from 19 Years of Observation.

Chapter Five
Inverted membrane shells

When the prestress was first applied the shell immediately rose along the whole length of the long section. The rise was fairly even over the larger section, about 20 mm but in the smaller section the rise was about 20 mm where it was connected to the larger surface and about 5 mm at the free edge. This rise is approximately 1/1500 of the shorter span of the larger shell surface. *Figure 5.16* reveals that over the 19 years from 1969 to 1988 the larger shell had actually risen further (up to a maximum of around 60 mm above its level when cast). However, the smaller part of the shell had dropped overall so that it was now up to 40 mm lower than its level when cast. The areas of greatest movement appeared to be at both ends of the long section but slightly

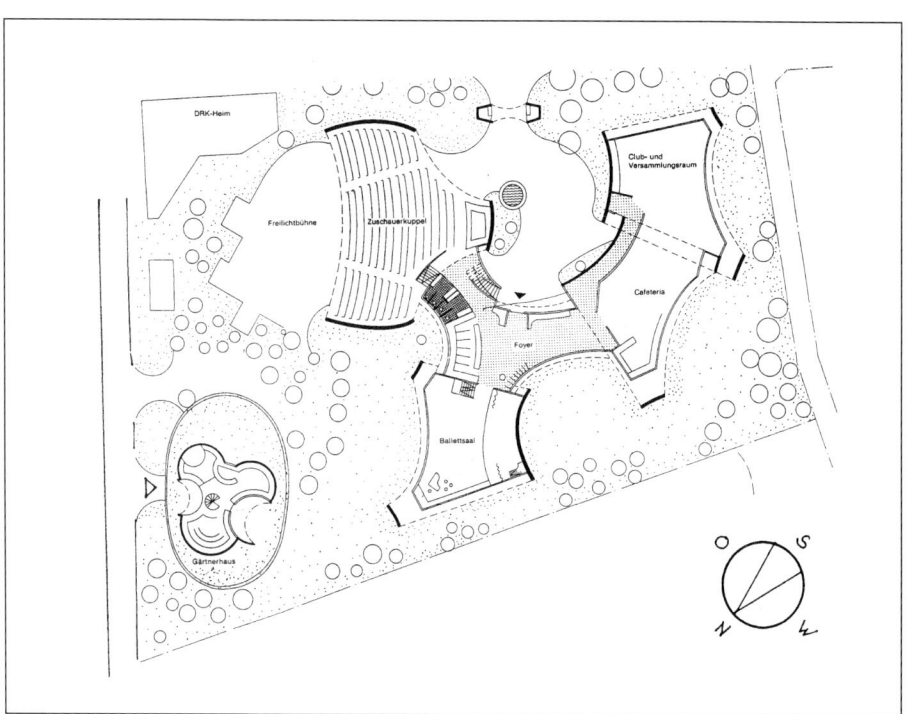

Fig. 5.17. Site plan of the complex of Isler shells at Stetten auf den Fildern, near Stuttgart, 1976.

Fig. 5.18. View of the whole Stetten complex.

inward of the free edges. Over the majority of the larger shell there seemed to be little movement. Isler was not too concerned about these movements as they appeared to be asymptotic but in 1985 there was a sudden unexplained change in their behaviour, when the smaller shell started to rise again! However, this movement caused by work on a neighbouring site,[80] has again become asymptotic. This study shows how important it is to record the actual behaviour of such non-conventional structural forms over long periods, so that their response to load, material properties and environmental conditions may be better understood.

Given the highly appealing sculptural form of these thin free-edged concrete shells, it is surprising that more similarly complex structures have not been built. Perhaps it is because architects feel their role as arbiters of a building's external aesthetic is threatened when the engineer dictates the dominant form; when the shape of the majority of the external envelope is derived entirely from the statics. An architect who does not feel so threatened is Michael Balz who has worked with Isler to create several free-form, free-edged shells that have been constructed near Stuttgart.

Fig. 5.19. View from the stage of the Stetten open-air theatre.

Fig. 5.20. The Ballet Salon shell, Stetten, showing its organic shape with a small surface area.

Fig. 5.21. The Ballet Salon shell permits large areas of glazing.

Chapter Five
Inverted membrane shells

Fig. 5.22. The Ballet Salon shell, corner view, as it contacts the ground.

Fig. 5.23. The Ballet Salon shell, interior view.

Open-air theatres at Stetten auf den Fildern, 1976, and Grötzingen, 1977
Architect: Michael Balz
Engineer: Heinz Isler

Stetten
The first of the shells in which Michael Balz and Heinz Isler collaborated was for a roof at the outdoor theatre, in Stetten auf den Fildern, near Stuttgart, in Germany. As well as being used for traditional plays and pantomimes, the open-air theatre at Stetten was also the venue for a very popular and successful annual series of summer weekend jazz concerts that attracted up to 10 000 patrons each year. The mainly amateur performers at the theatre being full of enthusiasm were not too deterred by the vagaries of the weather but it was thought that audiences might

Fig. 5.24. Plan of the Grötzingen outdoor theatre shell.

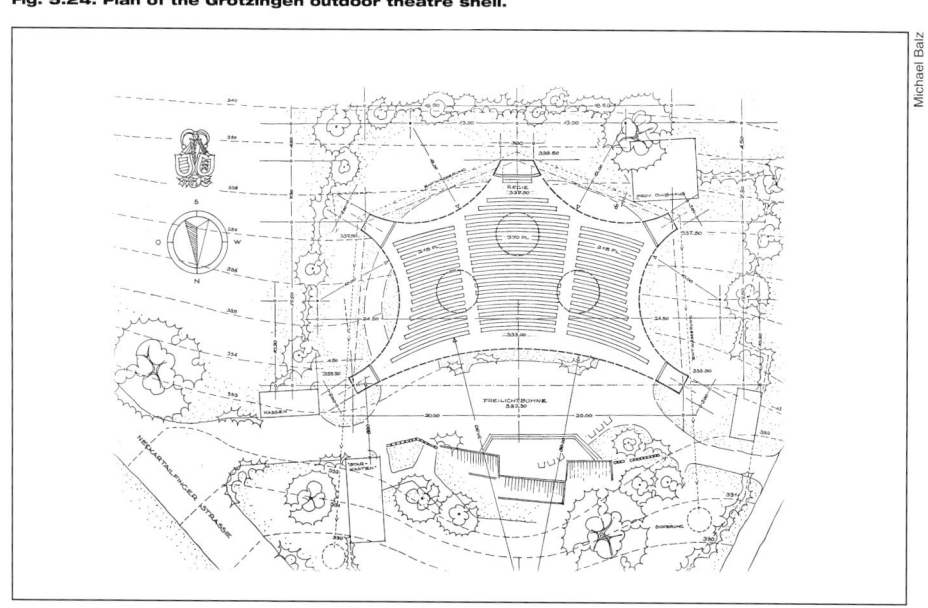

Fig. 5.25. Front elevation and section of the Grötzingen outdoor theatre shell.

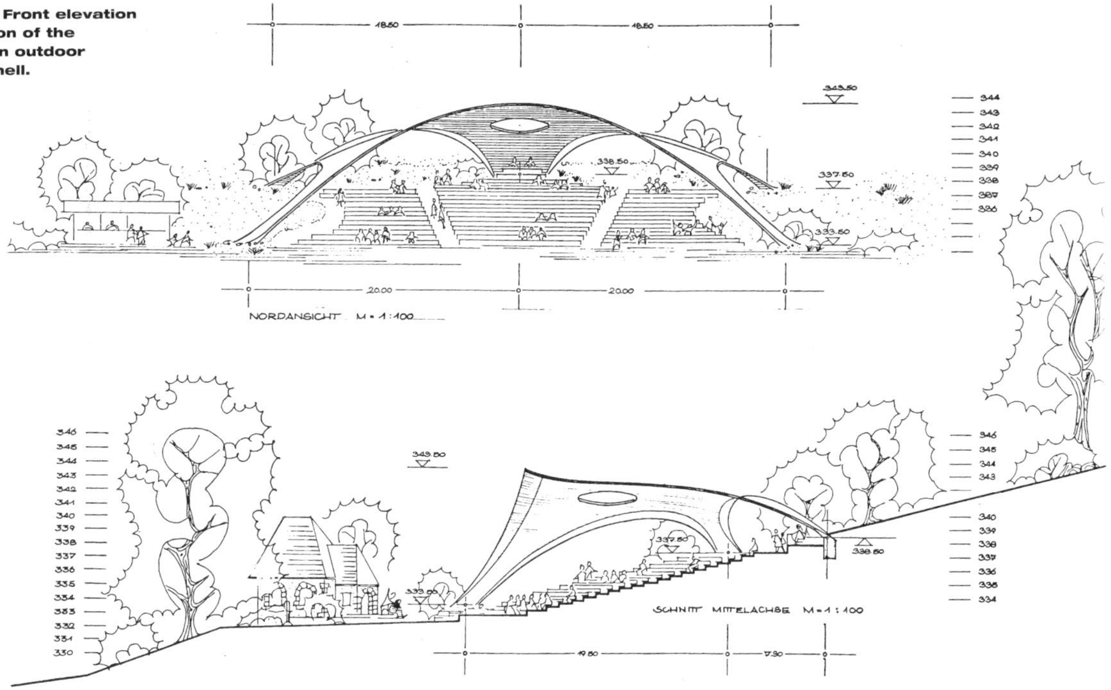

increase if some protection from the weather was provided for them. Therefore, to blend as much as possible into the natural setting of the theatre's surroundings, a concrete shell roof was commissioned to cover the 570 seats. This structural form was chosen as it combines a high loadbearing capacity with low material use and it was also assumed that, with time, the concrete would gradually weather to look like natural stone. Further the shell protects from aeroplane noise.

Maximum overall dimensions of the 500 m² free-form shell are 27·2 x 22·0 m with a single axis of symmetry. *Figure 5.17* shows the plan of the whole Stetten complex that incorporates several shells including the open-air theatre shell, which is to the top left of the plan. A general view of the complex is presented in *Fig. 5.18*, which shows, to the left, the architect Michael Balz's house, described in detail in chapter six, at the centre the theatre, and to the right the ballet salon, described below. Supported at three locations, the theatre shell has a truncated triangular plan form. The edge facing the stage is completely open, spanning 27·2 m and rising to 7·5 metres above the springing points. Along the sides of the raked seating the shell forms opposing, slightly curved, walls. At the rear of the seating the shell is supported on a third, shorter wall. The bases are connected underground by tie beams. In this case there is no stiffening beam or cantilever along the free boundary but the shell edge is turned up slightly, in a more sophisticated version of the cantilevers used in the Wyss Garden Centre shell (*see Figs 4.1 or 4.5*).

Fig. 5.26. Development model for the Grötzingen outdoor theatre shell.

Chapter Five
Inverted membrane shells

Fig. 5.27. Slender edge of the Grötzingen.

It may be noted that here, unlike in most of Isler's shells, the surface comes in contact with the ground over a considerable proportion of the perimeter, instead of being supported on a few slender buttresses (*Fig. 5.19*). This extra enclosure is due to the close proximity of Stuttgart Airport and is an attempt to limit the intrusion of aircraft noise into the auditorium. The shape of the shell, derived by inversion of a hanging model, was also designed to improve the acoustic qualities of the performance space. To assist in this, the wood-wool slabs usually used as permanent formwork and thermal insulation were also used here, although thermal insulation is obviously of little use in the open structure. In this case, the slabs act as acoustic absorbers, reducing unwanted sound reflections and preventing

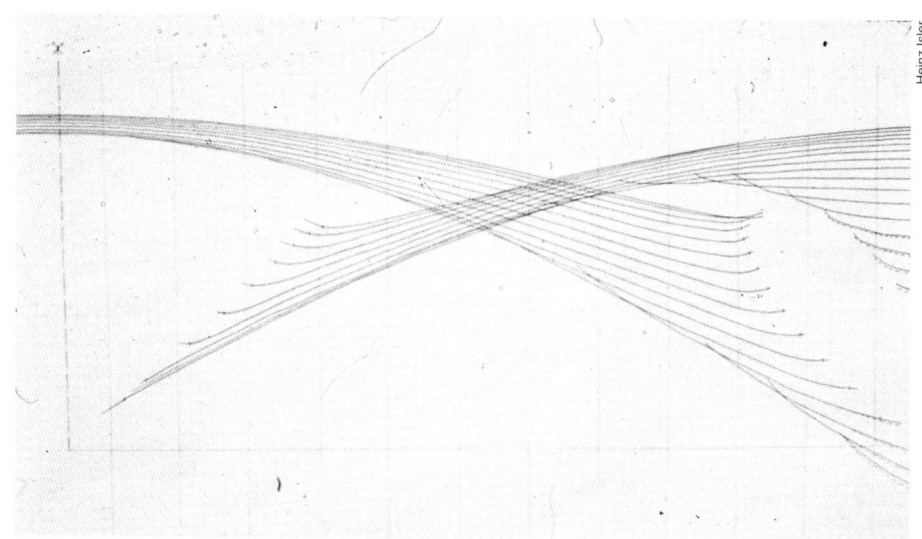

Fig. 5.28. (a) and (b) Drawings of the beam profiles.

Fig. 5.29. Interior view of the Grötzingen shell during a performance.

Fig. 5.30. Aerial view of the Grötzingen shell.

Fig. 5.31. Tennis halls at Heimberg, 1979.

sound focussing from the inner surface of the mainly synclastic shell.

Following the success of the theatre roof, which encouraged much larger audiences from its inauguration, Balz and Isler collaborated in the design and construction of additional shells at the same location. In 1979, a ballet salon was added. Seen in plan at the bottom centre of *Fig. 5.17*, this shell is totally free form and is supported on one curved wall and two point supports. Trapezoidal in shape it has a maximum span of 22 m. Although the organic shape of the ballet salon has a small surface area (*Fig. 5.20*), it still allows large areas of glazing to be incorporated as can be seen in *Fig. 5.21*. The way in which the shell elegantly contacts the ground is shown in *Fig. 5.22* and the light and airy interior in *Fig. 5.23*. Later, in 1988, a meeting room and rehearsal theatre were also constructed. These are at the top right of the site plan.

Grötzingen

In 1977, the architect Michael Balz collaborated again with Isler in the construction of a larger cover for the audience at an outdoor theatre in Grötzingen, also near Stuttgart. In this case the concrete shell was 600 m^2 in area, with maximum dimensions of 28 x 42 m and supported at five points at differing levels up the terraced seating. The shell form, seen in plan, elevation and section in *Figs. 5.24* and *5.25*, was again modelled using a hanging membrane (*Fig. 5.26*) and also had a single axis of symmetry. This larger theatre seats 800 people under the shell, which rises to 8·5 m at the centre of the side nearest the stage.

Once more edge beams are avoided as the thin shell free edges are turned up to increase their rigidity while maintaining their slender appearance (*Fig. 5.27*). The degree of surface modelling applied can be seen clearly in *Figs. 5.28(a)* and *(b)*, which shows how the curved timber board beams of the falsework turn up at the edge of the shell.

Here, as in the Stetten ballet roof, prestressing was applied by means of stressed tie beams below ground. No cracking is expected in the resulting compression structure, which although unprotected should remain watertight and maintenance free — an ideal solution for such a location. Given the greater span of this structure compared with the outdoor theatre at Stetten, it has a thickness varying from 90 to

Chapter Five
Inverted membrane shells

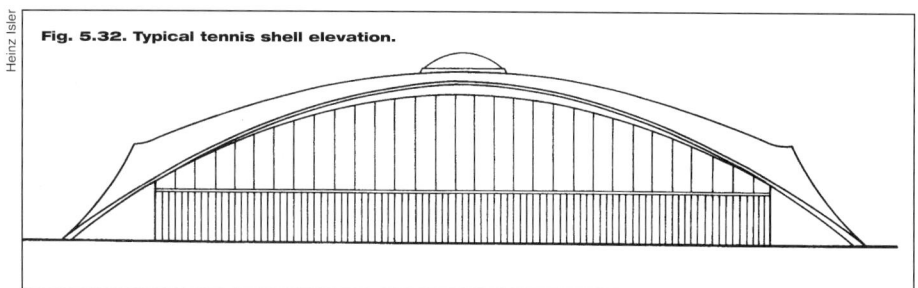

Fig. 5.32. Typical tennis shell elevation.

Fig. 5.33. Elevation of the Solothurn tennis hall shell.

Fig. 5.34. Interior view of the completed but, as yet, unclad tennis hall shell at Solothurn.

120 mm. As previously, the wood-wool slabs are retained as acoustic absorbers. General lighting is provided by rings of lamps (*Fig. 5.29*) which mimic the circular domed roof lights of many of Isler's other shells. Although not initially enclosed at the sides, the shell was constructed with provision for the installation of façades at a later date, if necessary.

When seen from above the overall elegance of the Grötzingen shell form, which is generated naturally and automatically by the effects of gravity on a membrane surface can be fully appreciated (*Fig. 5.30*).

Tennis halls and swimming pools
Tennis halls

One of Isler's most successful designs generated using hanging forms is that of his tennis or sports halls and swimming pool enclosures. These were first introduced in 1978 at Düdingen where three shells each 18·6 x 48·5 m overall were constructed. Typical concrete thickness is 90 to 100 mm. Since then similar tennis halls have been built all over Switzerland, mainly by the Haus + Herd Company, of Herzogenbuchsee.

It requires great skill and experience to design thin concrete shells with free edges without using heavy edge beams. To achieve this with shells of approximately square plan, where the structure is two-way spanning, is difficult but it becomes almost impossible to make a slender shell, without edge beams, as the plan becomes more rectangular in form. This is because the structure begins to want to span mainly in one direction, like a wide arch, so the benefits of the surface-active shell become less. The compression forces in the shell increase while the cross-section resisting them decreases. Hence, the stresses in the surface increase and buckling becomes more likely. However, following many hanging model experiments to find the ideal form, Isler achieved the almost impossible. The tennis and sports halls are long-span, rectangular, free-edged shells, that do not have edge beams. They are also highly efficient and economical structures and an elegant alternative to the conventional tennis hall. Large open volumes can easily be formed by joining several of the shells together, side by side. It is interesting to note that the roof form, determined from a hanging model, follows closely the trajectory of a tennis ball. Both the form and the trajectory are natural functions produced by the action of gravity, as can be seen by the typical elevation (*Fig. 5.32*) and the views of a completed but as yet unclad shell (*Figs 5.33 and 5.34*).

Fig. 5.35. Formwork for the tennis hall shells at Düdingen.

Fig. 5.36. Internal view of a typical tennis hall shell at Marin.

When the first tennis hall shells were constructed, Isler carried out what were effectively full-scale model tests, at Heimberg, by making four slightly different shapes. As each shell was prestressed, careful and detailed measurements were taken of the deformation of the structure. The third shell deformed the least, indicating that it was a more rigid form than the others, thus giving Isler valuable evidence about the structural efficiency of the four alternative forms. Subsequent tennis halls were of this form in two standard sizes 17·75 m and 18·6 m wide, now with 48 m span. The formwork for these shells creates a very elegant timber grid of glued-laminated beams (*Fig. 5.35*). Internally, the shells form a beautiful enclosure for indoor tennis (*Figs 5.36 and 5.37*) and the permanent wood-wool slab shuttering has a beneficial sound-deadening effect. Roof lights can be incorporated in the shells without problem but are not installed in the tennis halls, as the glare of such strong overhead light would dazzle the players.

Tennis hall shells have been built in considerable number since the late 1970s at Grenchen (4), Düdingen (3), La Chaux-de-Fond (2), Heimberg (4), Marin (4), Crissier (5), Burgdorf (4), Dreilinden Tennis Centre; Langenthal (4), Emmen Tennis Centre; Lucerne (4), 'Brühl' Sports Centre; Solothurn (6), 'Paradies' Tennis Centre; Allschwil/Basel|d (4), Sion (4) etc.

Fig. 5.37. Interior of the Solothurn tennis hall shell.

Chapter Five
Inverted membrane shells

Fig. 5.38. Exterior of Brugg Swimming Pool roof at Aarepark, Switzerland, 1981.

Fig. 5.39. Interior of Brugg Swimming Pool roof at Aarepark, Switzerland.

5.40. Shell form for the air museum extension in Dübendorf, 1987.

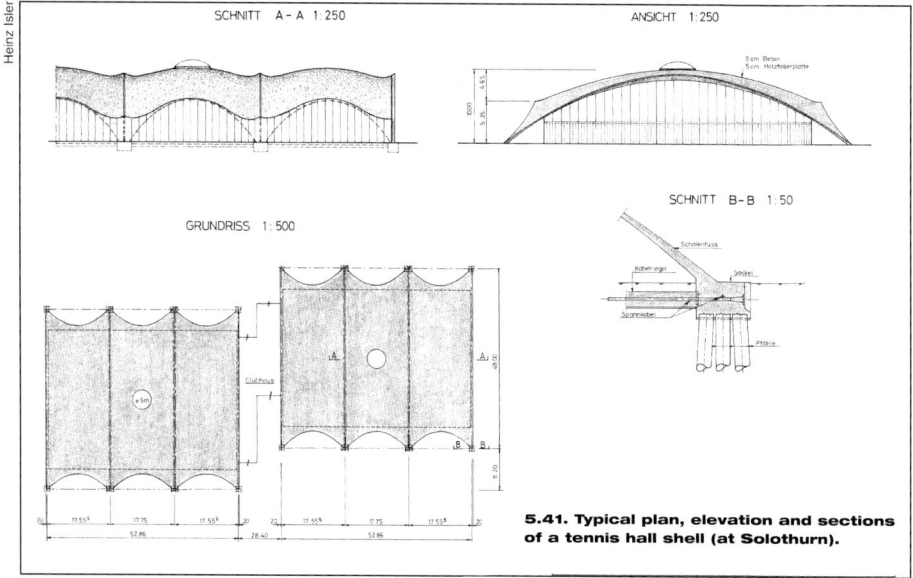

5.41. Typical plan, elevation and sections of a tennis hall shell (at Solothurn).

Swimming pools

At Heimberg a swimming pool was also built at the same time, adjacent to the tennis halls. This building was roofed with an elegant Isler free-form concrete shell with square plan 32·5 x 32·5 m only 90 mm thick. The dimensions and form of the structure are quite similar to the square hall, which is part of the seven point supported irregular shell constructed for the Sicli factory in Geneva, in 1969. However, in the swimming pool roof, the shell is turned up more at the free edges to provide more resistance to any potential buckling of the slender surface. In 1981, a similar form was used for a slightly bigger Brugg Swimming Pool roof at Aarepark, Switzerland. The exterior and interior of the pool hall are seen here in *Figs* 5.38 and 5.39 respectively. Again

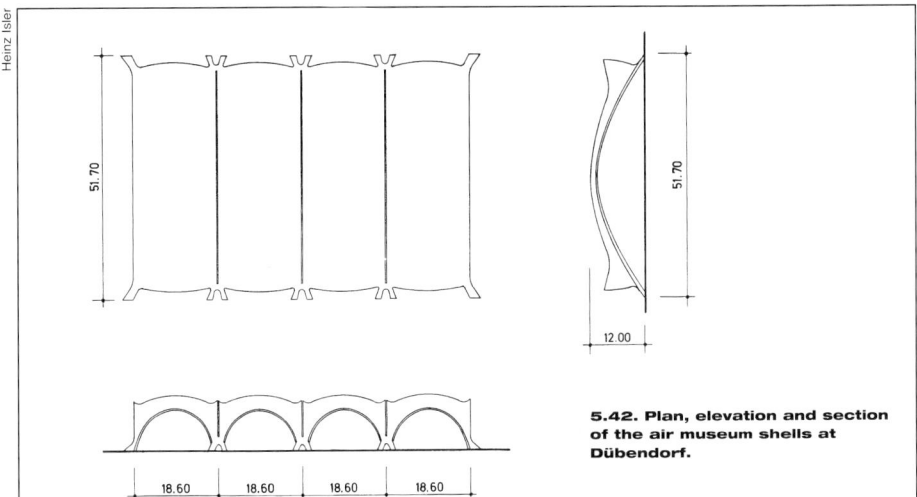

5.42. Plan, elevation and section of the air museum shells at Dübendorf.

5.43. Aerial view of the air museum shells at Dübendorf.

approximately square, of free form and with free upturned edges, the shell spans 35 x 35 m which gives a diagonal span of almost 50 metres. Comparing the shell thickness of 90 mm to the diagonal span of the roof gives a span to thickness ratio of about 550:1, relatively about one tenth the span/thickness ratio of an egg shell.

Aircraft Museum, Dübendorf, 1987
Architects: Haus + Herd
Engineer: Heinz Isler

The adaptability of Isler's shells is demonstrated by this project, which was for an extension to an existing aircraft museum in Dübendorf, constructed in 1987. Four rectangular shells were built, each 18·6 m in width and 51·7 m span, enclosing a total plan area of over 3800 m². In order that the same falsework and formwork could be used with only small modification, the shape of the shells (Fig. 5.40) was developed from that of the tennis halls. The width was the same but the length was increased by 3·7 m, while at the ends a much more pronounced upturned extension was included to give additional stiffness and increase the usable floor area. The difference in form can be seen clearly by comparing the plan and section of Figs 5.41 and 5.42, which show a typical tennis hall (at Solothurn) and the museum shell respectively.

One requirement for the building was that it should be able to house small aircraft and for this the shell form developed by Isler was perfect. As the shells are fully self-supporting over the 52 m span the whole of the end wall was available for door openings so that aircraft could easily be brought into the building after it was completed (Fig. 5.43). Similarly, if the client wanted to change the exhibits at a future date it would be possible to do so. Although the form of Isler's shells is most ideally suited to carrying its own self-weight (a distributed load), the shells are very rigid structures with considerable reserves of strength. Their thickness (and therefore their strength) is usually controlled by the static conditions and minimum thickness that can be placed while ensuring good quality, well-compacted, concrete. Therefore, because point loads are quickly dispersed through the surface of a double-curved shell, it was possible to hang small aircraft from the soffit (Fig. 5.44). The main checks that were required were that the local

Chapter Five
Inverted membrane shells

Fig. 5.44. Interior view of the air museum shells at Dübendorf.

Fig. 5.45. Dübendorf Air Museum - model used for the determination of the structural behaviour.

Fig. 5.46. Aquapark shell, Norwich Sports Village, 1990.

bending and punching capacities of the shell were not exceeded. If at a future date the museum were to be extended further, it would of course be possible to add new shells alongside those existing.

An interesting aspect of these shells is their rigidity. By form-finding and the model tests, Isler succeeded in getting a shape with minimal deformations. When the self-weight load is applied to the Aircraft Museum model (*Fig. 5.45*), it has negligible deformation.[81] This had been one of Isler's technical aims, to find a shape which did not deform appreciably under its own weight. Slight deformation was predicted but only in the region of 15 mm over a 52 m span, and evenly over most of the surface. By prestressing, a pre-camber of slightly higher magnitude was produced — as pulling the supports together caused the roof to rise. After 20 years, by gradual deformation due to creep and other factors, the roof is expected to return approximately to its original shape — then the theoretical deformation would be near zero. This is the way that Isler likes to play — with the physical law that says internal energy is equal to the external energy, playing prestress against gravitation.

Norwich Sports Village 1987–91

Architect: Copeland Associates (with Haus + Herd)
Engineer: Heinz Isler
Main Contractor: R.G. Carter Ltd., Norwich
Contractor for Shell Roof: W. Bösiger, Langenthal, Switzerland

Until the 1970s reinforced concrete shell roof

construction was quite common in the United Kingdom and there are some excellent examples by engineers such as Felix Samuely and Ove Arup. However, since that time, this form of construction has almost died out. Nevertheless, because of the previous favourable experience of the project architects, in 1987 it was decided to use shell roof enclosures at the new Norwich Sports Village. The project was being designed by local architects Copeland Associates working in collaboration with the Swiss architects Haus + Herd. Copeland considered that Isler shells would be just as economic to build in the United Kingdom as in Switzerland and commissioned the first, and to date only, examples to be built in the UK, at Norwich Sports Village.

Nine similar tennis hall shells were built in the first phase, which was opened officially on 12 September 1988. Each shell is 18·6 x 48·0 m in plan, and rises to a maximum height of 10·5 m above the supports. The shells were erected side by side in two blocks, one of three and the other of six shells to create two sports halls. These were situated on each side of a small hotel complex, which was also part of the development.

The second phase, opened in May 1991, is known as the Aquapark. It is a water sports facility providing

'…a 6-lane 25 m long swimming pool, leisure pools with water slides 76 and 88 m long, bubbling spas and water cannons, water and air jet loungers, a wild water channel, children's pool, a restaurant, bar and seating for 330 spectators'.[82]

Again one of Isler's shells was chosen to

Fig. 5.47. Falsework of glulam beams on lightweight trestles.

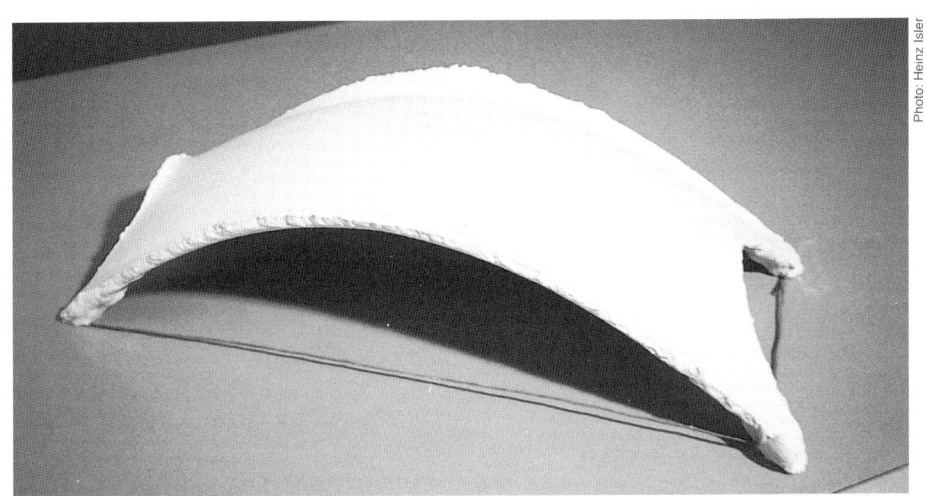

Fig. 5.48. Form-finding model for the tennis shells.

111

Chapter Five
Inverted membrane shells

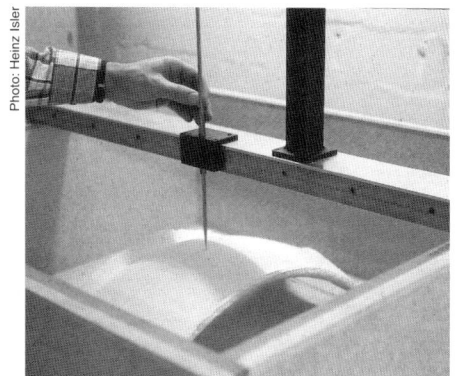

Fig. 5.49. A similar form-finding model being measured.

form the enclosure — a lightweight, free-form, reinforced concrete surface similar to the Heimberg and Brugg swimming pools. The 35 x 35 m square plan roof (*Fig. 5.46*) is supported only at four points and its centre rises to approximately 9 m above the corner supports. Bösiger was the contractor for shell construction for both phases of the development.

Thanks to the assistance of Heinz Isler, I had the good fortune to be present at the first day of concreting of the Aquapark shell. Having met Isler for the first time at the 30th Anniversary Congress of IASS,[83] where in his presentation he showed the recently completed sports halls at Norwich, and having shown interest in the imminent construction of the swimming pool shell, he contacted me the day before concreting began. In a hasty phone message one late morning in October 1990, he informed me that a room had been booked for me in the Sports Village hotel and that if I could get there that evening, concreting would begin early the next

Fig. 5.51. Double layer steel reinforcement of the Aquapark shell.

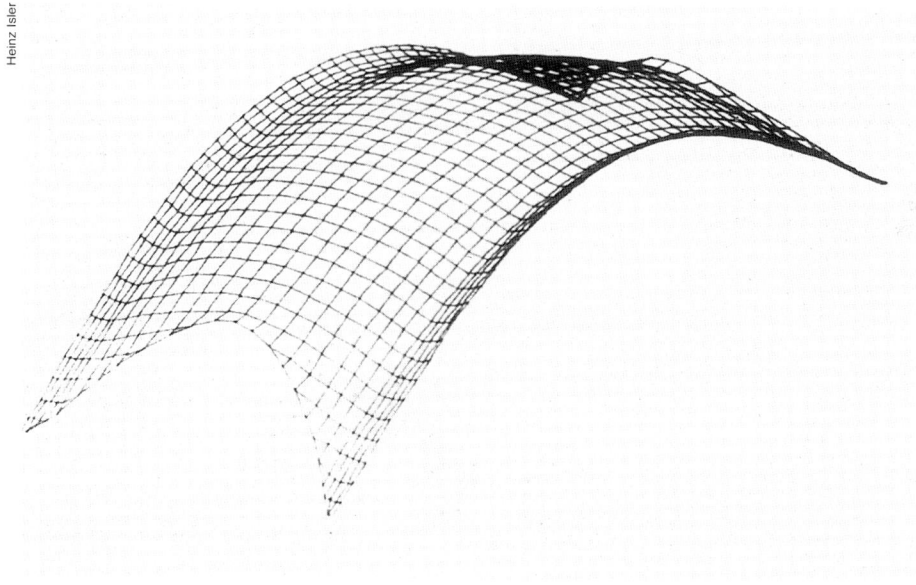

Fig. 5.50. Three-dimensional plot of the measured profiles.

Fig. 5.52. Additional radial and transverse reinforcement at the heavily stressed corner of the shell.

Fig. 5.53. The steep double-curved profile of the shell at the corner.

Fig. 5.54. Heinz Isler (left) inspecting the shell with the contractor Bösiger.

morning. This is an indication of the nature of the man who after more than one year had remembered my interest and took the trouble to invite me to see how his shells were built. Within an hour I had rearranged my appointments for the following day — how could such an opportunity be missed? The following account of how a modern Isler shell is constructed comes primarily from the information and experience gained on that day.

Formwork

The cost of the formwork and falsework necessary to support the wet concrete is perhaps the major constraint on the widespread use of reinforced concrete shells. Where free-form shell surfaces are involved, this restriction becomes even more pertinent. For the bubble shells described in chapter four, there is a considerable element of repetition in the use of the formwork and falsework as the shells are often constructed in a group of similar shells. Despite their more expressive form this is also true of the tennis hall and swimming pool shells. Heinz Isler has had a very long and mutually beneficial co-operation with the contractors, W. Bösiger of Langenthal. Because of this long relationship Bösiger's workforce are highly experienced in the construction of Isler's shell roofs. Together, this has permitted them to surmount the problem of cost, by reusing falsework and formwork wherever possible. Bösiger now maintains the stock of curved timber beams that can be adapted for various shell forms and Isler keeps the

Chapter Five
Inverted membrane shells

variations as close as possible to the standard profiles. These components may also be used for the free-form shells and this reduces their cost of construction. During assembly and dismantling of the falsework the timber beams become damaged and their expected life is between five and ten reuses.

The double-curved profile of the Isler shells is achieved using lines of curved glued-laminated (glulam) timber beams supported on adjustable height metal trestles (*Fig. 5.47*). The timber falsework builds up the 'skeleton' of the shell, which is reminiscent of the frames of traditional clinker-built boats. Centres between the beams are such that thin timber boards placed across them take up the appropriate profile. Each beam in the falsework for the shell is slightly different from its neighbour although depending on the shell form there may be some symmetry. Its form is made using the, suitably factored, precise measurements taken by Isler from his scale-model (*Figs 5.48, 5.49* and *5.50*).

In the case of the Aquapark shell in Norwich the thin boards were used to support a layer of wood-wool slabs and a final topping of sprayed polyurethane insulation. Vapour checks were provided between the separate insulation layers. On top of the insulation was fixed a double-layer of steel reinforcement. To guarantee that the wood-wool slabs would not become detached from the soffit of the completed concrete shell they were held in place by plastic fixings. The plastic fixings, which were used to reduce the cold bridging through the insulation, were connected to the steel reinforcement of the shell using stainless steel wire (*Fig. 5.51*).

Shell thickness

Generally, in the Norwich Aquapark shell, the concrete is 100 mm thick and reinforced with two separate layers of 6 mm diameter steel bars at 100 mm centres on a square grid. However, at the corners, the forces in the surface become concentrated into a section of reduced width, exactly where the total weight of the structure and imposed loads are being transferred to the foundations. Here the shell concrete needs to be thicker and additional radial and transverse

Fig. 5.55. Concrete being spread to the required thickness on the steeply sloping corner of the shell.

reinforcement is provided to cater for the higher stresses (*Fig. 5.52*). The steep double-curved profile of the shell in this area is seen in *Fig. 5.53*. Depending on his confidence in the quality of the concrete, Isler is prepared to reduce the thickness slightly and he has used a concrete thickness of just 80 mm for some of his shells in Switzerland.

Concrete

Durability of the concrete for an Isler shell roof is probably more important than its strength. Stresses under load are only a small proportion of those permitted by structural design codes, except in the regions near the supports. Because the forming of a shell is a time-consuming process, the concrete also has to remain workable for periods longer than normal. The large surface has to be of the correct thickness, properly compacted and with a reasonably smooth finish. Added to that it also has double curvature, which is also quite steeply inclined in some locations. Therefore, it takes additional time and care to form the concrete to the correct profile. Usually concrete with a 28-day strength of 35 to 40 N/mm^2 is used, with appropriate additions of plasticiser and retarder. The plasticiser is used to assist in compaction of the concrete round the network of reinforcement and prestressing ducts in the corners and to permit a drier mix of concrete so that it does not flow down the steep slopes so easily. Heavy retardation of the concrete is also required in order to allow for (possibly, very long) time differences between adjacent placements of concrete.

Here, approximately, 210 m^3 of 35 N/mm^2 strength ready mixed concrete were used, with appropriate additions of plasticiser and retarder, varying according to the location in the shell. This allowed pouring and hand finishing to take place over two days. Concrete was delivered by truck mixers from a local batching plant and placed from a skip using a tower crane with a jib long enough to cover the whole plan area of the shell.

Pouring the shell

In the case of the Norwich Aquapark shell, concrete was poured over a period of two working days. Previous to the day of the pour final checks had been made on the reinforcement,

Fig. 5.56. Flat vibrating plate and rotating vibrating plate compaction for the concrete of the inclined shell surface. Plasterers can be seen forming the rim of the shell in the lower half of the photograph.

plastic fixings for the insulation and the positioning of the prestressing ducts so that the concreting process could commence early the following morning. Heinz Isler is shown with the contractor Bösiger, inspecting the shell in *Fig. 5.54*. Shortly before the start, a team of plasterers arrived, contracted for a day's work. When told that they would be working on the shell (and when they began to appreciate how big the task was — a surface of over 1300 m^2), they almost got back in their van and drove off. Why were plasterers needed? Because the form of the shell is such that rainwater run-off converges on the corners and it is necessary to mould a rim along the edges to channel the water into the drainage system, rather than just let the water cascade off the edge. It had been found over the years that

Chapter Five
Inverted membrane shells

Fig. 5.57. First completed corner of the shell.

the forming of these channels was more easily carried out by hand, by skilled craftsmen, after initial compaction of the concrete.

Concreting commenced in one corner where first of all the thickest part of the shell, containing the prestressing anchorages was carefully filled and compacted with poker vibrators. The concrete was placed from a skip brought specially to the UK by Bösiger, which has been designed specifically for easy placing of the concrete with low water content that is required to prevent it from flowing down the relatively steep slope of the shell at the corners. Once the anchor block was full, concrete was placed on the sloping shuttering. After spreading (Fig. 5.55), this was then compacted using two methods, as seen in Fig. 5.56, one a flat vibrating plate and the other a rotating vibrating plate (much like an electric floor polishing machine). At this time the plasterers started working feverishly forming a lip at the edges to channel the rainwater into the large drainage hopper, tamping and smoothing the surface of the shell. This process, which can also be seen in the lower part of Fig. 5.56, was continued with the edge channel being formed up to a level where the upturned edge of the shell was sufficient to direct rain towards the corner drain. Then the concrete was placed more quickly and the surface was finished only by the plate compactors. All the time the thickness of the concrete was assessed by gauging whether the correct cover was being provided to the top reinforcement. Once the concrete at the first corner reached about one third of the way to the centre of the shell (Fig. 5.57), the construction team moved on to the next corner. Then the same procedure was repeated, at each corner in turn, where the shell is thickest, until all four were concreted to the same level. That was the end of the concreting for the first day.

The remainder of the shell was poured and finished on the following day. This is the reason for the heavy retardation of the concrete setting time at the joint, because there was a delay of about 18 hours between the final placing of concrete at the first corner and the first placing adjacent to it the next morning. Without the

Fig. 5.58. Unprotected surface of the Aquapark shell taken one year after concreting.

retardation a 'cold joint' would occur in the concrete which would create a weak and potentially pervious area in the surface. A similar method of working was used on the second day but the services of the plasterers were not required as an acceptable surface finish could be achieved using the plate compactors. The only tricky part of the operation occurs at the end. As the concreting progresses towards the middle of the shell, all the workers and equipment end up there and have to be removed by crane. Then the final area of concrete has to be placed and the final finishing completed by a tradesman on a working platform suspended from the jib of the crane.

Prestressing

Once the pour was completed the concrete was allowed to develop in strength for approximately three days before an initial prestress (approximately 25% of the final force) was applied to the shell. This was achieved by stressing the foundation beams along each side, which had the effect of pulling the corners in towards each other slightly. Then after the concrete had developed sufficient strength (about 21 days after pouring) the remaining prestress was applied using the same method. By pulling the corners of the roof inwards, the concrete shell is pre-compressed and rises, lifting the two layers of insulation from the supporting falsework. The supporting trestles curved beams and light boards were then dismantled and stored for future reuse.

Surface protection of the shell

No surface protection is applied to the exterior surface of this shell. Heinz Isler's experience over more than 30 years has shown that uncracked, well compacted concrete with an appropriate cement content is a durable and impermeable material. The unprotected surface of the Aquapark is shown in *Fig. 5.58*, which was taken about one year after concreting. Rainwater is channelled directly to large stone filled hoppers before entering the storm drainage system. Any surface treatment that has been applied to Isler's

Chapter Five
Inverted membrane shells

5.59. Interior view of the completed shell shows the light and airy atmosphere of the shell enclosure.

compression shells has usually been cosmetic. Literally hundreds of compression shell roofs have been constructed in Switzerland, since the mid-1950s, using the same methods. They show no signs of deterioration, having acquired a thin natural protective layer of lichens. Depending on the exposure and proximity of vegetation, in time, the colour of the untreated concrete roofs will tend to turn to grey like a natural stone. The shells at Norwich, constructed almost ten years ago, now show similar weathering characteristics, suggesting that this is a durable, impermeable, low maintenance form of construction.

Environmental considerations

Swimming pool enclosures are hot humid environments and ideally, when the pool is in use, the air within the envelope should be maintained at about 30ºC, with 55% relative humidity, in order to maintain the comfort of pool users. The free-form shell roof allows the owner the benefits of a large plan building with a minimum surface area. This reduces heat loss from the smaller envelope, and the lower internal volume also reduces the amount of air to be heated. If required, the elevations can contain large areas of glazing, which provide an agreeable internal environment that is predominantly naturally lit (*Fig. 5.59*). Other swimming pool enclosures built in Switzerland also have Isler's skylight polyester domes at the centre of the shell to provide more natural light. As the lighting and heating loads are decreased, because of the building form, the energy consumption is also reduced. Another benefit of the reduced surface area of the building is a lower use of construction and insulation materials.

Acoustically, swimming pool enclosures are generally noisy environments due to the hard reflective surfaces. However, the wood-wool slab thermal insulation used as a permanent former on the inside of the concrete shell has a beneficial effect. It acts as an acoustic absorber to moderate the high noise level. The thin but massive concrete shell also attenuates any loud external noise and prevents noise from leaving an enclosure, for instance when loud music is played for dances and parties in the restaurant area at the Aquapark.

This was probably the largest shell roof to be constructed in the UK for many years and it revived interest in this highly elegant form of structure. At the time of construction, Copeland Associates and Heinz Isler were working on several similar developments proposed for other locations in the UK but due to the economic situation of the mid 1990s these did not come to fruition. Since then a larger shell, of simpler form based on toroidal geometry, has been built for the American Air Museum at Duxford, near Cambridge. This double-layer shell, designed by architects Foster and Partners and engineers Ove Arup and Partners was constructed from precast concrete segments that had to be supported temporarily on heavy scaffolding.[84]

Chapter Six
Hypars, domes and sculptures

Chapter Six
Hypars, domes and sculptures

There are several very interesting projects designed by Heinz Isler that do not really fit into the categories described in the previous three chapters. Over the years he has produced some more conventional hyperbolic paraboloid and domed forms as well as acting as a consultant for the structure of several sculptural objects. However, when Isler has used a more conventional shell form, he has done so in his own unique way demonstrating his feeling for the forms and materials with which he works. Some of these non-conventional works are brought together in this chapter, starting with Isler's involvement in a rather beautiful modern church.

Holy Spirit Church at Lommiswil, 1967
Architect: Roland Hanselmann, Olten
Concept and Engineer: Heinz Isler

An inspirational example of Heinz Isler's contribution to contemporary architecture is the Holy Spirit Church at Lommiswil, near Solothurn. The church is located in a small quiet village, at the foot of the Jura Mountains (*Fig. 6.1*). Here Isler worked closely with architect Roland Hanselmann, of Olten, to produce an architectural jewel, small but dazzling.

The elders of the Lommiswil Church had been considering for many years the construction of a new building to replace the existing 14th century chapel. Many alternative schemes had been submitted by the architect, most involving the demolition of the existing chapel, which was at the time considered to be of little architectural

Fig. 6.1. The Holy Spirit Church at Lommiswil, near Solothurn.

Fig. 6.2. Original rough model made by Isler when he first proposed the form and location of the Lommiswil Church.

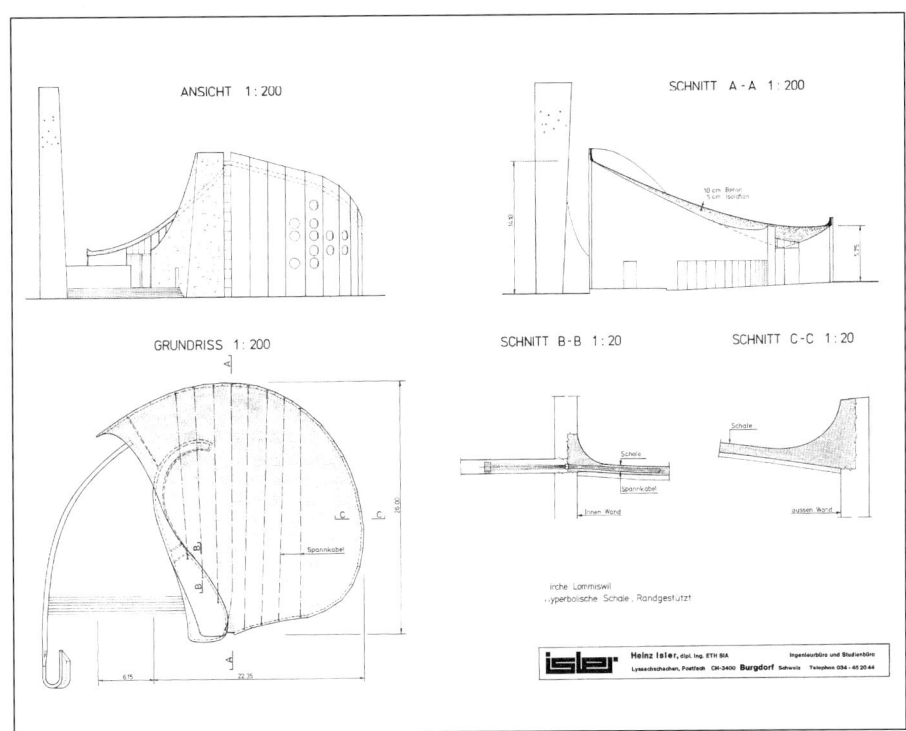

Fig. 6.3. Plan, elevation and sections of the Lommiswil Church.

significance. However, all of these proposals had been rejected by the parishioners. After the priest, by chance, had seen Isler's newly constructed shell roof for the Wyss Garden Centre at Solothurn (described above in chapter four), Heinz Isler was invited to the village in 1965 to offer his opinion on how the project might proceed. Confronted with the simplicity and elegance of the existing chapel, mounted atop a small rise, Isler proposed that this should be retained and that the new church should be built on a different site within the village. He felt that the new church should be subordinate to the ancient chapel leaving it the honour of first place. Drawn to a slight depression in the landscape near to the chapel, he suggested that the new church should be located there. At the centre of the depression there was a small cherry tree. Making a sweeping movement with his hand, indicating a roughly circular rotation encompassing the tree, Isler sowed the seed for the design of the new church.

Returning to the priest's house, Heinz Isler hurriedly assembled some small twigs from the fireplace, a lump of Plasticine and thick wool (for knitting winter socks) and made a rough model of his concept on a Plasticene model of the site, which included the old chapel. The twigs, roughly broken to provide 'columns' of varying length, were inserted into the base in a curved plan around a solid lump of Plasticine (which Isler conceived to be like a huge rock fallen from the Jura Mountains that form a dominant backdrop to the site). Around the curved plan, the columns gradually diminished in height. Connecting the tops of these columns with a network of straight wool threads generated the well-known double-curved form of a hyperbolic-paraboloid surface, which was to become the shell roof. Isler even suggested that the cherry tree might be retained within the new church. With the aid of this rather rustic model (Fig. 6.2), the priest and the board were convinced that here lay the solution and that a graceful and attractive building could be created.[85]

The architect, Roland Hanselmann, who had diligently produced all of the earlier proposals, unselfishly agreed to take on, refine and develop the original concept of Heinz Isler. Despite some objections by the local planning authority to details of the church, the main building work was completed in 1967 and, after consecration on 24 December, the first Mass was celebrated on Christmas Day of that year. However, the adjacent bell tower was not built until 1969. Isler's idea to incorporate the living cherry tree within the church[86] was not realised. However, the place where the tree once stood is now the site of the stone for the font containing the holy-water — the life coming symbolically from the tree.

In the project as built, the original simple curve had developed into three interlocking spiralling forms (see the plan of the church, shown in Fig. 6.3). The 'fallen boulder' had metamorphosed into a massive in situ concrete wall, curved in plan and tapering from a high

Chapter Six
Hypars, domes and sculptures

Fig. 6.4. Massive in situ concrete wall with highly textured finish produced by casting the concrete against rounded off-cuts of tree trunks.

point at its junction with the vertical slit window in the main perimeter wall to a low point near the main entrance door, where it penetrates into the main volume of the church. This wall houses small rooms and storage spaces. Externally, it has a highly textured finish produced by casting the concrete against rounded off-cuts of tree trunks (waste products from a local timber sawmill) nailed to the face of the shuttering (*Fig. 6.4*). This rough finish was the idea of the architect but had the whole-hearted support of Heinz Isler who considered that, with time, the 'rock' would acquire a natural mossy covering. However, now, over 30 years later this still has not come to pass, there being only a thin covering of lichens in the more shaded areas. The wall is the victim of the climate which, although wet in winter, overheats the wall in summer, killing most plants. Internally, the wall has a rough vertical board finish broken by vertical rebates.

The longer, main perimeter wall also curves and tapers in height from its junction with the slit window down to a small entrance that opens onto a small winding path leading to the old chapel. Although, initially, masonry was considered for this wall, it is constructed from precast reinforced concrete units, of varying height, that have a smooth external surface and an exposed local limestone aggregate finish internally. The internal texture was provided to improve the acoustic performance of the main space by reflecting certain sound frequencies

Fig. 6.5. Architectural model of original proposal which shows the tapered cleft window between the main walls and the original form of the bell tower.

Fig. 6.6. General view of the church and old chapel shortly after completion.

Fig. 6.7. View showing that the hypar shell surface is generally lower than the curved perimeter walls.

associated with speech (particularly the sound of the letter 'a'). Prefabrication was used in preference for these walls in order to save costs and speed construction. However, due to the need to construct a 5 m wide access road around the full wall perimeter to allow installation of the units, this solution ended up more expensive than in situ construction. Four of these units have 'porthole' stained glass windows (12 in total, representing the 12 apostles). Painter, René Acht from Basel, was commissioned to make the stained glass windows and it was his decision to represent the 12 apostles.

Between these two walls, at their high ends, there is a glazed vertical slot that Heinz Isler originally proposed should be a tapering 'V' shaped window. This proposal can be seen in the architectural model (*Fig. 6.5*), which also shows the original form of the bell tower. However, this tapered cleft in the walls was rejected by the local planning authorities, and a tall thin rectangular stained glass window was substituted to bring light into the church.

A third curved wall connects the bell tower with the main entrance, gently conducting the congregation towards the door. The original proposal for the bell tower was of more elaborate form (*see Fig. 6.5*) but again the local planning authorities objected to the design. They insisted that it should be redesigned to appear like a plain factory chimney when seen from the nearby main road. However, the side of the bell tower towards the mountains is of a freer form, hinting at the architect and engineer's original intentions. From photographs taken at the time of completion (for example, *Figs 6.1, 6.6 and 6.7*) it is obvious that the church tower was a prominent feature in the landscape but, with the years, new development and trees have surrounded the church and it is no longer so visible (*Fig. 6.8*).

The roof is a hyperbolic paraboloid (hypar) surface of irregular shape when viewed in plan. This means that the surface can be generated from two sets of orthogonal straight lines solely by varying the inclination of adjacent lines in a regular fashion (see *Fig. 6.9*, which shows a folding model used by Isler to demonstrate how a hypar surface is formed). Such a shell form usually has tensile stresses in the 'sagging' direction and compressive forces in the 'hogging' direction. However, Heinz Isler prefers to avoid

Chapter Six
Hypars, domes and sculptures

Fig. 6.8. General view of the church and old chapel in Aug. 1999.

Fig. 6.9. Generation of the hyperbolic paraboloid (hypar) form using straight lines.

tensile stresses in his reinforced concrete structures (and the consequent tensile cracks) in order to greatly improve their durability. Therefore, the shell is monolithically bound to the prefabricated elements of the supporting walls, so that the shell is clamped all round and the walls provide a stiffening ring. A system of prestressing is used to induce an initial compression in the whole roof surface, with the prestressing cables anchored in the tops of the precast wall units. The trajectories of these cables can be seen as dashed lines on the plan shown in *Fig. 6.3*.

Before construction of the shell roof, a very detailed investigation of its behaviour was carried out using the scale model shown in *Fig. 6.10*. This model includes the supporting walls as, with the two structures being bound together

monolithically, the roof interacts with them. The shell surface was very carefully and accurately modelled and the test rig allows vertical, horizontal and prestressing loads to be applied in various combinations (self-weight, full snow, half snow and quarter snow). Wind induced uplift loads can be modelled by changing the sign of the stresses (positive to negative and vice versa) induced by downward loads. Stresses in the model roof surface were recorded using electrical strain gauges.

The shell roof of the church is generally lower than the top of the perimeter walls, as can be seen in the views of the church taken from the rear, *Figs 6.6, 6.7* and *6.8*. However, the massive 'rock' textured wall dips steeply towards the entrance so that the shell comes above the wall,

separating from it and allowing a tapering band of glazing to be introduced between the two structural elements. Originally, a shell of only 100 mm thickness was proposed for the roof. Over and adjacent to the main entrance door its edge was intended to be unsupported by the in situ wall below, as the two structural elements follow different plans. However, during the testing of the model it was found that the compression forces present in the roof surface in that area required a thickening of the edge to prevent the shell from buckling. To avoid this edge thickening from becoming excessive, a slender steel prop was introduced at the point where the edge of the shell crosses the line of the wall below (*Fig. 6.11*). Although this prop is slightly thicker than the mullions within the glazing and despite it not coinciding exactly with a mullion location, the additional support is barely noticeable. The detrimental effect on the aesthetics of the building if the prop had not been included would have been worse.

Isler's interest in the long-term behaviour of his structures was discussed in chapter two. Surprisingly, one feature of the structure of this building that he particularly enjoys is some surface cracks in the precast wall units.[87] He thinks that they are wonderful as they are caused by differential thermal movement of the structure. Being monolithic, as the roof expands and contracts it is pulling and pushing on the walls and creating horizontal shear which creates the small diagonal cracks. He has asked that the cracks not be repaired because as he says

'…*they are innocent — it is just a slab, a vertical wall that always carries its load if it can take bending and this shear force does not harm it.*'

Isler likes the cracks to remain so that he can show them to students, to demonstrate how one can read the statics from them, considering the cracks to be 'the book of history, the record of the history of the building'.

Internally, the building is quite subdued as befits its external form. The furniture, designed by the architect, is absolutely simple, clean and there is no decoration. Heinz Isler is very complimentary about Hanselmann's treatment of the internal spaces.[88] To line the double-curved roof, an approximately square grid of large leather tiles has been used to improve the acoustics of the curved internal space. The edges of these tiles follow the orthogonal grid that generates the form of the hypar roof, so the tiles are not flat but have slightly warped surfaces.

This project shows an interesting interaction between engineer and architect where, unusually, the initial architectural concept came from the engineer, Heinz Isler, but was developed to a highly successful conclusion together with the architect, Roland Hanselmann, using his skills in spatial planning. Subsequently, the engineer used his expertise with three-dimensional surface structures to achieve the architectural spaces demanded. At all stages engineer and architect worked closely together with each willing to

Fig. 6.10. Scale structural investigation model of the church.

Fig. 6.11. Main door elevation of the church.

127

Chapter Six
Hypars, domes and sculptures

compromise where necessary. This was illustrated by the introduction of the single small prop supporting the shell's free edge near the main entrance where, if the architect had insisted on his original concept of having only glazing between the wall and the roof, the roof edge would have been much heavier. Thus compromise produced a lighter, more elegant solution.

Inflated 'ball' houses

Over 20 years ago, in 1977, Isler worked together with the architect J. Dahinden of Zurich, on the development of earthquake resistant housing for Persia (now Iran) before the overthrow of the Shah. The Persian Government of the day wanted to build a town of 3000 houses that were to be earthquake proof. Initial trials employed reusable inflatable balloon formers in order to produce shells. The aim was to make use of locally available materials, sand and stabilised soil, to manufacture the buildings. Preliminary experiments were carried out on some balloons of half the required diameter at Isler's experimental centre near Burgdorf. These were made with a sprayed gypsum/loam mixture or gypsum/cement mortar — a sort of modern adobe construction. The system permitted a flattened spherical balloon former to be used without adversely affecting the springing of the shell at its base. After leaving the shells to harden for some hours, the balloon former could be deflated, removed

Fig. 6.13. Collapse of experimental dome from effects of frost and rain.

Fig. 6.12. Half size dome house made from sprayed gypsum/loam mixture, 1977.

Fig. 6.14. Two of the full-size, frost resistant sprayed domes, over 20 years old.

Fig. 6.15. Each dome former was sprayed with three different materials.

and reused (*Fig. 6.12*). The material of the prototype was unable to tolerate the wet and later freezing conditions in Switzerland. It first swelled slowly out at its base and finally collapsed in on itself (*Fig. 6.13*). However, at the location where the shells were expected to be constructed the climate is different, there is only a dry cold, which the gypsum/soil mixture can tolerate. Unfortunately, due to the political overthrow of the Persian Government, that project was never finished. However, development continued and an experimental house of frost resistant material was made.

In the grounds surrounding Isler's offices there are still two of the full-size, frost resistant, sprayed dome shells that have been standing for 20 years. They were heated for the first winter but now lie semi-derelict and open to the harsh Swiss winter climate (*Fig. 6.14*). These were experiments to see how the basic forms could be combined to create larger dwellings and to investigate what types of opening could be produced. The first shell was cast on a balloon former, then the balloon was moved and a second was made. Each was sprayed with three different materials, first a layer of gypsum to provide a smooth inner surface, then polyurethane foam insulation and finally a fine concrete layer that provided weather protection (Fig. 6.15). After just one hour it was possible to remove the former under the gypsum layer and that layer then acted as the former for the subsequent sprayed insulation. The exterior concrete was sprayed in three layers to guarantee security, although just one would have been sufficient to deter intruders. These prototypes were made in one week.

This two-dome house could have been divided into between four and seven rooms — quite big enough to house a complete family. Inside the prototype there was just a small plinth and a box in order to modify the acoustics of the shell. Despite being neglected over some time, the only significant damage is to the gypsum lining, which is starting to fall down through the dual action of water and frost, but the rest of the shell is still in reasonable condition.

In the real situation they were to be built on a bed of sand then, in the event of an earthquake, the house would slide on the foundation but because of its very rigid form would not be destroyed. Usually with the ground

Chapter Six
Hypars, domes and sculptures

Fig. 6.16. The interior of one balloon shell, Ponthierry, near Paris.

Fig. 6.17. A group of 7 m balloon shells, Ponthierry, near Paris.

movements experienced in an earthquake, the building and the ground are connected by fragile columns that fail under the high horizontal shear forces produced by the relative movement, particularly if the frequency of the ground oscillation and the natural frequency of the building structure coincide. Whereas with Isler's domed shells, if they are built on sand then the floor will move beneath the house. Isler says that the shells, because of their double-curved shape, will not break.[89]

Isler and Dahinden had wanted to continue and had even started planning the incorporation of electrical and water services within the thickness of the shells (for instance, pipework ready for the installation of a shower). They were very keen to finish the development but when the Shah was deposed the project was abandoned by the in-coming administration. Seeing these shells in the Swiss woodland that surrounds Isler's offices it is interesting to speculate what future archaeologists will think of them in perhaps 500 or a thousand years time!

Following this setback Isler went on to develop the inflatable form shells even further in collaboration with his contractor Bösiger AG, of Langenthal, H. Schmid, of Kirchberg and Frutiger AG, of Thun. The aim of the continued development was to produce a standard range of 'balloon shells', for instance, for living spaces, studio workshops, club houses and motel rooms. These were to use the same principles of design and construction but were to be larger than the pneumatic shells of the prototypes. In this case, the balloon had a diameter of 7 m. Such shells have been used for a small group of studio workshops for craft workers in Ponthierry, near Paris (*Figs 6.16* and *6.17*), a motel in Mittleren Osten and a clubhouse in Aawangen. They have also been used for developments in Saudi Arabia.

Balz House, Stetten auf den Fildern, near Stuttgart, 1980
Architect: Michael Balz
Engineer: Heinz Isler
It is unusual for planning authorities to insist on the adoption of a non-conventional structural form for housing development but this was the case with architect Michael Balz's house at Stetten,

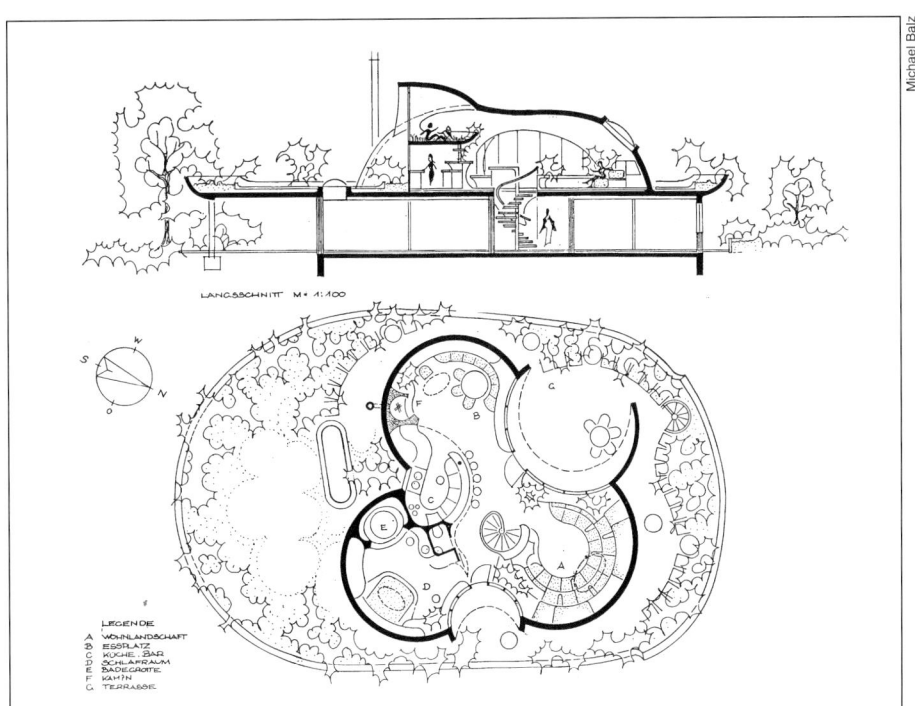

Fig. 6.19. Plan and section of Balz family house, Stetten showing 'clover-leaf' plan of the shell.

Fig. 6.18. Balz family house at Stetten auf den Fildern, near Stuttgart.

Fig. 6.20. Lounge/relaxation area of Balz house.

near Stuttgart, built in 1980. This may seem strange, however the house is situated adjacent to the shells of the dance workshop, cafeteria, club/meeting room and outdoor theatre (described in the previous chapter). These were all designed by Balz together with Heinz Isler and constructed between 1976 and 1979.

Being remote from the village, these buildings suffered from frequent vandalism and it was decided that a resident caretaker was required. Unusually, as a condition of the planning consent, the local plan prescribed that the new house had to be in the style of the adjacent shells. The result is a striking object that looks as if it has just arrived from another planet or solar system (*Fig. 6.18*). Having the approximate plan form of a three-leaf clover (*Fig.*

Chapter Six
Hypars, domes and sculptures

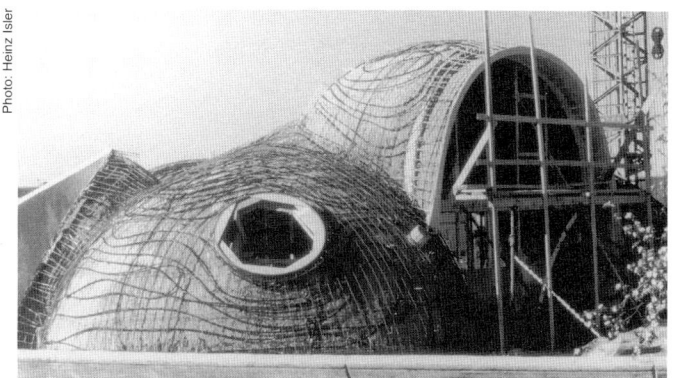

Fig. 6.21. Pipes used as a passive solar energy collector can be seen on the inner layer of the shell during construction.

Fig. 6.22. The villa near Geneva.

6.19), in elevation the house looks like most people's idea of a UFO or flying saucer. This remarkable shell is set on a conventionally built oval base with a maximum length of 17 m. While the lower part of the house contains more 'normal' rectilinear rooms, an office, children's rooms and a sculpture studio for the architect's mother, the upper part is completely non-conventional. A generous living space spreads over the whole area under the compound curved shell roof. This open plan space houses a large lounge/relaxation area (*Fig. 6.20*), a breakfast bar, kitchen, bedroom and bathroom alcove and was modelled in sympathy with the ground form. A continuous spiral staircase gives access to the lower floor. With the walls and roof merging seamlessly at the base of the shell, the architect decided that it was easier to integrate many of the normal household objects into the structure, including some furniture, a large sitting area in the lounge, wardrobes, bookshelves etc.[90] These were all accommodated within the rounded form. Difficulties in placing more traditional furniture within such a curvaceous envelope may be one of the reasons why more such dwellings are not constructed.

Vertical sliding glass doors open onto the sun- or viewing-terrace and allow sunlight to stream into the open-plan living space. The double-glazed roundel window and circular skylights sit seamlessly in the shell and bring additional brightness into the other parts of the living area. When it is dark, artificial light can be reflected from the inner surface of the shell to give a mellow illumination.

The shell was constructed in three layers over a pneumatically conceived form. The internal layer is of concrete surmounted by a layer of foam insulation and then finally an external skin of concrete. Similar techniques to those developed for the inflated 'ball' houses were used to make this more complex form.

Environmental aspects were also considered and that is shown in the design of the heating system. The whole complex, with 145 m² of surface in the lower floor and 95 m² in the shell, needs little heating of the traditional kind. Plastic pipes are situated in the concrete parapets of the lower plinth and in the shell itself to absorb the heat from the sun and pass it into the heating system. The pipes can be seen on the inner layer

Photo: Heinz Isler

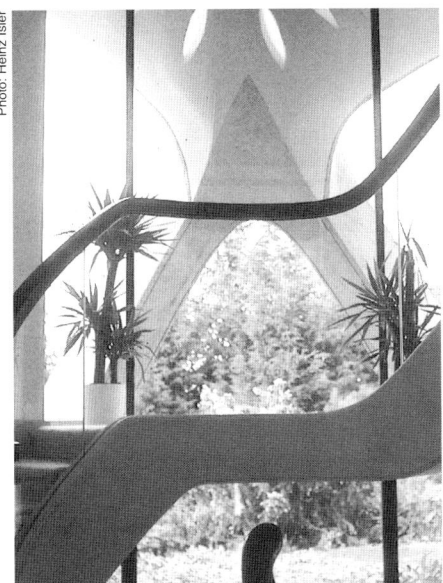

Fig. 6.23. Interior of the villa, near Geneva.

of the shell during construction in *Fig. 6.21*. Using a heat pump, energy is extracted from the environment and by means of a further controlled network of pipes is distributed to the interior of the building (as background heating). The excellent thermal mass of concrete is therefore of assistance to this heating system. Any surplus heat is stored under the floor of the lower part of the house and enters the distribution system on demand. During the heating period 1980/81 the system yielded a heating cost of only 10 DM / m^2. Although, Isler's shells do not contribute directly to the energy efficiency of this house, the rounded form does so indirectly. The surface of the shell is better oriented to collect solar energy than vertical walls would be and, because there are few angled corners, there is

Fig. 6.24. (a) Plan and elevation of the villa with (b) a single axis of symmetry for the roof along one diagonal, through the largest and smallest quadrants of the shell.

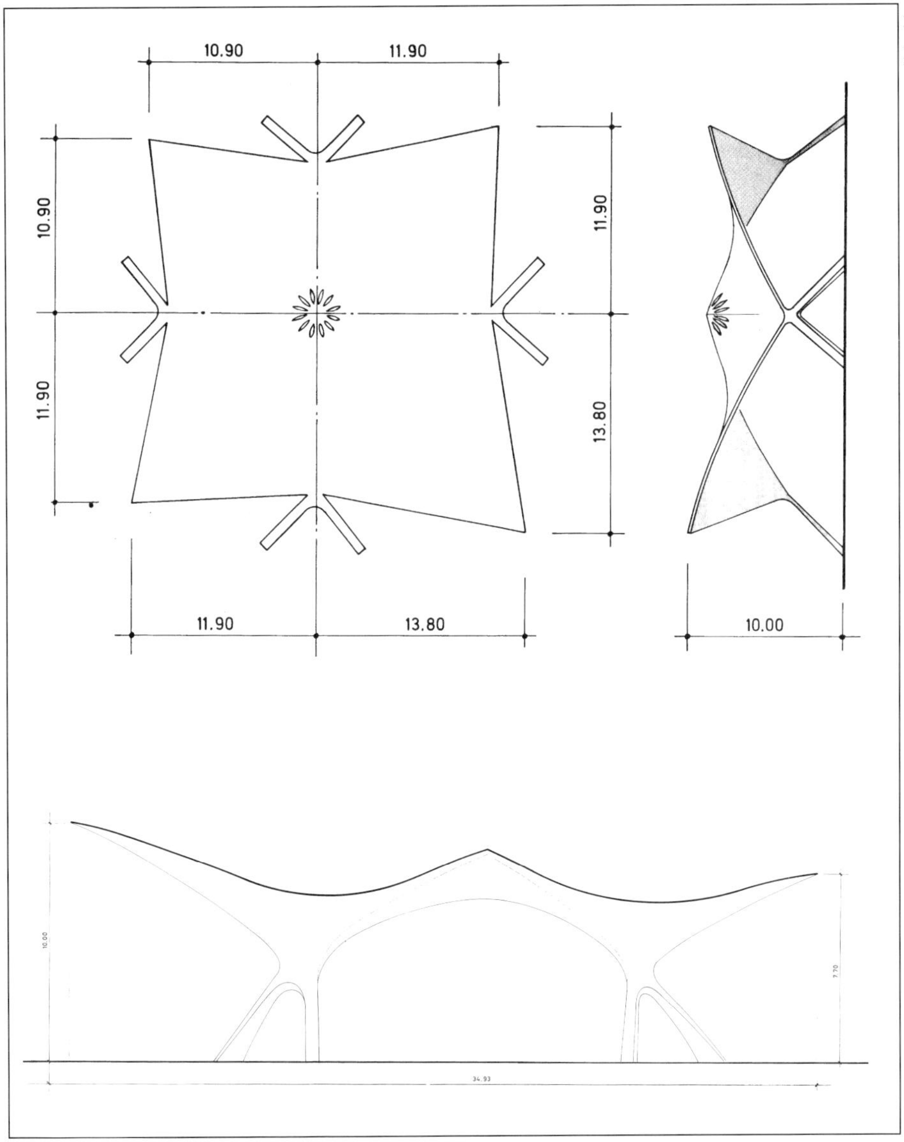

Heinz Isler

Chapter Six
Hypars, domes and sculptures

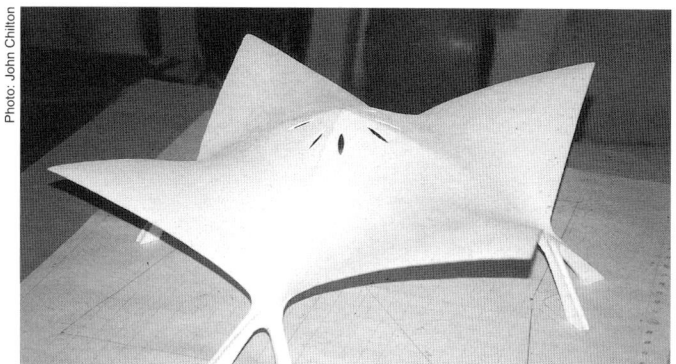

Fig. 6.25. Aerial view of a model of the villa in which the actual shape of the shells can be seen more clearly.

Fig. 6.26. The new Church in Cazis, 1996, under construction.

little self-shading. In addition, the volume within that needs heating and the surface area that requires insulation are both minimised by the form of the shell.

Villa, near Geneva, 1986
Architect: Pierre Camoletti
Engineer: Heinz Isler
This villa is located near Geneva, and has a magnificent view over the lake. The non-conventional, curvilinear roof form of shells is a challenge to architects. However, the architect Pierre Camoletti, who had previously had some experience of the planning of architectural spaces under shell roofs, was able to organise the volumes and functions with great skill. With him, Isler created a slender and striking form (Fig. 6.22) and elegant interior (Fig. 6.23).

Sitting on four inclined split columns, of inverted 'V' form, are four shells linked to form one large surface. As can be seen in the plan (Fig. 6.24(a)), there was just one axis of symmetry for the roof along one diagonal, through the largest and smallest quadrants of the shell (Fig. 6.24(b)). Although the overall distance of lines joining facing supports is equal, the point of intersection of these lines is not at the centre of the roof, giving one quadrant 13·8 x 13·8 m, another 10·9 x 10·9 m and two of 11·9 x 11·9 metres. The roof is self-supporting with the four cantilevering shells delicately balanced on the four supports. Its form, which at first glance appears to be four linked hyperbolic paraboloids, was initially determined arbitrarily on the drawing board.

From Fig. 6.25, which shows a model of the structure, the actual shape of the shells can be seen more clearly. In each quadrant both the cantilever section and the part inboard of the supports have mainly synclastic curvature[91] and are linked by a smoothed valley section of reversed curvature.

With this geometry, Isler was able to avoid the use of edge beams and he achieved free edges of the shells that are extremely slender. An additional architectural feature of the design is the provision of small 'petal-shaped' openings at the centre of the roof to bring daylight to the internal spaces. This villa is a fine example of Isler working with an architect as structural artists.

Fig. 6.28. Rubber model of the Church in Cazis.

New Church in Cazis, 1996

Client: Evangelische Kirchgemeinde, Cazis, CH-7408 Cazis/GR

Architect: Werner Schmidt, Mag. Arch. SIA/GSMBA, CH-7014 Trun/GR

Engineer: Heinz Isler

Cazis is a small community in the Grison part of Switzerland, at the entrance of the famous gorge of Via Mala. In 1994, needing a new church, the community invited seven architects to submit proposals. Two years later they chose the project

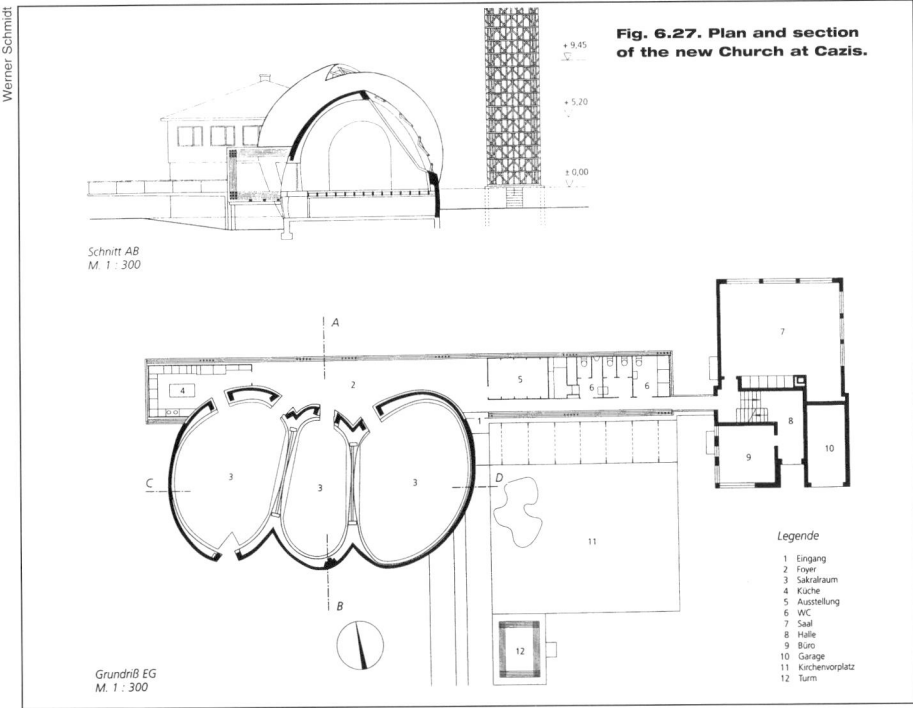

Fig. 6.27. Plan and section of the new Church at Cazis.

Fig. 6.29. (a) and (b) Glazed openings of the Church in Cazis.

Chapter Six
Hypars, domes and sculptures

of the architect Werner Schmidt, from Trun, which consisted of three egg-like structures (*Fig. 6.26*), shown in plan and elevation in *Fig. 6.27*. The concept model, which won the competition, consisted of just three rounded stones.[92]

In 1995, Isler was asked to collaborate with Schmidt to solve the problem of discontinuity in the shells, as the architect wanted to have large windows cutting into the three rounded volumes. Schmidt wanted glass with the minimum of structure, so Isler had to calculate the effect of the openings, which were detrimental to the stability of the pseudo-spherical bodies. As Isler points out, a football is very stiff but when you cut out a big portion it is no longer. He had to find a way to transmit forces across the openings with a minimum of structure. Then he was inspired by his shoelaces and expecting initially that the forces would be in tension, he provided ties, or structural 'shoelaces', across the window apertures, like stitching across a wound. These would transmit the forces from one side of the shell to the other. At first he was absolutely sure that the elements must be tension, as they were in his shoe, but when finally he analysed the structure he found that the force depended on the position of the element. In the event, the final shape of the three volumes was chosen arbitrarily by the architect according to his vision. Isler just had to give the boundaries within which the architect was free to develop his forms. The shape was elaborated on models then finally defined in

Fig. 6.30. The interior of the Church in Cazis, which is not yet finished.

Fig. 6.31. (a) and (b) Climbing form sculpture, 1974, at the swimming baths in Tramelan.

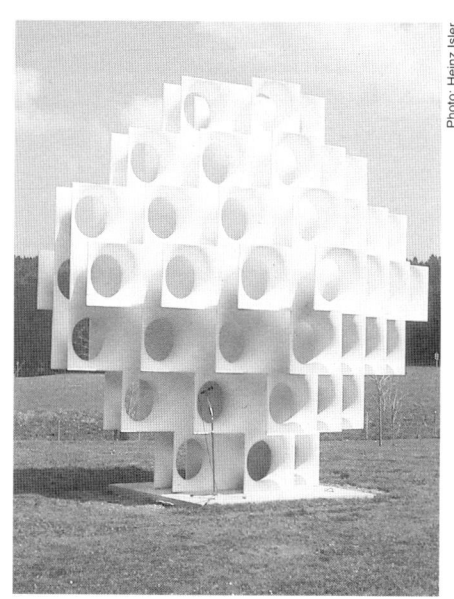

a computer, while the statical behaviour was checked by models and computers.

Isler first came to realise how the forces were acting around the window openings in the rounded shell surfaces through his model (*Fig. 6.28*). This model was not made of plaster or some form of plastic or foam but rubber.[93] Isler believes that rubber has excellent properties for use in structural models. Of the correct thickness, the rubber has sufficient self-weight that there is no need for apparatus to apply this load to the model. When the form is thin enough or big enough it is even possible to see how it buckles. In this case, with the holes in the shells, it would not be possible, but in an enclosed form, all that is required is slight decompression. By removing a small volume of air from the enclosed form one can see exactly how it will buckle — so simple. Similarly, with the rubber model one is able to apply various loads quite easily and see physically what is happening in the structure. For instance, in the case of the church shell model, when Isler pushed on it he saw exactly what was occurring. He literally saw the compression in some of the struts across the window apertures as the model had small cords across the openings to represent the glazing bars. When he pushed on the shell some of the cords (near the top) went loose, whereas near the bottom of the model they were stretched and obviously in tension.[94]

At the higher level in the form there was compression and at the lower levels tension. In the model the members were colour-coded red

Fig. 6.32. Children on the sculpture in Tramelan.

for compression and blue for tension. The preliminary proposal had been to use MacAlloy bars in a tube as the tension elements across the apertures and Isler thought that he would now have to change to heavier structural sections. However, on determination of the forces present in the elements, he realised that he just had to dimension the bars and the tubes that would be in compression to resist buckling. Although, in terms of material use, this solution is less efficient than using perhaps tubular members alone, the use of bars plus tubes gave a more slender appearance, as preferred by the architect (*Figs 6.29(a) and (b)*).

One problem to be overcome was the anchorage of the bars. The architect offered to provide the co-ordinates for the locations and the

Fig. 6.33. Sculpture at St. Guérin School, Sion, 1977.

Chapter Six
Hypars, domes and sculptures

Fig. 6.35. Sculpture at Gewerbeschule, in Langenthal, 1979.

angles of the bars, so that Isler could detail the different anchorages. But he said that he would prefer to have one standard detail that could be used for all the nodes. His solution was a 'brush anchor', which he had used before on other projects. In such an anchor the end of the threaded steel bar is held in a socket which has several (in this case 12) smaller steel reinforcing bars welded to it. This means that a common detail can be used for each location. Isler was just able to go onto site and demonstrate to the steel fixers how they should bend the small diameter bars, like a brush or fan, to distribute the main bar force into the concrete shell. With one single element he had solved the anchorage problem. Undoubtedly this was a much cheaper solution than having an individual anchor block for each end of each bar, for every direction, and every force, 36 in number.

The three volumes of the church can be used as separate rooms, or as an integral space. They can be united or separated by intermediate walls, which can be lowered into the ground. Each of the three spaces has a large opening where light and sunshine can enter and a splendid view to the mountains around is offered. The interior of the church is not yet finished; however, the building is used very frequently for all sorts of concerts, exhibitions and numerous discussions besides the normal church activities (*Fig. 6.30*). This project demonstrates admirably how the structural art of a creative architect and Heinz Isler may contribute to contemporary architecture.

Sculptures

Over several years Heinz Isler collaborated as structural consultant with the Spanish sculptor Angel Duarte, of Sion, assisting him in the

Fig. 6.34. A 9 m high double-sail sculpture at the Haven von Pully, by the shore of Lake Geneva, 1978.

realisation of several large objects. Isler was responsible for verifying the strength and stability of the structures, for specifying the materials and supervising their manufacture. This fruitful association produced several interesting examples. In 1974, at the swimming baths in Tramelan, a climbing form sculpture 5 m high was assembled using multiple units of a single module type. It was of sandwich construction using fibre-reinforced polyester (*Figs 6.31(a)*, *(b)* and *6.32*). A second large sculpture was erected at the St. Guérin School, Sion, in 1977. This consisted of three hyperbolic wing forms made of ferro-cement placed on wire mesh moulded appropriately (*Fig. 6.33*). By the shore of Lake Geneva, a 9 m high double-sail object was positioned at the Haven von Pully, in 1978. Balanced on three points this again was based on hyperbolic paraboloid surfaces generated by straight elements (*Fig. 6.34*). A final example of Isler's collaboration with Duarte is a sculpture erected outside the Gewerbeschule, in Langenthal, in 1979. Here four hyperbolic wing-like surfaces of ferro-cement stand vertically on a four-point support (*Fig. 6.35*).

Isler was structural consultant for a further interesting sculptural object in 1983, when he assisted the designer Meret Oppenheim with her fountain, in Waisenhausplatz, in Bern. The city of Bern, capital of Switzerland is noted among other things for its impressive collection of fountains that adorn the streets, particularly Kramgasse. Waisenhausplatz is not on that street but quite

Fig. 6.37. Detail of the vegetation growing on Meret Oppenheim's fountain.

Fig. 6.36. Fountain designed by Meret Oppenheim, in Waisenhausplatz, Bern, 1983.

nearby. The fountain (*Fig. 6.36*) is unusual in that it is designed so that water trickles slowly down a series of steps, spiralling about a central pillar. It was designed so that over the years vegetation would start to grow on the steps thus softening the form of the fountain and providing a haven for small wildlife in the city environment (*Fig. 6.37*). The structure, calculated by Isler is a vertical tubular concrete shell which had to resist possible freeze–thaw cycles in winter and be as light as possible, so as not to impose excessive additional point loading on the roof of the underground car park below.

Chapter Seven
Translucent shells of ice and plastic

Chapter Seven
Translucent shells of ice and plastic

Fig. 7.2. Demonstrates the size and transparency of a 5·5 m dome.

Fig. 7.1. One of the first sky domes being installed, by just three workers.

As Heinz Isler recently outlined in a conference paper,[95] to form shell structures the ideal material is initially a liquid but then becomes solid and, for economy, this hardening process should take place under normal atmospheric conditions of ambient temperature and atmospheric pressure. Concrete satisfies these requirements as it is prepared by mixing gravel, sand, cement and water to form a semi-liquid, which then hardens with time due to chemical reactions and no high temperature or pressure is usually applied. This is the material that Isler uses for his large shells, but as he pointed out there are other groups of materials that satisfy the same requirements, for example, two component plastics such as polyester or epoxy-resins. These are originally liquid but if hardener is then added the chemical reaction of polymerisation starts and a solid material is produced. As with concrete, this process is easy and cheap as the polymerisation process occurs under normal atmospheric conditions. These resins on their own are not particularly appropriate for structures but, to improve their structural performance, they can be reinforced by fibres, usually glass fibres, just as concrete is reinforced by steel bars.

Such resin materials are cold poured (as is concrete) which allows large areas to be produced without seams or joints. As the material is initially liquid it flows into the details and surface modelling of the formwork to which it is applied so almost unlimited shapes are possible. One drawback to the wide use of polyester and epoxy resins is their high cost compared to that of concrete. They are sold by the kilogram or litre, whereas concrete is sold by the cubic metre, as its components are quite plentiful and therefore cheap. Given their high cost, in order to make their use economic the resins must be utilised in highly efficient structures, therefore, double-curved thin shells are an ideal application. One important property of the resins (that concrete lacks) is highlighted by Isler, 'resins not only are weather resistant, watertight and durable but also light-translucent, they can be applied for skylights of all kinds'.[96] This is the property that Isler exploits when he incorporates large skylights into his concrete shells and from very early in his career (1956 onwards) he was using reinforced polyester resins to form the large shell domes that he uses for this purpose.

Fig. 7.3. Skylights of 7 m diameter in a canopy over a factory loading bay.

Fig. 7.4. The same domes seen from above.

Sky domes and vaults

When Isler first set out to cover large openings in his concrete shell roofs he found that no manufacturer was able to supply translucent domes of the appropriate size. This required that he had to develop his own system for the manufacture of large sky domes made from glass reinforced polyester. The domes are fabricated in one piece with no joints, are designed as shells and are extremely light as can be seen from Fig. 7.1. Typically a translucent polyester shell with a thickness of just 4 mm, such as that seen in Fig. 7.2, can be used to cover a 5 m circular opening. Such a shell is capable of supporting the snow load on its 20 m² surface or several people standing upon it.[97]

In such a dome the material thickness is very small, just 1/1250 of the span and this is due to the high structural efficiency of the surface stressed shell. As the material is so thin, the translucence is excellent and it produces a diffused light, which is often desirable from the architectural point of view. Due to their economy and efficiency these skylights have been installed in great numbers (and still are). For prolonged use, Isler says that they have to be cleaned regularly (about every five to seven years) and an acrylic coating has to be applied to protect the polyester material from the effects of ultraviolet light. If untreated, with time, the material becomes darker and less translucent.[98]

Chapter Seven
Translucent shells of ice and plastic

Fig. 7.5. Vaulted polyester shell of 6 m span that could be carried by four people.

Fig. 7.6. Sand mound former for the shells shown in Fig. 7.5.

In some of Isler's earlier domes a small circular opening was required by the authorities, as a smoke vent in case of fire (as can be seen in the domes shown in *Figs. 7.1 and 7.2*). As one might expect, smaller translucent domes were also used to cover these openings. In later domes the smoke vent was not required, as the skylights were mounted on hydraulic jacks.[99] These permitted the skylight to be lifted, as a whole, by 100 mm, thus producing an opening of about 2 m².

Larger skylights, such as the 7 m diameter domes of the cantilevered canopy shown in *Figs. 7.3 and 7.4*, are too big to be transported by road. Therefore, they were fabricated on site using a sectional transportable mould. As Isler's sky domes increase in diameter, the material of the shell also has to be made thicker and this reduces their translucency to an unacceptable level. Therefore, Isler started to search for a way to make a double skin shell and after two years he found a method using linked hollow blocks made from polyester. This method proved to be so efficient that he did not need to build domes with it. Even though the structural performance of double-curved shells is far superior to that of flat plates he found that the plates were more than adequate for the required purpose. Using flat plates, Isler could achieve clear spans of up to 15 m.[100] Some of the projects realised using the double skin flat plate are described in the next section.

Another development from the domes was vaulted polyester shells (*Fig. 7.5*). The vaults, which spanned 6 m, had synclastic curvature to give maximum strength with minimum weight and were formed on a sand mound (*Fig. 7.6*). Isler experimented with these shells as part of a modular storage system for the Swiss military. In the late 1950s and 1960s there was much concern about the possibility of nuclear war in Europe. Therefore, the Swiss authorities wished to construct vapour and moisture proof storage bunkers in long tunnels in the mountains, to house emergency food and medical supplies, ammunition etc. By assembling the prefabricated wall and vault units, which could each easily be carried by no more than four people, absolutely vapour proof warehouses were constructed (Figs 7.7(a) and (b)). The units had to be manhandled into position, as the size of the angled tunnel

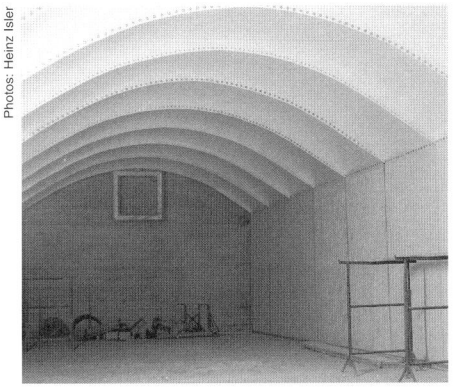

Fig. 7.7. (a) and (b) Vapour and moisture-proof storage sheds of vaulted polyester shells.

Fig. 7.8. Polyester roof for weekend houses being turned over during fabrication.

entrances was deliberately restricted so large vehicles could not enter.

Translucent plates

Several of Isler's projects made with double-layer polyester units are described in articles written by him in 1968[101] and 1977.[102] In 1959, a roof 4·5 x 9·0 m was made for a weekend house but there were difficulties during its fabrication. Firstly, a large flat reinforced polyester sheet was made on the floor then a two-way square grid of flat beams was laminated to it. Once rigid, the grid, still open on one side, was then lifted, turned over and placed onto a second, still liquid, layer of reinforced polyester (*Fig. 7.8*). It was expected that a good bond would be made between the grid and the unset polyester sheet but despite

145

Chapter Seven
Translucent shells of ice and plastic

Fig. 7.9. On site fabrication of polyester roof canopy for Moser petrol filling station, Thun, Switzerland, 1960.

Fig. 7.10. The roof being lifted into place in one piece.

heavy ballasting there was only about 30% contact and a weak connection. Patiently and laboriously the missing seams had to be remade through hand holes in the outer surfaces. Once completed the whole roof was transported to site on the back of a lorry.

Following these early problems the techniques were refined and, in 1960, a roof of 14·5 x 22·0 m was designed and manufactured for the Moser petrol filling station in Thun, Switzerland. The polyester structure 320 m², standing on eight columns, was made on site under a tent roof (Fig. 7.9) and then lifted into place in one piece (Fig. 7.10). In this case prefabricated boxes were fixed to the base sheet then a second layer of inverted boxes were fixed to the first layer and weighted down. Finally, the joints between the boxes were filled and an overall layer of reinforced polyester was used to link them all together. To transfer the roof load into the columns large bearing pads were required to prevent punching shear. These can be seen in Fig. 7.11, which also demonstrates how sunlight penetrates the roof.

Similar techniques were used in 1965 to make the five translucent plates, shown in Figs 7.12(a) and (b). These plates, each 12 x 13 m, are on top of the turbine hall of a power station in the middle of the River Rhine at Säckingen. Each roof is one piece and can be rolled to one side by one person, however the roofs have to be securely fixed in position to resist wind uplift, as the plates are extremely light. In fact they weigh only 18 kg/m², having two outer skins each with a thickness of just 4 mm. When viewed from inside, there is little glare from the plates but periodic maintenance is again required to maintain their translucency.

A folded plate structure was constructed using the same methods at the Realschule Geislingen in 1969 (architect V. Gmelich). The roof (Fig. 7.13) consists of 16 triangular plates made using the hollow box system. It covers a recreational area in a gymnasium and has a span of more than 20 m. The triangular plates are connected monolithically in order to transfer the shear forces between the plates. The final example of this type of construction is a circular roof of 7 m diameter for a church in Stuttgart-Fellbach (architect K. Franz). Here hexagonal

Fig. 7.11. Large bearing pads were required to transfer the roof load into the columns.

Fig. 7.12. (a) and (b) Translucent reinforced polyester plates from a power station at Säckingen.

shaped boxes were used as they accorded better with the circular plan. Once again the roof was made as one piece and lifted into position by crane (Fig. 7.14).

Translucent cantilever shells

In the basement laboratory of Isler's offices can be seen the test carried out on some double-curved, reinforced polyester cantilever structures (Fig. 7.15). One is broken and Isler asks, 'Can you explain that to me? Please explain it'. He describes how the load was hanging at the end of the cantilevers for months (with the units held at the back with three screws) but one day he entered his laboratory and one was broken at the mid-length of one lower edge. The explanation was a buckling failure in the outermost unit, in the top edge of the upstand, which forms the gutter on the unit and stiffens the lower edge. In the units loaded as cantilevers there is tension running from the loaded end towards the centre fixing at the top, and compression in the bottom, i.e. the gutters. The upper edge of each gutter is unrestrained in compression and therefore liable to buckle unless gutters are bolted together to connect the adjacent units. Buckling failure usually occurs at the mid-length of an unrestrained edge and this is what had happened in this case.

These appropriately shaped double-curved shells were used to solve the problem of how to form a translucent cantilever of 4 m (Figs 7.16(a) and (b)). The self-supporting shell elements needed no other structural elements, no ties, beams, or trusses. They were fixed simply by two sets of bolts, those at the top resisting tension and those at the bottom resisting compression with snow load or maintenance load (and vice versa to resist upward wind forces). The shape is self-cleaning, with dirt being washed into the gutter. It was expected that after a short time the gutters would become dirty and discoloured so they were painted so that the dirt is not visible. These cantilever shells demonstrate admirably the simplicity that results when function, statics, production and minimal material are united in one design idea. It is the right shape, the correct form, which gives the right answer — similar cantilevers made from cylindrical single-curved vaults would be much weaker.

Chapter Seven
Translucent shells of ice and plastic

Fig. 7.13. Folded plate structure at the Realschule Geislingen, 1969 (architect V. Gmelich).

Fig. 7.14. Circular roof of 7 m diameter for a church in Stuttgart-Fellbach (architect K. Franz).

Structures in ice

A cheaper and more readily available material that is at first fluid and then becomes solid is water, when it freezes in wintertime. Eskimos have been building igloos, their domed shell houses of frozen snow, for generations. Arctic buildings, military stations and temporary buildings in Japan,[103] have also made use of the same or similar techniques.

In an earlier chapter it was remarked that an element of play is probably essential within the creative process. Isler's enthusiasm for making magical grottoes and hanging forms of ice in the garden of his country farmhouse on cold winter nights is just such a form of play. He has been experimenting with such ice forms since 1955. Initially, he sprayed bushes and branches, then trees, nets, cloths, strings, cords and balloons. In

Fig. 7.15. Test of some reinforced polyester cantilever structures in Isler's laboratory - the broken piece can be seen to the left.

Fig. 7.16. (a) and (b) Translucent 4 m reinforced polyester cantilever shells.

Fig. 7.17. Form generated by Isler spraying water onto plants in his garden.

his keynote presentation at the Colloquium of the IASS Structural Morphology Group held in Nottingham in 1997 he described the inspiration he feels as follows

'When in a cold winter night — well protected by a warm, watertight overall — you begin to experiment with the gardener's hose, you really enter a new world. Your wildest imagination is modest compared with the richness nature can produce'.[104]

He explained that there is one quality that is indispensable when trying to play in this area — one has to listen and obey what the water/ice wants to do![105]

In the basement of the traditional farmhouse where Heinz Isler and his wife live there is a storeroom well stocked with materials for making ice structures — a wide selection of fine and

Fig. 7.18. Form generated by Isler spraying water onto plants in his garden.

149

Chapter Seven
Translucent shells of ice and plastic

coarse cloths and netting, ropes and cords, hoses and connectors, lights and cables and all the other paraphernalia that he needs to create his world of icy wonder.

The wealth of form generated by Isler's ice-shells is incredible. Depending on the way they are supported, the direction of the wind, the temperature, the way of spraying the water (by hand or by automatic sprinkler) gives a huge variety of different structures. And yet it is just clear drinking water. Thin films of water are practically transparent and under certain conditions so is ice, or at least translucent. Even in caves within glaciers a tinge of blue light may be detected through quite thick ice. Therefore, all the structures that Isler creates are bright in the daytime, reflecting the sunlight, and warm inside like a greenhouse. At night, when lit from inside, they shine like jewels, radiating their warm glow into the winter darkness and they gleam fabulously in the twilight.

There is a process of evolution in Isler's experiments as each winter he broadens the scope of the objects he creates. New captivating and diverse structures emerge. Often he achieves a stable structure with an ice layer just 1 mm thick.

There is a metamorphosis of the structures as they are warmed by the sun by day, causing a gradual melting and change of form. This is somewhat equivalent to the creep that occurs in concrete structures with time, but here the process takes place at high speed and can readily be observed.

This magic of this world is best displayed by photographs rather than verbal description. However, the following illustrations are used to describe the principal techniques that Isler uses for the creation of his ice structures (perhaps better described as ice sculptures as they have a great ephemeral beauty). These are just a sampler of the infinite variety of forms that could be produced and as Isler has said, 'it would fill a book to show all the discoveries, failures as well as successes'.[106]

Isler's experiments with ice are very cheap to perform but require a lot of dedication and energy. A distinct advantage that he has is the climate in the district around his home where, sometimes for more than a week, there are temperatures permanently below zero. Isler had observed what is produced by nature, without the intervention of the human hand — the sculptural forms made by wind-blown snow and ice formations frozen onto natural objects. Imitating this, his early experiments consisted of spraying water onto plants in his garden and many beautiful forms resulted (see Figs 7.17 and 7.18). With more intervention simple forms can be made by hanging a system of cords from a tree or

Fig. 7.19. Flower of Ice.

Fig. 7.20. The 'Münster' (or Minster) of 1985.

Fig. 7.22. Once the balloon is deflated the form is supported on a diverse colonnade of icy stalactites.

Fig. 7.21. Balloons inflated and sprayed with a fine mist of water until their form becomes entombed in ice.

high support and soaking them with water. For example the 'Münster' (or Minster) of 1985 (*Fig. 7.20*), in which a rigid 6 m high space structure was created from hanging frozen cords, sprayed with water, over two nights when the temperature was 19°C below zero.

Balloons of any size and shape may be inflated and sprayed with a fine mist of water until their form becomes entombed in ice (*Fig. 7.21*). On deflation of the balloon there remains an ice cave or grotto, perhaps supported on a diverse colonnade of icicles or icy stalactites of variable shape and size (*Fig 7.22*). In 1981 Isler created an Ice Palace from a three-sided group of balloon ice shells, in which it was possible to accommodate 40 people within the five rooms. The topmost balloon shell can be seen melting in *Fig. 7.23*.

Chapter Seven
Translucent shells of ice and plastic

Fig. 7.23. Ice Palace (1981), a three-sided group of balloon ice shells.

Fig. 7.24. Beautiful 'ice-flowers'.

Fig. 7.25. A structure made from frozen fine garden netting.

Cloth may be hung in many different forms. The simplest can be hung at low level and draped on the ground. Once frozen they create beautiful 'ice-flowers' that may then be displayed in trees and bushes (*Figs 7.19 and 7.24*). A structure made from frozen fine garden netting is shown in *Fig. 7.25*. Two similar forms were combined to create a slender and elegant roof over a bench (*Fig. 7.26*). In *Fig. 7.27*, three such forms have been suspended by cords from a central pole, which was later removed. The cords remain standing above the ice shell structure. All of these structures are fully self-supporting despite being only a few millimetres thick. Every year Isler tries something different with the similar technique. The ice steeple, shown in Fig. 7.28, was made by suspending bird protection netting from a central pole. The ice structure so formed, which was 6 m high and of ice 20 mm thick, was self-supporting when the central pole was removed.

Sadly, these enchanting ice structures all have one thing in common — they no longer endure except in the memory, in photographs, in videos and the wide knowledge that Isler has acquired from them about qualitative behaviour and beauty of thin shells (*Fig. 7.29*). Perhaps that is part of their charm, their ephemeral existence that lasts maybe just a few days, or with good luck in cold winters maybe a few weeks. Their fleeting presence depends totally on the vagaries of the weather. Huge effort, artistry and skill go into their making but quickly they are gone.

Fig. 7.27. Three such forms have been suspended by cords from a central pole, which was later removed.

Fig. 7.26. Two similar forms were combined to create a slender and elegant roof over a bench.

Fig. 7.28. An ice steeple made by suspending bird protection netting from a central pole was self supporting when the central pole was removed.

Fig. 7.29. The beauty of the 'Christmas Village' ice shells is displayed by internal illumination at night.

Chapter Eight
Influence of Heinz Isler's work and the future of thin concrete shells

Chapter Eight
Influence of Heinz Isler's work and the future of thin concrete shells

Heinz Isler's contribution to contemporary architecture

Over the last few chapters we have seen many examples of Heinz Isler's skill as an engineer and more particularly his art of form-finding by a variety of different methods. This is probably his greatest contribution to contemporary architecture — the demonstration of what beauty may be achieved through the sensitive use of thin double-curved shell surfaces. Compared with the shells of Isler, those of the other shell builders sometimes appear rather mechanical and unnatural. This follows from their designer's use of geometrical forms and precise mathematical formulae to describe their surfaces. When these methods are contrasted with Isler's more intuitive processes of form generation, for instance following the example of nature and using gravitational forces to mould his models, the reason for the appeal of his shells is immediately apparent. Such organic shapes fascinate many architects who respond to the rounded profiles that map the flow of forces within the shell — form following force.

As remarked earlier, in chapter five, the allure and influence of Isler's work has been confirmed by the recent furore about the plans of the oil company BP to demolish the magnificent triangular shell roofs at their filling station on the N1 Motorway at Deitingen Süd in Switzerland. Here, unprompted, the general public and a group of eminent architects rose up to defend his work, citing its elegance and beauty as their reason for its retention. Few engineers receive such popular support for their accomplishments and this demonstrates without doubt the esteem in which Isler's work is held.

Working with architects

Isler believes that he works with three or four different types of architects in the realisation of buildings and each type has a different attitude to the engineer's contribution to and involvement in the project. The first and most rewarding is a collaborative relationship, where the aspirations of both engineer and architect are subordinated to the object that is being designed, with neither trying to impose their will. Here the design develops from an interchange of ideas between both professions within a mutually stimulating environment. This, Isler considers, produces some of the best results and yields more inspiring shells.[107]

The second type of professional relationship is where the architect is less willing to respond to Isler's counsel or has insufficient interest in, understanding of or empathy with Isler's design philosophy. In this case Isler considers that the result is sometimes uninspired and lacking in the elegance achieved in projects where engineer and architect are working together towards the same end. In the third case, the architect does not collaborate at all, dictating the form of the shells that Isler is then expected to realise in the most aesthetically pleasing and structurally efficient way that he can. Here, the shells are perhaps the least successful as they tend not to be of the most appropriate form, unlike those that Isler generates through his own form-finding methods.

Finally, the fourth situation is when Heinz Isler acts as both engineer and architect, with full responsibility for the design. Isler has never been formally trained as an architect yet he has an eye for beauty and elegant form, which stems from his appreciation of nature and love of painting and sketching. This characteristic, connected with his passion for efficient and refined structures, as produced by his various form-finding and modelling techniques, is perhaps the secret of his successful designs. It is significant that when people select the most enchanting and beautiful of the many projects with which Isler has been involved over almost half a century, they are inclined to choose projects where Isler has been the sole designer. He accepts such compliments with modesty.[108]

IASS and structural morphology

For many years Heinz Isler has influenced architects and engineers alike through his inspirational lectures and presentations (more than 1000) world-wide. Many of these have been at conferences and symposia organised by the International Association for Shell and Spatial Structures (IASS). When, during the IASS Symposium held in Copenhagen in 1991, it was proposed to set up a working group in the field of structural morphology,[109] Heinz Isler was present at the inaugural meeting. He enthusiastically welcomed the establishment of the group. This is a field of study dear to his heart and in which he has experimented for all of his working life, therefore, he was delighted to have the opportunity to encourage young architects and engineers to follow in his footsteps.

Since that very first meeting, held in the back room of a bar in Gammel Dok, Copenhagen, Isler has given the group his full support and has attended all of their events. For instance, at the Structural Morphology Colloquium held at the University of Nottingham, in August 1997, he was one of the two keynote speakers at the opening session, where he presented a paper on *Transparent structures of fibreglass and ice*.[110]

Isler's support of this working group has been invaluable. Because of his reputation as an inspired designer he is respected by all. This has given him the opportunity to show many young and enthusiastic architects and engineers that structural modelling is an art that can transcend the current domination of computer analysis and create beautiful, functional, efficient and enduring objects. This is a considerable contribution both to contemporary architecture and to architecture in the future.

Future of shells

A discussion of the contribution of Heinz Isler's work to contemporary architecture cannot be divorced from an assessment of whether there is a future for thin concrete shells, given the architectural profession's current affection for very lightweight, transparent structures. In terms of physical weight, when compared to most concrete construction, thin shells are without a doubt lightweight. However, because they lack the transparency of glass-clad steel, aluminium or timber structures, this lightness is often difficult to appreciate. The thin edges presented by many of Isler's concrete shells and the thin translucent reinforced polyester domes that frequently surmount them go some way to counter these objections. As one might expect, Isler has his own opinions on the subject.

In his invited address to the 40th Anniversary Congress of the IASS, Heinz Isler explained how that learned association, founded by the engineer and shell builder, Eduardo Torroja, had widened its perspectives, in the late 1960s, to take in all types of spatial structure. While welcoming the stimulation that this brought to IASS, given the popularity and widespread use of steel, timber and membrane spatial structures, he asked whether there still existed a future for thin shells.[111]

Answering his own question, Isler stated that it was a fact that there were now fewer applications of thin concrete shells. However, he then presented eight points, as follows

'However the following facts are also true:
- *shells use a minimum amount of material*
- *shells provide maximum bearing capacity*
- *shells have a great simplicity, being bearing structure and space enclosure at the same time*
- *our office designs and builds in Europe 2 to 12*

Chapter Eight
Influence of Heinz Isler's work and the future of thin concrete shells

- shells every year
- India and South America are producing shells continually
- real glass shells are increasingly built
- universities make continuous progress in computer programs on statics, form and optimisations for shells
- two events in recent past: in an international competition for the new Stuttgart Main Station a shell proposal was the winner and the new American Air Museum in Duxford (GB) is a concrete shell'.[112]

The first three of these points are presented as reasons why designers should continue to use shells and the remaining five are given as evidence that shell structures are not yet as dead as many people may think. There is a current fashion among architects for using earth-covered roofs for buildings, so that they blend more naturally into the environment. This, potentially, should give a new lease of life to thin concrete shell structures, especially of the type built by Isler. He has demonstrated, using the roof of his own offices, how well-made unprotected concrete in compression may support a layer of vegetation[113] without allowing water or roots to penetrate. His refined shell forms, ideal for supporting relatively heavy uniformly distributed loads, also merge effortlessly into natural surroundings. Although they sometimes look less comfortable when completely surrounded by man-made buildings based on orthogonal geometry.[114] Thermal and acoustic insulation of such forms is easy, as the insulation material can be used as permanent formwork for the shell. The surface area of the building envelope that has to be insulated and the volume to be heated are also minimised. Combining these beneficial properties should encourage designers to realise appropriate small to medium span buildings in locations where development is often rejected on environmental grounds.

The fact that Isler's own office designs and builds several shells in Europe each year in itself shows that thin concrete shell building is not defunct. Further, as the final point in the list quoted above from the report of his lecture,[115] Isler mentions two highly prestigious building projects. The first of these is the roof of the new Main Railway Station in Stuttgart, designed by architects Ingenhoven Overdiek und Partner, of Düsseldorf working with engineers Happold Ingenieurbüro, Berlin and Leonhardt, Andrä und Partner, in Stuttgart.[116,117] This concrete vaulted structure has its geometry derived from the inverted form of a hanging tensile membrane. The second is the American Air Museum in Duxford, designed by architects Foster and Partners with engineers Ove Arup and Partners, the roof of which, completed in September 1996, is a synclastic double-layer shell, with shape generated by a segment cut from a toroid. A third recent high-profile project is at the Universal Oceanographic Park, in Valencia (L'Oceanografic) where there are two fine hyperbolic paraboloid shells being constructed, which were the last work of Félix Candela. Structural design for these shells is by Prof. A. Domingo and Eng. C. Lázaro of the Universidad Politécnica de Valencia.[118]

The acceptability of shell forms for these high profile schemes show that there are still opportunities for thin concrete shells in modern architecture. One of the reasons for that acceptability is the influence also that Isler's own quietly magnificent structural art has exercised on the architectural profession.

To support his opinion that there is a relatively promising future for thin concrete shell structures, Heinz Isler quotes the words of the current[119] President of IASS, Prof. Stefan Medwadowski

'Concrete thin shells continue to offer the advantages of strength and beauty of form, and will remain a viable structural system in the future. …they will continue to be used, both for smaller, more utilitarian projects, but also for the prestigious realisations that will attract significant attention among the designers and the public…'[120]

In the same seminar Stefan Medwadowski also referred specifically to Heinz Isler's shells, commenting on his 'unique approach to the design of shell roofs'.[121] However, perhaps the most significant remark in Medwadowski's paper comes when he comments on the relative stagnation in the design and construction of thin concrete shell structures since their heyday in the 1950s and 60s, when he says

'Since the sixties, the field of design and construction of concrete thin shell roofs has been

somewhat stagnant — the work of Isler being the notable exception.'[122]

This recognises that Isler's shells have something that others do not and that this difference has maintained their popularity at a time when concrete shells were being displaced by space grids and tensile membranes. The distinguishing feature is the humility of the form-finding processes that Isler employs — letting gravity and nature find the form for him (with a little bit of assistance and much care and patience). The resulting forms are unassuming but at the same time uplifting to the spirit.

Thanks to the inspiration that Heinz Isler's shells have provided for architects and engineers throughout the world, the future is bright and it is shell shaped!

Endnotes

Chapter One

1. Having endured for almost two millennia, the 43·5 metre diameter coffered dome of the Pantheon in Rome is constructed from brick and a lightweight concrete.

2. The masonry dome of Hagia Sophia is 32·5 metres diameter and has a thickness that varies from 0·7 metres at the springing to 0·6 metres at the crown. This gives a span to thickness ratio of 46·4:1 at the base and 54·2:1 at the crown.

3. Both Brunelleschi's dome in Florence and Michelangelo's in Rome have a span of approximately 42 metres and are double shells. In Florence the inner shell is 2 metres thick and in Rome both are around 1·2 metres thick.

4. A typical fabric membrane weighs only 1 or 2 kg/m^2 but even Felix Candela's exceedingly thin concrete shells, only 40 mm thick, weigh around 90–100 kg/m^2.

5. Heinz Isler, in conversation with the author, August 1999.

6. Heinz Isler, in conversation with the author, August 1999.

7. Billington D. (1983), *The Tower and the Bridge – the new art of structural engineering*, Princetown University Press, p 222. In 1980, Prof. Billington created an exhibition on '*Heinz Isler as Structural Artist*' which travelled to numerous universities in the USA and Japan.

8. Heinz Isler, in conversation with the author, August 1999.

9. 'Then I began to change to the curve. I did not want a straight line. I began to sketch a continuous blend of radii and finally I got to this hill-like shape but I had to do it on the drawing board and it is a task which cannot be solved.' [Heinz Isler, in conversation with the author, August 1999.]

10. Isler H.: Discussion IIIb, Instability of thin pre-stressed shells; in: *Second Congress of the Fèdèration Internationale de la Prècontrainte*; Amsterdam (1955); p736.

11. Isler H.: Discussion Shell Research; in: *Proceedings of the Second Symposium on Concrete Shell Roof Construction*; Teknisk Ukeblad Oslo, Norway; July (1957); p 327.

12. Isler H., (1960), New shapes for shells, *IASS Bulletin* No.8.

13. Isler (1960).

14. Isler (1960).

15. 'Mr. Isler: You know, you can make up this form just in a primitive way, by using a cylinder, a sphere and a cone. That is the first analogy; and you know that the buckling stability of the cylinder is rather poor, whereas the sphere is highly better, because the double-curvature is very good. Here the second curvature is very flat; and by correcting this, we got an improvement of buckling stability of about 7% to 10%. By avoiding the cone the local improvement was about 100%.' [Heinz Isler in the discussion of Isler paper in *IASS Bulletin* No. 8.]

16. The architects for this project, completed in 1959, were Camelot, de Mailly and Zehrfuss.

17. 'The second thing to which I want to draw attention is that in practice, when we talk about new forms of shells, which are often built [for] more spectacular buildings, churches and so on, it is very often the architect who in the first place decides the shape of the shell, which is a most unfortunate state of affairs, if he does not know much about it, because he will propose some shapes which are maybe useful functionally — one must hope that — but very expensive and unpractical to build ;....' [Ove Arup in the discussion of Isler paper in *IASS Bulletin* No. 8.]

18. Billington D. (1983), *The Tower and the Bridge – the new art of structural engineering*, Princetown University Press, p 224.

19. Arup O.N. and Zunz G.J., Sydney Opera House, *The Structural Engineer*, Vol. 47, No. 3, (1969), p 99–132, provides a detailed description of the design development and construction of these roofs.

20. '...because if a snail-shell stands up, it does not mean that if you blow it up a thousand times and make it of concrete, that it will also stand up. This point ought to be made quite clearly to architects,...' [Mr. Flint in the discussion of Isler paper in *IASS Bulletin* No.8.]

21. Constructed from GRC for the Bundesgartenschau (Federal Garden Exhibition) in Stuttgart 1977.

22. 'Any conventional engineer, including Schlaich himself, would have told Behnisch that the free-form cable net envisaged in his competition model could not possibly work. If this had happened, the present roof would not now exist....' Holgate A., *The Art of Structural Engineering: the work of Jörg Schlaich and his team*, Edition Axel Menges, Stuttgart/London, (1997), p 64.

23. 'I was shocked because I felt that I had found really a treasure. A treasure that nobody had found, then suddenly....' [Heinz Isler, in conversation with the author, August 1999.]

24. Isler considers that perhaps the closest emulation has been achieved (provided the detailed result is known before) by Professor Ekkehard Ramm and his research team, at the University of Stuttgart.

25. Isono Y., Looking for the structures of R. Maillart and Heinz Isler in Switzerland, Appendix of the *6th Prof. Y Tsuboi Memorial Seminar on Shell and Space Structures*, Tokyo, 21 (May 1998). Intended mainly for travelling students this is written in Japanese and English.

26   '…and I have a hobby at home, you know. Maria will now laugh … always when I eat something I make experiments. One of the most wonderful materials is Emmental cheese. You can do wonderful things with material like that to understand reinforced concrete.' [Heinz Isler, in conversation with the author, August 1999.]

27   Heinz Isler, communication with the author, February 2000.

Chapter Two

28   '…everything in nature, whatever you find is organic shape, is double curvature, nothing plane.' [Heinz Isler, conversations with the author, August 1999.]

29   A similar method was also used by the great Catalan architect Antoni Gaudí for the design of many of his great works including the structure of the cathedral of Sagrada Familia in Barcelona and the crypt of the chapel at Colonia Guell. However, Gaudí used arch elements whereas Isler uses membranes.

30   Concrete has about one twentieth the strength in tension that it has in compression.

31   The name 'Buckelschale' Isler borrowed from 'Buckel-Blech', a steel element in bridge design.

32   Synclastic is the term used for a double-curved surface when the principal curvatures at all points on the surface are of the same sense (i.e. both either concave or convex). A surface where they are of opposite sense (i.e. one concave and the other convex) is termed an anticlastic surface.

33   'That was the first and from that…that was rather successful. We could do many of these shells.' [Heinz Isler, conversations with the author, August 1999.]

34   'That is a phenomenon, …when you do it in the plane you get a counter curvature here, in the corner. This is, of course, for my purpose, not good because here the pressure line cannot go backwards.' [Heinz Isler, conversations with the author, August 1999.]

35   'That is the harmonious shape inflated, there I have rectangular and here we have the square. Here I avoided the problem of the counter curvature by making it round….' [Heinz Isler, conversations with the author, August 1999.]

36   Isler H., New shapes for shells, *IASS Bulletin* No. 8, (1960).

37   A uniformly loaded flat slab resting on four walls would transfer 100% of that load to the walls.

38   '..a very important fact in shell shapes — that the spherical is the best.' [Heinz Isler, conversations with the author, August 1999.]

39   'I have no frame around — I do not want a frame — but finally I found that the corner support is a good one, ...' [Heinz Isler, conversations with the author, August 1999.]

40   'One day on my shell I saw a piece of cloth hanging in the reinforcement and because the light was very low I saw the shadow and it was a shape, a beautiful perfect shape. That brought me to the idea that I need not a balloon to create the shape, … a hanging membrane is doing automatically a very similar shape. And this can be square, can be rectangular, in the round, whatever you like — an automatic shape. I saw that and said we have another one, another way to find three-dimensional shapes, no more by inflation, by air pressure, but by gravitation.' [Heinz Isler, conversations with the author, August 1999.]

41   Working Group 15 of the International Association for Shell and Spatial Structures (IASS) is known as the Structural Morphology Group. It was formed in 1991 at an IASS symposium in Copenhagen. Heinz Isler was at the inaugural meeting, became a founding member and gives the group his every support.

42   Resin that sets when exposed to ultra-violet light.

43   'So just by changing the point of support I got the counter curvature, which finally makes it really stiff — it's beautiful.' [Heinz Isler, conversations with the author, August 1999.]

44   'So if I am wrong in my calculation, if I'm 100% wrong, I'm still only at 30%.' [Heinz Isler, conversations with the author, August 1999.]

45   'I can just easily within minutes solve this.' [Heinz Isler, conversations with the author, August 1999.]

46   'I start with models which are too thin and then all the effects, all the problems are exaggerated.' [Heinz Isler, conversations with the author, August 1999.]

47   Isler H., The stability of thin concrete shells, in *Buckling of Shells*, ed. E. Ramm, Springer, Berlin (1982), p 647.

48   'For instance, that is the height. If I take the difference of the height that is the slope. If I take the difference between the slope here and the slope here I get the curvature. The curvature must change regularly, not with bumps. So when I take the second variation I have the curvature. This must be continuous and smooth. When I get a bump in it there was either an error in the measurement, or an error in the man who measured it.' [Heinz Isler, conversations with the author, August 1999.]

49   Isler H., The stability of thin concrete shells, in *Buckling of shells*, ed. E. Ramm, Springer, Berlin, (1982), p 662–3.

Endnotes

50 Isler H., Third decade of structural shells, in *Ten Years of Progress in Shell and Spatial Structures*, (eds F. del Pozo and A. de las Casas), CEDEX, Madrid, (1989), Vol. 1, no page numbers.

51 Carbonation occurs due to the gradual neutralisation of concrete's natural alkalinity through chemical attack, such as by acidic rain.

52 '…about what is happening after the birth, after the taking off of the scaffolding. There is not a single thought and not a single word and nearly no publication except about our big dams in the Alps.' [Heinz Isler, conversations with the author, August 1999.]

53 Isler H., Is the physical model dead?, in *Structural Morphology – Towards the New Millennium*, (eds Chilton J.C. et al), Nottingham, (1997a), pp 270–274.

54 'No one would like to wait for hours or days to get a simple reservation or confirmation for a seat in a plane.' Isler (1997), p 270.

55 '… you touch it, you feel it, you see it from all sides. And sometimes you hear it, the buckling for instance, before the model breaks.' Isler (1997a), p 270.

Chapter Three

56 '…the concentration of the forces is in the corners therefore there I need material. …and also the prestressing cables are concentrated in the corners, …so there is needed material to put in the forces, whereas the membrane itself can be rather thin.' [Heinz Isler, in conversation with the author, August 1999.]

57 'Very interesting — when you see the buckle here don't believe it.' [Heinz Isler, in conversation with the author, August 1999.]

58 Client: Formex AG, CH-4416 Bubendorf; Architect: Widler & Partner AG, CH-4515 Oberdorf; Structural Engineers: Blattner AG, Sissach and Duppenthaler & Wälchli, Langenthal; For Shells: Heinz Isler, CH-3401 Burgdorf; Contractor: Spaini Bau AG, Basel; For Shells: W. Bösiger AG, CH-4900 Langenthal.

59 Architects: Rolf and Hotz, Architekten BDA, D-79100, Freiburg; Engineers: Dr. F. Ebner, Prüfingenieur, D-77652 Freiburg and Heinz Isler, CH-3401, Burgdorf for the shells; Contractors: Fischer bau Gruppe, D-77652, Offenburg and Bösiger AG, CH-4900 Langenthal for the shells.

60 Half a metre of snow weighs perhaps 35 or 40 kg/m^2 but the same depth of sand weighs about 1000 kg/m^2.

Chapter Four

61 Isler H., Aplicactiones recientes de cascarones representativos, *Journal of IMCYC* (Mexican Institute for Cement and Concrete), Mexico D.F., Vol. 5, No. 30, Jan-Feb (1968a), p 1.

62 '…the preparation of the shuttering of the foot. No, in order to design that, it would have been a rather difficult problem because you cannot design something in space on the place where you draw.' [Heinz Isler, conversations with the author, August 1999.]

63 'Today with computers you can simulate it but it is not real. You just have the aspect of it but you can't touch it you cannot see the stresses. But here you see it.' [Heinz Isler, conversations with the author, August 1999.]

64 'The cupola came down with the insulation and they met in one line. I didn't want to have a profile or a thickness, just one line. I think that gives it the cleanness that you see, and there is not a single thing too much.' [Heinz Isler, conversations with the author, August 1999.]

65 'When I can do something with one line, if I use two lines, then I have 100 % too much — that's not good.' [Heinz Isler, conversations with the author, August 1999.]

66 'They don't have the feeling for it or the value. Today they make all different colours, they throw colours on the glass and they make it loud and ugly, whereas I take "de-materialising" to the utmost…' [Heinz Isler, conversations with the author, August 1999.]

67 'It is now 35 years old and still intact. The only thing that is no more good, all around they have built heaps of additional things so it is just disappearing in a heap of rubbish. That's then the real problem for me.' [Heinz Isler, conversations with the author, August 1999.]

68 'The form reflects the pure geometry of the sphere. As in other instances, the problem lay in deciding whether a shell ought to assume a form chosen beforehand, or whether the form should be dictated by the distribution of forces.' Jürgen Joedicke, *Shell Architecture*, Reinhold, New York, (1963), p 126–130.

69 Eero Saarinen quoted in Jürgen Joedicke, *Shell Architecture*, Reinhold, New York, (1963), p 127.

70 Isler H., 'The stability of thin concrete shells', in *Buckling of shells*, ed. E. Ramm, Springer, Berlin, (1982), p 662.

71 Ramm E. and Schunck E., *Heinz Isler Schalen*, Karl Krämer Verlag, Stuttgart, (1986). This is the catalogue (in German) of a very fine exhibition about Isler's shells, created by Prof. Ekkehard Ramm and Prof. Eberhard Schunck, of the University of Stuttgart. Having previously been shown in 27 European universities it is soon to start to tour again, visiting new locations.

72 '…somewhere where we could say that it should have been free-form (maybe) but the architect forced it not to be?' [Heinz Isler, conversations with the author, August 1999.]

73 Taillibert R., 'Centre Sportif', *L'Achitecture d'Aujourd hui*, Vol. 45, No. 168, July/Aug (1973), p 98–101.

Chapter Five

74 'In my opinion these shapes give the highest efficiency, very small deformations, initial and long-term, no cracks, no corrosion, high safety against buckling.' Isler in *Buckling of shells*, ed. E. Ramm, Springer, Berlin, (1982), p 667.

75 'Then the storm began from outside not from myself and I have never experienced such a thing. The publicity and the media were so interested in doing it — every day and every night some television, some radio, some newspapers even special newspapers produced it. I was just astonished. I had only one explanation — it was in the summer in a week when they had no other subject.' [Heinz Isler, in conversation with the author, August 1999.]

76 The five architects that gave their support were - Mario Botta, Roger Diener, Theo Hotz, Tilla Theus, and Peter Zumthor. Sonntagszeitung, 18th July 1999, Kultur, page 45.

77 This translates as 'Because of its beauty the construction has absolutely to be saved'.

78 Subsequently, the results of the investigation into the shell concrete turned out to be positive. There was extremely little carbonation of the concrete and no other deficiencies were found. [Heinz Isler, personal communication with the author, February 2000.]

79 Isler, H., Long term behaviour of shells, *Proceedings of the Seiken-IASS Symposium on Non-linear analysis and design for shell and spatial structures*, Tokyo, October 19-22, (1993), pp 9–16.

80 The rise was caused by grout injection of the soil under a neighbouring building, which made the foundation of one shell foot rise several centimetres.

81 '…which is moving with the absolute minimum at every point.' Heinz Isler, conversations with the author, August 1999.

82 Chilton J.C., Shell comeback, *Concrete Quarterly*, No. 173, Summer (1992), pp 24–26, ISSN 0010-5376.

83 Where Isler presented his 21- page paper 'Third decade of structural shells', Isler published in *Ten Years of Progress in Shell and Spatial Structures*, eds. F. del Pozo and A. de las Casas, CEDEX, Madrid, Vol. 1, (1989).

84 Evans B., Concrete in flight, Architects' Journal, Vol. 206, No 17, (November 6) (1997), pp 51–54.

Chapter Six

85 'Half an hour after we met on the site and everybody was so enthusiastic about it.' [Heinz Isler, conversations with the author, August 1999.]

86 The Hungarian architect, Imre Makowicz, has actually included living and dead trees within some of his buildings.

87 'But what I like, look at that, I like these cracks.' [Heinz Isler, conversations with the author, August 1999.]

88 'Finally, he made the finish, the inside finish and that is absolutely perfect, also in detail….' [Heinz Isler, conversations with the author, August 1999.]

89 '…the earth can shake however it likes and it cannot break, it cannot fall in, it cannot be destroyed.' [Heinz Isler, conversations with the author, August 1999.]

90 Balz M. and Isler H, *Haus und Gehäuse* Publikation Naturtheater, Ballettsaal und Schalenhaus, Architekt M. Balz. Beton – Prisma, 43 – 8, (1982).

91 The shells have double curvature of the same sense in the principle directions, unlike a hyperbolic paraboloid surface, which is anticlastic, having principle curvatures of opposite sign.

92 '… they just took gravel put them together and had a model of that size and won the competition for the church.' [Heinz Isler, conversations with the author, August 1999.]

93 When asked how he made the form, Isler replied, 'This has been 'moulded' by the architect. I told him the limits within which he was free. He made many models till he had the shape he wanted and then he gave me one of his models over which I poured the material.' [Heinz Isler, conversations with the author, August 1999.]

94 'You can see it. It's amazing.' [Heinz Isler, conversations with the author, August 1999.]

Chapter Seven

95 Isler H., Transparent structures of fibreglass and ice, in *Structural Morphology – Towards the New Millennium*, (eds Chilton J.C. et al), Nottingham, (1997b), p 3.

96 Isler (1997b), p 3.

97 Isler (1997b), p 4.

Endnotes

98 Isler (1997b), p 4.

99 Isler (1997b), p 5.

100 'Free spans of up to 15 m could be solved with mere plates!' Isler (1997b), p 5.

101 Isler H., Tragende Bauteile aus Kunststoff, in *Schalen in Beton und Kunststoff*, Bauverlag GmbH, Wiesbaden, Berlin, (1968b), p 113.

102 Isler H., Erfahrungen mit selbsttragenden Kassettenplatten aus GF-UP; in: *Plasticonstruction* 3 (1977).

103 Kokawa T. and Watanabe K, Ice shell – contemporary 'igloo' or 'kamakura', in *Structural Morphology – Towards the New Millennium*, (eds Chilton J.C. et al), Nottingham, (1997), pp 286–292.

104 Isler H., Transparent structures of fiberglass and ice, in *Structural Morphology – Towards the New Millennium*, (eds Chilton J.C. et al), Nottingham, (1997b), pp 3–10.

105 'Even simply freezing water has its own laws and rules: Physical strict laws. You cannot produce anything against them. But you can experience the full creativity if you try to perceive the rules and to follow them.' Isler (1997b), p 7.

106 Isler (1997b), p 8.

Chapter Eight

107 'Good co-operation with the architect — that is the good one.' [Heinz Isler, conversations with the author, August 1999.]

108 '…I was not proud of it. I knew that I had the idea that I did not quite understand, but in recent time I see that it was not so bad at all.' [Heinz Isler, conversations with the author, August 1999.]

109 Working Group 15 of IASS, Structural Morphology, was set up at the instigation of Ture Wester (its present chairman), René Motro, Pieter Huybers and Jean-François Gabriel and is currently one of the most active working groups of IASS. Structural morphology is sometimes described as the bridge between structural engineering and architecture.

110 Isler H., 'Transparent structures of fibreglass and ice' in *Structural Morphology: Towards the New Millennium*, (eds Chilton J.C., *et al.*), University of Nottingham, (1997b), p 3–10.

111 'Today the question arises if the original scope of IASS, namely, if the shell constructions are out.' Isler H., 40 years of IASS, in the *Journal of the International Association for Shell and Spatial Structures: IASS*, Vol. 40, No. 131, (1999), p 154.

112 Isler H., 40 years of IASS, in the *Journal of the International Association for Shell and Spatial Structures: IASS*, Vol. 40, No. 131, (1999), pp 154–5.

113 There are actually delicate trees, up to 10 m high, on the Isler office roof.

114 This by no means signifies any criticism of Isler's shells but merely highlights the fact that they are more at home in an environment that embraces curves, as does nature.

115 Isler H., 40 years of IASS, in the *Journal of the International Association for Shell and Spatial Structures: IASS*, Vol. 40, No. 131, (1999), p 151–1.

116 Special consultant, Prof. Frei Otto, Warmbronn.

117 In this Stuttgart Railway Station project Heinz Isler is acting for the client as expert for the vaulted shell construction.

118 Domingo A. and Lázaro C., La ciudad de las artes y de las ciencias de Valencia: the expressive force of the structures, in the *Journal of the International Association for Shell and Spatial Structures: IASS*, Vol. 40, No. 131, (1999), pp 169–78.

119 At the time of writing, April 2000.

120 Medwadowski S., Concrete thin shell roofs at the turn of the Millennium, in *Current and Emerging Technologies of Shell and Spatial Structures*, eds J. Abel, R. Astudillo and N.K. Srivastava, IASS, Madrid, (1997), p 20.

121 Medwadowski (1997), p 15.

122 Medwadowski (1997), p 16.

Selected List of Works

1952
Development of northlights cylindrical shells with straight prestressing cables.

1954-55
Concert hall at the Hotel Kreuz, Langenthal, Switzerland – cylinder shell with dome-shaped ends.

1956-59
33 Bubble shells from 14 m x 20 m to 22 m x 22 m span.

1956
Application of the northlights shells developed in 1952.

Development and construction of first skylight dome from polyester; 5 m diameter; licensed to the firm of Eschmann, Thun, Switzerland.

Free formed swimming pool from polyester and glass fibre for the Motel Losone, Tessin.

1960-64
163 Bubble shells predominantly 20 m x 20 m and 22 m x 22 m; some with integral crane beams.
Development of the shell types "Free-form 29".

1960
COOP, Wangen bei Olten, Switzerland
Bubble shell 54.6 x 58.8 m

1962
Flower shop and display area 650 m²; Wyss Söhne AG, Solothurn, Switzerland

1963
Retail shop, Cooperativa di consumo, 440m², Biasca.
Architect: Sigg, Basel

1964
Retail shop, Migros Ticino, 961m², Bellinzona.
Architect: Chiesa, Bellinzona and Büchler

1965-66
72 Bubble shells
Continuing development of free-forms

1965
Factory building for Kilcher (Building Insulation), Solothurn, Switzerland
Free-form shell 25.3 m x 25.3 m with free edges on four point supports.
Collaborating architect: Paul Wirz, Solothurn

Flower shop and display area, Florélites L. Clause SA, RN12, Plaisir, Paris; newly developed pentagonal free-form, diagonal span length 39.0 m.
Collaborating Architect: Dresse, Paris
Collaborating Engineer: Summer, Paris

1967-69
124 Bubble shells between 15 x 15 m and 30 x 30 m, some with crane beams.

1967-68
Collaboration in the Design Competition for the Sports Facilities for the Olympic Games in Munich with Behnisch and Partner and Jürgen Joedicke. During the execution collaboration in the Stadium and the roof construction.

1967
Church at Lommiswil/SO, Switzerland
Hyperbolic paraboloid shell.
Design and engineer: Heinz Isler
Architect: Roland Hanselman

1968
Laboratory and research facility: Grips – Union Bex.

Motorway Service Station; Deitingen – Süd, Switzerland
Two, three-point supported pre-stressed concrete shells 26 x 31 m.

Private house roof; Knoch R.; Klagenfurt, Austria
Hyperbolic paraboloid shell of 140 m².

1969
Factory; SICLI SA, fire extinguisher manufacturer, Geneva, Switzerland
Free-form prestressed concrete shell of irregular plan form with seven point support.
Architect: C Hilberer, Geneva
Engineer: Heinz Isler (form and statics)

Retail and display centre, Florélites Clause SA; RN 20, La Ville du Bois, France; prestressed concrete shell, pentagonal ground plan, span 46.6 m on the diagonal.

General engineering construction; single and multi-family housing, primary school, Kindergarden; PTT Building for Telefonzentrale.

1970-71
151 Bubble shells; development of new crane beam system.

New development of a hexagonal plan shell for Daimler Benz AG; diagonal span 51.0 m.

Villa Camoletti, Geneva; hyperbolic shell, 20.0 m span.

Swimming and sports facilities; Chamonix, nine triangular shells with side lenghs from 22.0 to 60.0 m.
Architects: Roger Taillibert, Paris
                     BET Europé Etude, Paris
Engineer (shells):   Heinz Isler

Retail and display garden centre; Bürgi, Carlo; Camorino/TI square, free-form shell with unstiffened edge, span 27.2 m.

1972-74
117 Bubble shells up to 34 x 34 m span.

Roof over indoor swimming baths; Hotel Splendide Royal, Lugano, Switzerland
Free-form shell 16 x 16 m.

Roof over indoor swimming baths; Marisella SA, Immobilare Cassarate – Lugano, Ponte Capriasca, Switzerland, 30.8 m span.

Ski centre; Chamonix, 10 triangular shells with side lengths from 22.5 to 45.0 m.
Architects: Roger Taillibert, Paris
                     BET Europé Etude, Paris
Engineer (shells):   Heinz Isler

Retail and display centre; Florélites Clause SA; Rennes, France
Free form pentagonal shell.

Construction E.N.S.A.; Chamonix, France
Five triangular shells with side lengths from 22.5 to 31.0 m.
Architects: Roger Taillibert, Paris
                     BET Europé Etude, Paris
Engineer (shells):   Heinz Isler

Retail and display centre; Florélites Clause SA; Bordeaux, France
Free-form pentagonal shell, 31.0 m span.

General engineering construction; Static calculations for the steel construction for the retractable fabric umbrella roofs for the Bundesgartenschan, Cologne, Germany
spread when opened 17.0 m height about 8.0 m.

1975-79
43 Bubble shells.

1975
Retail and display centre; Florélites Clause SA; RN 1, Moiselles, France
Free-form pentagonal shell, 46.6 m span.

Community centre with library; Chamonix, France
Four triangular shells with side lengths from 22.5 to 37.0 m.
Architects: Roger Taillibert, Paris
                     BET Europé Etude, Paris
Engineer (shells):   Heinz Isler

Leisure centre and dance school; Chur, Switzerland
Square free-form shell span 27.9 m.

1976
Monument in Hafen von Pully; sculpture by M. Angel Duarte Sion, shell from 'ferro-cement' in the form of sails.
Sculpture by M. Angel Duarte Sion; 3 hyperbolic shells from 'ferro-cement'.

Display centre; Florélites Clause SA, RN 7, Ponthierry, France
Free-form shell, pentagonal plan, diagonal span 46.6 m.

Selected List of Works

Open-air theatre roof; Stetten auf den Fildern, Germany
Free-form shell 27.2 x 22.0 m.
Architect: Michael Balz

Retail and display centre; Florélites Clause SA, Laval, France
shell with pentagonal plan, diagonal span 31.0 m.

1977
Retail and display centre; Florélites Clause SA, Villeparisis, RN 3, France
Pentagonal shell with diagonal span 46.6 m.

Artist's studios; Ponthierry, RN 7, France
Six ball/sphere shells of 70 m^2 each, 2 of 34 m^2 each, patented balloon (inflated) shells.

Markethall; Riyadh, Saudi Arabia
43 ball/sphere shells each 6 x 6 m, sprayed concrete balloon shells.

Open-air theatre roof; Grötzingen, Germany
Inclined free-form shell of 42.0 m span
Architect: Michael Balz

1978
Tennis halls:
Düdingen, Switzerland
Three shells each 18.6 x 47.0 m.
La Chaux-de-Fond, Switzerland
Two shells of 18.6 x 47.0 m.
Heimberg, Switzerland
Four shells of 18.6 x 47.0 m.
Swimming pool, Heimberg, Switzerland
Free-form shell of 32.5 x 32.5 m.
Clubhouse; Tennis club, Aarwangen, Switzerland
Ball/sphere shell.

1979
Ballet hall; Stetten auf den Fildern, Germany
Free-form, trapezoidal shell, span 22.0 m
Architect: Michael Balz

Sculpture; M. Angel Duarte Sion; Langenthal, Switzerland.
"Hard", 8 hyperbolic shells of ferro-cement, for vocational school.

1980-85
43 Bubble shells of different sizes.
Development of transparent canopies in glass-reinforced polyester 4.0 m cantilever.

1980
Tennis hall; Crissier VD, Switzerland
Five shells each 18.6 x 47.0 m.
Tennis hall; Burgdorf, Switzerland
Four shells each 17.75 x 47.0 m.
Dreilinden tennis centre; Langenthal, Switzerland
Four shells each 18.6 x 47.0 m.

1981
Retail and display centre; Foncierère Agricole de Servon, Servon, RN 19
Pentagonal, free-form shell.

Swimming pool; Brugg, Switzerland
Square, free-form shell of 35.0 x 34.0 m.
Emmen Tennis Centre; Lucerne, Switzerland
Four shells each 18.6 x 47.0 m.

1982
'Bruchl' Sports Centre; Solothurn, Switzerland
Six shells each 17.75 x 47.0 m.
'Paradies' Tennis Centre; Allschwil/Baselld, Switzerland
Four shells each 18.6 x 47.0 m.

1983
Tennis and squash halls; Sion VS, Switzerland
Four shells each 18.6 x 47.0 m.

Consultant for Meret Oppenheim's Fountain; in Waisenhausplatz, Bern, Switzerland

1986
Villa; Geneva, 4 self-reciprocally supported shells.

Book: *Heinz Isler Schalen* by Ramm + Schunck (in German)

1986 - 1990
46 Bubble shells of various spans from 18 x 18 m to 25 x 25 m

1987
Air museum, Dubendorf: 4 shells 18.60 x 51.70 m
Architects: Haus + Herd

1987
Broadland Sports Village, Norwich, United Kingdom:
Nine tennis hall shells of 18.60 x 47.00 m
Architect: Copeland Associates (with Haus + Herd)
Engineer: Heinz Isler
Main Contractor: R.G. Carter Ltd., Norwich
Contractor for Shell Roof: W. Bösiger, Langenthal, Switzerland

Residence Oberonz, Switzerland
Five doubly-curved vaults

1988
Cultural centre, Stetten, Stuttgart, Germany
Free form, trapezium 22 x 19 m
Architect: Michael Balz

1991
Broadland Sports Village, Norwich, United Kingdom
Covered swimming/leisure pool, square plan 35.00 x 35.00 m
Architect: Copeland Associates (with Haus + Herd)
Engineer: Heinz Isler
Main Contractor: R.G. Carter Ltd., Norwich
Contractor for Shell Roof: W. Bösiger, Langenthal, Switzerland

1991 - 1999
32 Bubble shells

1994
Formex AG, Budendorf, , Switzerland
Two shells 39.10 x 39.10

1996
SWEG, Sudwestdt. Verkehrs AG, Lahr D
Two shells 30.87 x 31.68 m

1993
Europapark, Rust, Germany
Three shell roofs (4-leaf cloverleaf)
Four point supports, 9.20 x 8.40 m

Tennis hall Grenchen, Switzerland
Extension with two shells 17.30 x 47.00 m

1996
Evangelical Church, Cazis, Switzerland
Three pebble-shaped shells, 11.30 m, 9.30 m and 8.80 m high

1998
New office building, W. Bösiger AG, Langenthal

1999
Hyperboloid entrance canopy, Langenthal, Switzerland
Two-point support, 9.40 x 12.00 m, architect Michael Balz

1998
Special adviser for shell construction
Deutsche Bundesbahn, Stuttgart Station Competition Project Gmbh, Stuttgart 21

1999 – 2000
Special adviser for shell construction
Deutsche Bundesbahn, Stuttgart Station Competition Project Gmbh, Stuttgart 21
Detailed design, Stuttgart New Station ca. 30000 m^2

Bibliography

Arup O.N. and Zunz G.J. (1969). Sydney Opera House. *The Structural Engineer*, **47**, 3.

Balz M. and Isler H. (1982). *Haus und Gehäuse*. Publikation Naturtheater, Ballettsaal und Schalenhaus, Architekt M. Balz, Beton–Prisma, 43–8.

Billington D. (1983). *The Tower and the Bridge — the new art of structural engineering*. Princetown University Press.

Chilton J.C. (1992). Shell comeback. *Concrete Quarterly*, 173, Summer.

Domingo A. and Lázaro C. (1999). La ciudad de las artes y de las ciencias de Valencia: the expressive force of the structures. *J. of the International Association for Shell and Spatial Structures*. IASS, **40**, 13.

Evans B. (1997). Concrete in flight. *Architects' Journal*, **206**, 17, (6 Nov.).

Holgate A. (1997). *The art of structural engineering: the work of Jörg Schlaich and his team*. Edition Axel Menges, Stuttgart/London.

Isler H. (1955). Discussion IIIb, Instability of thin prestressed shells. In *Second Congress of the Fèdèration Internationale de la Prècontrainte*, Amsterdam.

Isler H. (1957). Discussion Shell Research. In *Proc. of the Second Symp. on Concrete Shell Roof Construction*. Teknisk Ukeblad Oslo, Norway, July.

Isler H. (1960). New shapes for shells. *IASS Bulletin* 8.

Isler H. (1968a). Aplicationes recientes de cascarones representativos. *J. of IMCYC* (Mexican Institute for Cement and Concrete), Mexico D.F., **5**, 30, Jan–Feb.

Isler H. (1968b). Tragende Bauteile aus Kunststoff. In *Schalen in Beton und Kunststoff*, Bauverlag GmbH, Wiesbaden, Berlin.

Isler H. (1977). Erfahrungen mit selbsttragenden Kassettenplatten aus GF–UP. In *Plasticonstruction*, 3.

Isler H. (1982). The stability of thin concrete shells. In *Buckling of shells*, E. Ramm (ed.), Springer, Berlin.

Isler H. (1989). Third decade of structural shells. In *Ten years of progress in shell and spatial structures*, F. del Pozo and A. de las Casas (eds), CEDEX, Madrid, **1**.

Isler H. (1993). Long term behaviour of shells. In *Proc. of the Seiken–IASS Symp. on Non-linear analysis and design for shell and spatial structures*, Oct. 19–22.

Isler H. (1997a). Is the physical model dead? In *Structural morphology — towards the new millennium*, J.C. Chilton et al. (eds), University of Nottingham.

Isler H. (1997b). Transparent structures of fibreglass and ice. In *Structural morphology — towards the new millennium*, J.C. Chilton et al. (eds), University of Nottingham.

Isler H. (1999). 40 years of IASS. In *J. of the International Association for Shell and Spatial Structures*, IASS, **40**, 131.

Isono Y. (1998). Looking for the structures of R. Maillart and Heinz Isler in Switzerland. Appendix of the *6th Prof. Y Tsuboi Memorial Seminar on Shell and Space Structures*, Tokyo, 21 May.

Joedicke J. (1963). *Shell architecture*. Reinhold, New York.

Kokawa T. and Watanabe K. (1997). Ice shell — contemporary 'igloo' or 'kamakura'. In *Structural morphology — towards the new millennium*, J.C. Chilton et al. (eds), University of Nottingham.

Medwadowski S. (1997). Concrete thin shell roofs at the turn of the millennium. In *Current and emerging technologies of shell and spatial structures*, J. Abel et al. (eds), IASS, Madrid.

Ramm E. and Schunck E. (1986). *Heinz Isler Schalen*, Karl Krämer Verlag, Stuttgart.

Taillibert R. (1973). Centre Sportif. *L'Achitecture d'Aujourd hui*, **45**, 168, July/Aug.

Sonntagszeitung, 18 July 1999, Kultur, 45.

Index

20th Anniversary Congress of the IASS	20
30th Anniversary Congress of the IASS	112
40th Anniversary Congress of the IASS	21, 157
aesthetics in shell structures	19
Aircraft Museum, Dübendorf	109, 5.40-5.45
American Air Museum at Duxford	119, 158
Aquapark, Norwich Sports Village	111, 112, 114, 115, 117, 119, 5.46, 5.51-5.59
Arup, Ove	12, 17, 18-20, 111
Avag Garage, Solothurn	3.8
Ballet Salon, Stetten auf den Fildern	5.20-5.23
balloon former	128, 129
Balz House, Stetten auf den Filden	130-134, 6.18-6.21
Balz, Michael	36, 101-103, 105, 130, 3.29
Bellinzona, supermarket	77, 83, 4.7-4.9, 4.11-4.14
BET Europé Etude, Paris	86
Billington, David	20, 27
Blaser	16, 1.6
Bösiger AG, of Langenthal	58, 115, 116, 130
Bösiger offices	53, 3.7, 3.27-3.29
Botta, Mario	96
Brugg Swimming Pool roof at Aarepark, Switzerland	108, 112, 5.38 5.39
brush anchor	138
bubble shells	15-17, 24, 33, 35, 50, 54, 60, 62, 65, 2.2, 2.3, 3.1-3.3, 3.5, 3.6
buckling behaviour	42, 55, 84, 4.21, 5.15
Buckling failure	147
buckling resistance	42, 3.14
Bulletin of IASS	17
Bürgi Garden Centre, Camorino	70, 86, 4.23-4.26
Bus depot at Müllheim, in the Schwarzwald	58, 61, 3.22-3.26
Camoletti, Pierre	134
Candela, Félix	12, 20, 158
Centre National des Industries et Techniques (CNIT)	19
Chamonix	70, 92, 4.27-4.29
Chiesa, Bellinzona and Büchler	77
Church in Stuttgart-Fellbach	146, 7.14
Clubhouse in Aawangen	130
coating the concrete	44
computers	23, 32, 38, 46, 72, 99, 137
conceptual models	18
concreting	3.17, 4.14, 5.55-5.57
COOP, Wangen bei Olten	54, 3.13-3.18
Copeland Associates	110, 111, 119
crane beams	3.11, 3.12
Creative play	28
curved timber beams	113
Dahinden J., of Zurich	128, 130
deformation	42, 45, 80, 99, 110, 5.16
Deitingen Süd	36, 66, 92, 156, 5.1-5.7
demolition	66, 67, 95, 3.30-3.34
Design philosophy	22
domed roof lights	52, 58
domed shells	128-130, 148, 6.12-6.17
Domingo, Prof. A.	158
double skin shell	144
double-layer polyester units	145
Duarte, Angel of Sion	138, 139
Düdingen	106
efficiency of thin shell structures	32
Emmental cheese	28
Equillan, Nicolas	12, 17, 19
Eschmann, of Thun	16, 50
ETH, Zürich	14, 21, 45, 66
Evangelische Kirchgemeinde, Cazis	135-138, 6.26-6.30
exotic materials for modelling	28
expansion forms	35
façades	52, 74, 106, 3.25, 4.4, 4.26
fire	2.13
Flint, A. R.	20
form active structures	32
Formex AG at Budendorf	58, 60, 3.19-3.21
formwork and falsework	62, 2.15, 3.15, 4.2, 5.47
Foster and Partners	119, 158
Franz K. architect	146, 7.14
free-form shells	35, 37, 70
Frutiger AG, of Thun	130
Gammel Dok, Copenhagen	157
Garden Centre Florélites Clause SA. St. Appoline, Paris	80, 4.15-4.17
general equation for shell buckling	41
Gewerbeschule, in Langenthal	139, 6.35
glazing	73, 74
glued-laminated timber beams	19, 43, 56, 71, 107
Gmelich V., architect	146, 7.13
Grötzingen, outdoor theatre	36, 102, 105, 106, 5.24-5.30
growth forms	35, 2.6
Günter Behnisch and Partners	22
HABA Uster	66
Hangai, Prof.	27
hanging forms	36
hanging membrane	105, 2.7-2.10
Hanjal-Konyi	19
Hanselmann, Roland of Olten	122, 123, 127
Happold Ingenieurbüro, Berlin	158
Hauri, Hans	20
Haus+Herd Company of Herzogenbuchsee	106, 109-111
Haven von Pully, Geneva	139, 6.34
Heimberg	107, 108, 112, 5.31
Hilberer C., Geneva	97
Holy Spirit Church at Lommiswil	122-128, 6.1-6.8, 6.10, 6.11
Hotel Kreuz	14, 1.2
Hypalon coating	77
hypar	125, 127, 3.28, 6.7, 6.9

IASS Structural Morphology Colloquium in Nottingham	46	
IASS Structural Morphology Group	149, 156	
IASS Symposium held in Copenhagen in 1991	156	
ice flowers	152, 7.24	
Ice Palace	151, 7.23	
ice steeple	152, 7.28	
ice structures	28, 38, 150, 152, 1.9, 7.17-7.29	
l'Ecole Nationale de Ski et d' Alpinisme (ENSA)	89	
inflated membrane	50, 2.3-2.5	
Ingenhoven Overdiek und Partner, of Düsseldorf	158	
instability	41, 44	
International Association for Shell and Spatial Structures (IASS)	16, 156	
International Association for Shell and Spatial Structures 30th Anniversary Congress	44, 112	
International Association for Shell Structures	16	
Isler offices	24, 25, 1.13, 1.14	
Isler, Maria	21, 43	
Isono, Y.	27	
Jakob, Jules	21	
Joedicke, Jürgen	22, 78	
Kilcher Factory, Recherswil, Solothurn	83, 86, 4.18-4.22	
Kresge Auditorium at (MIT), Massachusetts Institute of Technology	78, 4.10	
Lake Geneva	139	
Lardy, Prof. Pierre	14, 15, 21	
Lázaro, Eng. C.	158	
Leonhard, Andra und Partner, in Stuttgart	158	
Leonhardt, Fritz	22	
licence to construct	65	
long-term behaviour	18, 40, 42, 45, 99, 5.16	
Lyssachschachen, near Burgdorf	16, 24	
measuring the form	42, 43, 2.14, 5.49, 5.50	
Medwadowski, Prof. Stefan, President of IASS	158	

Menn, Christian	14	
model testing	40, 2.12, 2.13, 4.17, 4.21, 5.4, 5.45, 6.10	
modular storage system	144	
monitoring the long-term shape	44	
Moser Company	25	
Moser petrol filling station in Thun	146, 7.8-7.11	
Moser, Lyssach	54, 3.9, 3.10, 3.12	
Motel in Mittleren Osten	130	
Motorway Service Station, Deitingen Süd	36, 66, 92, 156, 5.1-5.7	
Munich Olympic Stadium	22	
Münster' (or Minster)	151, 7.20	
natural protection and erosion	44	
Nervi, Pier Luigi	12	
Norwich Sports Village	66, 111, 112, 114, 115, 117, 119, 5.46, 5.51-5.59	
Oceanographic Park, in Valencia (L'Oceanografic)	158	
office roof	27	
Open air theatre, Stetten auf den Fildern	102, 5.19	
Oppenheim, Meret	139, 6.36, 6.37	
Ove Arup and Partners	119, 158, 1.11, 1.12	
Paul Wirz of Solothurn	83	
physical models	32, 40, 42, 47, 71	
polyester cantilevers	147, 7.15, 7.16	
polyester plates	145-147, 7.8-7.14	
polyester shell domes	16, 98, 118, 1.3	
polyester shell vaults	144, 7.5-7.7	
Ponthierry, near Paris	130, 6.16, 6.17	
Power station, River Rhine at Säckingen	146, 7.12	
President of IASS	158	
prestressing	35, 37, 40, 44, 80, 84, 89, 93, 100, 110, 115, 117, 126, 3.3, 3.16, 4.12, 4.13, 4.15, 5.1, 5.2,	
R.G. Carter Ltd., Norwich	110	
Ramm, Prof. Ekkehard	27	
Ramseier + Jenzer, Biel	1.7	

Realschule, Geislingen	146, 7.13	
René Acht, of Basel	125	
Research Institute EMPA Dübendorf	66	
resistance to buckling	19, 40	
roof of Isler office	25	
rubber membrane	33, 34	
rubber model	137	
Saarinen, Eero	78, 4.10	
Schlaich, Jörg	20, 22	
Schmid H., of Kirchberg	130	
Schmidt, Werner (Mag. Arch) of Thun	135, 136	
Schunck, Prof. Eberhard	27	
Sculptures	138, 139, 150, 6.31-6.37	
shell and sky domes	142, 143, 7.1-7.4	
Sicli SA factory, Geneva	36, 108, 5.8-5.16	
Sigg of Basel	76	
simple hand calculation	38, 2.11	
Soc. Migros, Bellinzona	77, 83, 4.7	
Sonntagszeitung	96	
Sports and Sky Centre, Chamonix	86	
St. Appoline, Paris	83	
St. Guérin School, Sion	139, 6.33	
Stetten auf den Fildern	36, 102, 103, 130-134, 5.17-5.23, 6.18-6.21	
Structural Morphology Colloquium held at the University of Nottingham, in August 1997	157	
Structural Morphology Group of IASS	36	
Stuttgart Main Station	158	
supermarket at Biasca	76, 4.6	
swimming baths in Tramelan	139, 6.31, 6.32	
swimming pool enclosures	98, 106, 108, 113, 118, 5.38, 5.39, 5.59	
Sydney Opera House	20, 1.11, 1.12	
Taillibert, Roger	70, 86, 92	
tennis and sports halls	36, 106, 107, 109, 111, 113, 5.31-5.37, 5.41, 5.48	
Torroja, Eduardo	12, 14, 17-21, 157	

169

Index

Trösch Bützberg, 1955 62
Tsuboi, Prof. Y 27

Utzon, Jørn 20

vertical stressing 84
Villa, near Geneva 134, 6.22-6.25
Ville du Bois, RN 20, suffered a severe fire 81

W. Bösiger AG, Langenthal 62, 64, 65, 110, 113,
Waisenhausplatz, in Bern 139, 6.36, 6.37
weather-resistant and impermeable shells 22
wood-wool slabs 104, 107, 114
Wyss Garden Centre 70, 76, 77, 80, 103, 121, 4.1-4.5